Social Development
in Latin America

WW Woodrow Wilson Center
Current Studies on Latin America

Published with the Latin American Program
of the Woodrow Wilson International Center for Scholars
Joseph S. Tulchin, Director

Social Development in Latin America

The Politics of Reform

edited by

Joseph S. Tulchin
Allison M. Garland

LYNNE
RIENNER
PUBLISHERS

BOULDER
LONDON

Published in the United States of America in 2000 by
Lynne Rienner Publishers, Inc.
1800 30th Street, Boulder, Colorado 80301
www.rienner.com

and in the United Kingdom by
Lynne Rienner Publishers, Inc.
3 Henrietta Street, Covent Garden, London WC2E 8LU

Library of Congress Cataloging-in-Publication Data
Social development in Latin America : the politics of reform /
   edited by Joseph S. Tulchin and Allison M. Garland.
   Includes bibliographical references and index.
   ISBN 1-55587-843-1 (pbk. : alk. paper)
   1. Latin America—Social policy—Case studies. 2. Latin America—
Social conditions—1982—Case studies. 3. Latin America—Politics and
government—1980—Case studies. 4. Latin America—Economic policy—
Case studies. 5. Latin America—Economic conditions—1982—Case studies.
I. Tulchin, Joseph S., 1939– . II. Garland, Allison M., 1965– .
HN110.5.A8 S6263   2000
361.6'1098—dc21   00-023074

British Cataloguing in Publication Data
A Cataloguing in Publication record for this book
is available from the British Library.

Printed and bound in the United States of America

⊗   The paper used in this publication meets the requirements
    of the American National Standard for Permanence of
    Paper for Printed Library Materials Z39.48-1984.

5 4 3 2 1

Contents

1

The Politics and Administration of Social Development in Latin America

Allison M. Garland

In response to the debt crisis of the 1980s, countries throughout Latin America instituted sweeping monetary, fiscal, and financial reforms, adopting neoliberal policies to reduce the size of the state and liberalize trade in order to participate more competitively in the global economy. These programs stabilized macroeconomic indicators, brought low rates of inflation, restored economic growth, and allowed countries in the region to return to international capital markets. In spite of these advances, rates of poverty and indigence, which rose dramatically during the "lost decade" of the 1980s, only recently regained the levels held in 1980. While the percentage of poor households in Latin America decreased from 41 percent (200 million) to 36 percent (204 million) between 1990 and 1997, levels remained nearly the same as those attained in 1980, 35 percent (136 million).[1]

Even more disturbing, income inequality in the region did not improve during the 1990s and remains as high today as it was two decades ago. On average, the Latin American and Caribbean region is the most unequal region in the world in terms of income disparities. The poorest 30 percent of the population receive 7.5 percent of all national income, while the wealthiest 10 percent receive 40 percent.[2]

Economic restructuring and reform programs that have allowed countries to compete in international markets have also resulted in greater disparity between the beneficiaries of globalization and those left behind. Widening income differentials between skilled and unskilled workers contribute further to inequality. Countries that successfully tackled serious inflation problems continue to be plagued by joblessness and an erosion of real wages. Unemployment, which dropped from the mid-1980s to the early 1990s, began to rise in the mid-1990s as a result of the 1995 Mexican peso crisis, and again in

1

1997 in response to the Asian financial crisis.[3] A survey of regional economic performance found that unemployment in Greater Buenos Aires reached 20 percent in 1995.[4] Another report issued in the same year found that real wages in Argentina, Mexico, and Costa Rica had not recovered to their 1980 value and that average real wages in Peru were down to just 47 percent of their 1980 value.[5] The hardest hit by these trends in the labor market are women, young people, and the poor.[6]

Changing socioeconomic conditions have created a tremendous sense of instability and uncertainty among the citizens of Latin America. Unequal growth and development have further polarized the region, eroding social cohesion. Difficulties in gaining access to health care, education, and employment generate perceptions of social defenselessness in a world that is increasingly competitive and challenging. In this context, crime and violence have found fertile ground for growth.

Throughout the region, social issues—unemployment, income distribution, poverty, and insecurity—have risen to the top of the political agenda and have come to pose a serious threat to the consolidation of democracy. The inability of governments to respond to social problems threatens to undermine public confidence in democratic institutions. There is a growing sense in the region that growth alone cannot address these problems without a powerful political commitment to poverty alleviation and redistribution of the nation's resources. Many observers have asked why it has been so easy to conceptualize and implement a new economic model for the region while social sectors remain untouched. Why has the social question been so difficult to deal with in Latin America?

There is a growing realization within the hemisphere, and in financial centers of industrialized nations, that social reform is a condition upon which economic and political stability rests—that the still tenuous economic and political successes in the region over the past decade may be undermined by poverty and inequality. An increasing sense of social exclusion threatens the consolidation of democracy in Latin America. Old patterns of distribution created a system based on patronage and clientelism, relying on massive welfare bureaucracies to manage social demands channeled in a highly centralized fashion through political parties and labor unions. That system has been rendered anachronistic by the dual transition to a market economy and to political democracy. It is no longer a viable system: It is corrupt, inflexible, and inefficient. Now, welfare reforms must carefully be devised to improve access to and the quality of social services, while at the same time contributing to the strengthening of democratic institutions. As the region's governments redefine their role, the state's relationship with citizens is being transformed. Ultimately, success hinges on the ability of governments to restructure social-sector agencies, overhauling and modernizing organizational processes; to reallocate funds to reflect priorities; and to safeguard reforms from political interference.[7]

The Challenge of Institutional Reform

During the economic adjustment of the 1980s, many countries of the region witnessed a decline in investment in public services. Today, however, most analysts agree that the problem in Latin America is not the amount of resources allocated to social-sector expenditure, but the distribution and poor performance of social programs due to weak public-sector institutions. In fact, social spending in Latin America compares favorably with other regions of the world.[8] Pouring additional funds into the current system will not improve social conditions because of structural flaws within government institutions and because of public-spending policies that favor the wealthy and the politically powerful.

Much of the literature about social policy and public-sector reform in Latin America emphasizes the need to look first and foremost at large, ineffective social ministries as obstacles to progress. In many countries, efforts to implement more-constructive approaches to the delivery of essential public goods and services pale in comparison with the central role played by national systems. For example, Venezuela's Ministry of Education is by far the country's largest single employer, followed by the Ministry of Health and the social security system.[9]

As the sole providers of social services, ministries administer public goods in a highly centralized structure that rarely consults beneficiaries or bodies responsible for program implementation at the local level. As a result, the central monopoly over social services has had a crowding-out effect on local government and other actors. Organizational processes have yet to be modernized and are plagued by strong institutional inflexibilities. The administrative structure lends itself to excessive influence and interference of interest groups. Ministry units dealing with services for the poor are "less sophisticated and well connected than units responsible for higher education or for hospitals." Doctors usually control policy choices in health ministries, which are "virtually an agent of the profession in some countries."[10] Social ministries do not enjoy high status and those chosen to head them are not strong leaders nor do they have political clout. High turnover at the top translates to both a lack of continuity in leadership and increased influence of bureaucratic interests.[11]

Health and education ministries in particular are often deeply divided internally and have failed to tackle the challenges of sectoral integration and coordination of policies. Most countries in Latin America offer a wide range of social services and programs, often with overlapping objectives. Rarely do those involved in the design and delivery of services come together to organize efforts in a clearly defined set of national priorities for an overall strategy toward poverty alleviation and social equity.

Problems rated in this lack of integration and coordination are compounded by failures in program design and evaluation. Uncertain objectives and ambiguity in criteria for selection of program beneficiaries can often be attributed to an absence of specific diagnostics of the population's needs. A 1995 assessment of antipoverty strategies employed throughout the region finds that "there are no in-depth evaluations of the programs' impact on the living conditions of their beneficiaries, nor studies to determine the actual coverage of the target group or to identify sectors that are excluded."[12] Unlike economic progress, it is very difficult to measure and monitor input and output of social services; it is impossible to assess the impact of policies without sufficient data. "Countries spend a great deal to measure inflation, the fiscal deficit, output, and the balance of payments accurately. Poverty, income distribution, and social indicators are never measured with equal care," concludes Nora Lustig in another comprehensive study of social policies.[13]

Without accurate data collection or sophisticated program design and coordination, deep-rooted patterns of social exclusion, clientelism, and corruption continue to pervade state services, reflecting a system ruled by corporate interests and political patronage. In spite of stated policies of universalism, large segments of the population are excluded from social services, particularly rural workers and urban poor employed in the informal sector. Social policies formulated in this context have had a regressive effect on income distribution in Latin America. Reforms to address equity in the distribution of public goods will invariably challenge vested interests and traditional patterns of political power.

In spite of powerful interests to protect policies that have been biased toward Latin America's elite and the middle class, there is widespread consensus today for the need to tackle institutional and structural obstacles to equitable growth. Reform of the state now means much more than downsizing or policies of liberalization, privatization, and deregulation. Political leaders, with the encouragement of international lending institutions, have shifted beyond efforts to reverse policies founded on populism and import substitution to pursue a course toward institutional development.[14] Focus on social-welfare issues has brought public attention away from mediating the costs of adjustment to deeper concerns about the quality of and access to social services, particularly health and education. However, the region lacks a model for addressing more difficult second-generation reforms.

This volume addresses the challenges of implementing second-stage, deeper reforms that consolidate democracy by changing institutions. The authors reflect upon the ways in which social reform in particular has been politically and technically more complex than the introduction of radical changes in economic policy. While macroeconomic reform was rapidly implemented in the context of crisis, often in a top-down technocratic or autocratic manner, social reform has proven to require a lengthy process involving ongoing monitoring and adjustment that can open opportunities for opponents to block change. Democratization in Latin America has made it difficult for political leaders to institute reform by decree or other executive measures, requiring greater public participation, consensus building, and compromise around reform. Success has been achieved with the creation of stakeholders and the mobilization of new constituencies through greater involvement of civil society.

Strategies for Change

Many policymakers, with enthusiastic support from multilateral development banks, have embraced decentralization as a tool both to improve services and strengthen democracy by bringing decision-making closer to the citizen. In response to political and fiscal decentralization, local governments have assumed greater responsibility and are held more accountable for service provision. A 1996 World Bank study details how innovations at the local level can be harnessed to drive the next stage of reform. The report illustrates decentralization efforts that brought improvements in administrative performance and the quality of public services; strengthened fiscal management; enhanced private-sector development; and increased participation in local and regional decisionmaking.[15]

While there is uniform eagerness to increase the involvement of civil society at the local level, decentralization is not a panacea. Studies that trace the effects of decentralization show mixed results. Decentralization has given rise to conflict in the allocation of responsibility and finance among the federal, state, and municipal governments. In some cases, municipalities shoulder increasing responsibilities for social development without an increase in transfers from the central government. In others, states have received sizable revenues for social services, but their efforts to deliver services have been rife with inefficiencies and financial disarray. At issue here is the ability of municipalities to build capacity as well as an independent tax base to support locally delivered social services. Inefficiencies and weaknesses encountered in the central government similarly appear in local-level public institutions with the same implications for quality, productivity, and effectiveness of social services. Finally, decentralization can "create problems of equity within countries, in the absence of central quality monitoring and financial and technical aid for poorer districts."[16]

In the same vein, there is a need for more empirical evidence to support the current enthusiasm for privatization. Advocates argue that the contracting-out of social services has introduced competition, providing users with choice as a tool to leverage quality and responsiveness. Yet evidence from ten years of privatized schools in Chile suggests little improvement in test scores.[17]

In spite of concerns about scale, capacity, quality control, and administration, decentralization and privatization have opened up opportunities for nongovernmental organizations (NGOs) to join local governments and the private sector as growing providers of social services. As national governments scale back to accommodate international rules of finance, local actors have increased their influence over the design and implementation of social policies. Furthermore, NGOs and community-based organizations are playing an expanded role in channeling the demands of civil society as they become more actively involved in articulating the political interests of the poor. Shifts in administrative patterns inevitably precipitate changes in political forces. As new actors are empowered in administrative terms, new political players are created.

Social policy research suggests that significant reforms in addressing poverty and inequality are possible only when issues of political economy are tackled. While traditional actors such as political parties, bureaucracies, and labor unions still play a crucial role in the fate of social reforms, their influence has waned with the rise of new political players.

The costs and benefits of adjustment have by no means been distributed equally among Latin America's social classes. Many of the social reforms proposed today pit working-class interests, traditionally represented by labor unions, against the interests of the poor. While labor unions have played a significant role in corporatist urban Latin America, their response to the reconstruction of a centralized state is uncertain. Financial constraints imposed by the global economy have further reduced the room for maneuver of labor unions and workers.

Social service sectors employ large numbers of people who are organized in strong unions and enjoy civil service rules that offer broad protections and benefits. In many cases, single unions bargain with national ministries charged with wide-ranging powers to make personnel decisions, creating a strong stake in the old system. Labor laws seriously compromise the possibility of restructuring the public sector, particularly social-sector agencies. Often, labor unions representing social sectors are affiliated with political parties, contributing further to a system of patronage.[18]

Latin America's political parties have similarly served as a vehicle for the expression of middle-class demands. Yet, democratic institutions, particularly political parties and legislative bodies, are increasingly perceived as corrupt, ineffective, unresponsive, and ultimately to be discredited. Research surrounding the administration of social policies and the political expression of social demands raises serious questions about the implications of social reform for the consolidation of democracy. The failure of traditional forms of representation to channel social demands, and the inability of the state to address the basic problems of poverty and inequality, erode citizen faith in the democratic process and threaten stability in the region.

Recent episodes of social unrest in Latin America, such as in Chiapas, Mexico, offer insight into the frustrations of the poor. Without basic standards of social equity, the fabric of Latin American society is beginning to unravel, manifest in political protest and violence, ultimately threatening the consolidation of democracy in the region.[19] Successful economic and social policies have created new stakeholders who serve as powerful advocates for reform, but absent among the participants in the policy process are the poor, whose voice remains diffuse and poorly organized. Opportunities for the formation of citizenship and creation of connections between vulnerable social groups and the state or its intermediaries remain limited.

In a drive to prove their ability, some governments have implemented social-welfare reforms in a very undemocratic fashion. The most successful social programs, such as social-emergency or investment funds, have been created outside of social ministries and are administered by small, highly skilled technical groups. Institutional bypassing undermines efforts to strengthen national governments and their democratic institutions. This is a particularly sensitive concern for a region with a legacy of authoritarian rule.

Social reforms, like economic reforms, are easier to implement when they are safeguarded against interference from partisan politics and political clientelism. However, these protections may increase efficiency at the cost of transparency, accountability, and ultimately, public participation. In order to be successful, social reforms require the support and involvement of a wide range of actors within the government, across ministries, and within various levels of state and local governments. More importantly, these government actors must, in turn, gain the support of the citizenry for policy proposals.

Political leaders must learn how to communicate clearly the policies they advocate and persuade the public of their value. The media, NGOs, and citizen-based organizations share in this responsibility to inform the public, mediate demands, shape reforms, and help make connections between the state and society. Only in this way will citizens, particularly the poor and the marginalized, become empowered to participate meaningfully in the policy process.

As federal governments in Latin America redefine their role, some analysts have expressed concern that the collapse of the overcommitted state threatens to result in the "under-engaged state."[20] Central governments have a critical role to play in providing coordination, technical support, and information as well as in ensuring equity.

The Structure of This Volume

Analysis of public-sector reform efforts in Latin America has primarily focused on strategies to redefine the role of the state in the economy. This volume examines social reform as a facet of larger public-sector reform efforts currently underway in the region. These changes will significantly alter the relationship between the state and its citizens; yet, there has been little serious consideration of the political, social, and economic consequences of the trends. Better understanding of these issues in governance is at the top of the research agenda for Latin America.

The chapters in this volume explore the issues that make the social question so difficult to solve, identifying lessons learned or "best practices" from research and analysis in comparative perspective. Examining the political economy of social reform, chapter contributors explore how the costs and benefits of economic adjustment and growth can be more equitably shared.

This book is organized into two parts. Part 1 offers a broad perspective of the challenges facing social reform in the region. Addressing deeply held beliefs and traditions concerning entitlements, the role of government, and its responsibilities to citizens, the contributors consider the dynamics that aid or impede the implementation of effective reform strategies.

Part 2 looks beyond general conclusions about the politics and administration of social policies in the region to explore more critically specific country studies. The cases of Chile, Venezuela, Argentina, and Mexico are by no means intended to provide a comprehensive review of welfare reform in Latin America, but rather were selected to highlight some of the major issues facing the region as it approaches the issues of poverty and inequality.

Part 1

In Chapter 2, Merilee Grindle outlines a social agenda that emerged by the mid-1990s in response to more than a decade of disturbing trends in poverty and inequality in Latin America. A broad consensus from a variety of perspectives developed around the need to reform social-sector policies, programs, and delivery systems. In this context, the capacity of traditional interest groups, such as public-sector bureaucracies and unions, to obstruct reform has been overstated, according to Grindle. The real challenge to reform, she argues, can be found in the inherent problems of second-generation institutional and administrative reforms. She concludes that organizational design and management that vex the agenda-setting and implementation phases of the policy process deserve much greater attention in the analysis of the political economy of social-sector reform.

In Chapter 3, Joan Nelson concurs with Grindle that there is remarkable convergence in the recognition that social-sector reform is imperative to the consolidation of economic adjustment and democratic opening in Latin America. Why then, she asks, has systematic reform in social sectors been so difficult? In contrast with macroeconomic reforms that were implemented by a small group of technical experts in a context of crisis, social reform entails the involvement of a number and variety of actors in a gradual, participatory approach. Progress has been most visible in pension system reform, Nelson argues, because the Chilean model offers a sound alternative around which debate in the rest of the region could be shaped. In contrast, the absence of a clear model has slowed efforts to introduce systemic reform in the health and education sectors.

A popular way to evade formidable opposition to institutional change and shifts in resources is to set up programs outside of mainline ministries. Safety net programs and social funds offer flexible, rapid, and highly visible means to deliver social services in a less politically charged environment. In chapter 4, Carol Graham considers the lessons learned from social safety net programs for reform of social-sector institutions over the longer term. The effectiveness of safety nets illuminates the need to target social policies to the truly disadvantaged rather than the politically powerful and vocal. Experience also demonstrates the importance of incorporating the participation of beneficiaries and local institutions to create new stakeholders, improve local capacity, and ultimately enhance the sustainability of poverty reduction efforts. Safety nets, Graham warns, must not divert attention from necessary public-sector reform, but should be implemented within a sound macroeconomic policy framework designed to generate growth over the long term.

Judith Tendler shares Graham's concern that resources and attention are directed toward social funds rather than the larger task of public-sector reform and institution building. In Chapter 5, Tendler raises questions about the current enthusiasm for social funds, suggesting that the international development community and national governments should consider other models for permanently organizing and providing services for poor communities. Tendler challenges assumptions about the superiority of the features of social funds—decentralization, partial privatization, and demand-driven approaches to service delivery. Research finds little evidence that social funds have achieved stated goals of creating sustainability and ownership, or of reducing unemployment and poverty. Remedies such as increased monitoring and supervision, transparency, training, and public information would drive social-fund programs into a more costly, supply-driven direction, leaving little to distinguish them from traditional government programs. The more successful social funds, such as the Chilean FOSIS, Tendler points out, are integrated into line ministries and receive the majority of their funds from national governments instead of international donors.

Part 2

In Chapter 6, Dagmar Raczynski details the case of Chile, which leads the way in human development in Latin America and is often referred to as a model for integrating a far-reaching and sophisticated social policy system with economic growth strategies. Raczynski follows the development and impact of social policies in Chile as they were shaped by seventeen years of military rule and then, beginning in 1990, by the Concertación governments of Presidents Patricio Aylwin and Eduardo Frei. While the neoliberal policies of the military regime left the country with macroeconomic stability, poverty levels were higher than they had been twenty years earlier, income distribution was more highly concentrated, and deteriorating public services were underfunded. Social policy under democratic rule was modified, but without altering the country's capitalist, free-market approach to economic development. The government initiated a process of negotiation and consensus building to build support for significant investment in sectoral policies based on community participation, targeting, decentralization, and public-private-NGO cooperation. While human development indicators and service delivery have improved, Racznyski offers additional strategies that could be employed to overcome an enduring imbalance between traditional administration—centralized, vertical, and sectorally segmented—and flexible, decentralized, participatory approaches that effectively respond to diverse local demands. What are the ultimate objectives of the model being constructed in Chile, she asks, referring to the unmet challenges of equity and social integration.

A close examination of housing programs in Chile by María Elena Ducci in Chapter 7 further illustrates some of the unintended consequences of a policy widely considered successful. Improving upon the programs of the military regime, Chile's democratic government increased the number of units available to low-income families, reaching the poorest segments of the population through careful targeting. Provision of basic water, sewage, and health services along with housing brought about a dramatic improvement in human development indicators. However, state policies have created ghettos, or cities within cities, to which the poor are confined. Located on poor-quality land in the outskirts of urban areas, housing projects have created highly concentrated enclaves of poverty which isolate residents from jobs and family networks in a rapidly deteriorating environment. Small-sized housing, excessive regulation, the allotment system, and a paternalistic approach have further eroded family and social relations, solidarity, and homegrown initiatives to improve settlements. Ducci attributes the spread of drugs, alcohol, and violence and an increase in women's mental-health problems to inadequate and poor-quality housing. In comparison with the experience of other Latin American countries, Ducci concludes that policies in Chile have not only prevented housing from becoming an asset in promoting economic stability and reducing the vulnerability of the poor, but have also destroyed social capital fundamental to development.

Drawing from the case of Mexico City, Susan Eckstein illustrates in Chapter 8 how different communities respond to political and economic change at the macro level. Comparing the experience of three urban neighborhoods in the aftermath of neoliberal economic reform, Eckstein finds that center-city residents were better placed to adapt to local informal-sector opportunities than dwellers in a planned housing project or in a squatter self-built shantytown. The center city had a long history of commercial networks on which to build, she explains. Residents also effectively organized to obtain vending and credit opportunities. Eckstein then explores the interplay of administrative and political reforms with informal local political dynamics in the three neighborhoods. Formal democratization, she concludes, is not perceived by the urban poor as providing more effective channels to express political demands or to access government resources and decisionmaking.

In Chapter 9, Juan Carlos Navarro details how political and administrative decentralization in Venezuela led to an unintended transformation of social policy. The introduction of direct elections of governor and mayors in 1989 established new political conditions that had a dramatic impact on the organization and management of public social services. In response to direct social demand, newly elected heads of state and municipal governments allocated a larger proportion of their budgets to social priorities, assuming a greater proportion of Venezuela's total social expenditure at the subnational level. Autonomous decisionmaking and a new system of incentives stimulated a wave of institutional innovation and significant sectoral reform. Furthermore, the priorities assigned to different social sectors and the substance of reforms introduced by different state and municipal government are very diverse, indicating a greater alignment of policies with the needs and characteristics of each jurisdiction. Still, Navarro concludes, sectoral reforms initiated from below exist in a vacuum and are not a part of national policy. Effective decentralization of social policies requires a strong and capable central government that can ensure equity and provide coordination, technical support, and information.

Neoliberal reform in Argentina, as in the rest of Latin America, has been accompanied by growth in inequality, unemployment, and the informal sector. In Chapter 10 Laura Golbert assesses the changes in social protections offered by labor market and pension system reforms introduced in Argentina over the past decade. Benefits that accompany new employment and retirement policies do not reach wide sectors of Argentina's population, while the circumstances of those workers who are affected by the reforms have not appreciably improved. Golbert finds a high degree of uncertainty as well as pronounced differences in access to and the quality of social services, exacerbating social heterogeneity. The politically and economically marginalized lack appropriate channels of expression and the organizational capacity to fight for inclusion. Protecting the most vulnerable requires consensus among all social actors—political parties, labor unions, the private sector, and NGOs—around priorities, resources, and appropriate tools, Golbert concludes.

Notes

1. Comisión Económica para América Latina y el Caribe (CEPAL), *1998 Social Panorama of Latin America* (Santiago: United Nations Publications, 1999), p. 18.
2. Inter-American Development Bank, *Facing Up to Inequality in Latin America* (Baltimore: Johns Hopkins University Press, 1998), pp. 11–15.
3. CEPAL, *1998 Social Panorama*, p. 77.
4. Economic Commission for Latin American and the Caribbean (ECLAC), *Social Panorama of Latin America 1995* (Santiago: United Nations Publications, 1995), p. 22.
5. CEPAL, *Preliminary Overview of the Latin American and Caribbean Economy, 1994* (Santiago: United Nations Publications, 1994).
6. CEPAL, *1998 Social Panorama*, p. 79.
7. Moisés Naím, "Latin America's Journey to the Market: From Macroeconomic Shocks to Institutional Therapy," Inter-American Dialogue Policy Brief no. 2.
8. Inter-American Development Bank, *Facing Up to Inequality*, p. 181.
9. Ricardo Hausmann, "Sustaining Reform: What Role for Social Policy," in Colin I. Bradford, Jr., ed., *Redefining the State in Latin America* (Paris: OECD, 1994), p. 178.
10. Joan Nelson, "The Politics of Social Service Reforms in Developing Nations" (paper prepared for discussion at the International Political Economy Workshop of Columbia University, 22 February 1996).
11. Naím, "Latin America's Journey" and Nelson, "The Politics of Social Service Reforms."
12. Dagmar Raczynski, "Strategies to Combat Poverty in Latin America," in D. Raczynski, ed., *Strategies to Combat Poverty in Latin America* (Washington, D.C.: Inter-American Development Bank, 1995), p. 15.
13. Nora Lustig, ed., *Coping with Austerity. Poverty and Inequality in Latin America* (Washington, D.C.: Brookings Institution, 1995), p. 35.
14. Shahid Javed Burki and Guillermo E. Perry, *Beyond the Washington Consensus: Institutions Matter* (Washington, D.C.: World Bank, 1998).
15. Tim Campbell, "Innovations and Risk Taking: The Engine of Reform in Local Government of LAC," Draft Report, (Washington, D.C.: World Bank) 3 September 1996.
16. Nelson, "Education and the Multilateral Development Banks," Summary of ODC Workshop, 21 ODC, Washington, D.C., 21 June 1995.
17. Ibid.
18. Nelson, "The Politics of Social Service Reforms" and Naím, "Latin America's Journey."

19. John Walton and David Seddon, *Free Markets and Food Riots: The Politics of Global Adjustment* (Cambridge, Mass.: Blackwell Publishers, 1994).

20. Jonathan Hartlyn, "Democracies in Contemporary South America: Convergences and Diversities," in Joseph S. Tulchin and Allison M. Garland, eds., *Argentina: The Challenges of Modernization,* (Wilmington, Del.: Scholarly Resources, 1998).

PART 1

SOCIAL POLICY REFORM
IN LATIN AMERICA

2

The Social Agenda and the Politics of Reform in Latin America

Merilee S. Grindle

It must be considered that there is nothing more difficult to carry out, nor more doubtful of success, nor more dangerous to handle, than to initiate a new order of things. For the reformer has enemies in all those who profit by the old order, and only lukewarm defenders in all those who would profit from the new order, this lukewarmness arising partly from the fear of their adversaries, who have the laws in their favor; and partly from the incredulity of mankind, who do not truly believe in anything new until they have had the experience of it.

—Niccolò Machiavelli
The Prince, 1513

Did Machiavelli say it all? Students of the political economy of policy reform might usefully reflect on this question. Indeed, much that has been written about the politics of reform reiterates the insights of the first modern analyst of power in the early sixteenth century.[1] Beginning with a premise that policy change threatens entrenched interests, today's analysts are quickly led to Machiavelli's conclusion that any initiatives to alter existing policies will be met with obstruction, protest, and resistance. Reformists, from this perspective, face daunting odds. Their task is defined as the management of opposition and constraints in order to achieve goals that, however much heralded as beneficial in the future, impose burdens on politically important sectors of society or on large numbers of citizens. To add to their problematic task, reformists can expect few friends in the short term, as their innovations must demonstrate results before they attract support. Notwithstanding growing evidence of the widespread adoption of significant policy changes, analysts continue to approach the politics of reform by exploring factors that are likely to inhibit it.[2]

Assessing the politics of social-sector reform is no exception. The political-economy research agenda is dominated by questions about who is likely to be hurt through reform, who is likely to resist, and why the process of change will be difficult and potentially destabilizing. Nor is there a paucity of hypotheses to put forward in answer to these questions: Public-sector unions and public-sector bureaucracies will resist reform because they will lose power, access, jobs, and control if proposed reforms in health, education, and pension systems are put in place; populist politicians will oppose change because new and more efficient systems will rob them of vitally important spoils to distribute and make it difficult to garner votes; organized labor will protest the loss of its protected status; opposition parties will welcome opportunities for lambasting government for its unresponsiveness, neoliberalism, and narrow technocratic approach to human need and suffering. And indeed, these hypotheses about sources of opposition to social-sector reform can be readily researched. In the 1990s, evidence accumulated about opposition to a wide variety of reforms in a wide variety of countries. In the future, the literature on why reform won't fly is likely to increase as reformers continue their efforts to introduce significant change.

Yet what is remarkable about current discussions of the social agenda in Latin America is the extent to which there is broad consensus that current systems are ineffective, inefficient, and unable to respond to the needs of largely poor populations. A very large number of citizens, politicians, bureaucrats, policy and management specialists, development professionals, and academics seem to be in strong agreement: Public-sector delivery of health care, education, and other welfare-enhancing programs is deplorable and must be changed. Many voices have contributed to an emerging consensus that "something must be done" to improve radically the design of social-sector policies and the delivery of social-sector programs.[3]

Increasingly, also, a consensus has emerged that the problems of Latin America's social services go far beyond the need to invest in the social sectors. The problems are deeply embedded in service delivery models and systems constructed in the past. Consequently, many agree that reform must attack the basic way in which social-sector services are conceptualized and delivered if they are to be improved.[4]

Equally interesting, reformism is very popular. The discussion of innovation in social-sector delivery systems has generated an array of new models and approaches that have been adopted in public, private, and not-for-profit service delivery programs and then widely publicized.[5] Stories about how things can be done better have appealed to both public and specialist audiences.[6] Reformist politicians and social-sector entrepreneurs report their successes in headlines, and their stories appear in the "boxes" of policy agenda setters such as the *World Development Report* and the *Human Development Report*. Some governments have promoted their reputations for having introduced successful reforms in education, health, community problemsolving, and decentralized service delivery.[7] Interestingly, the popularity of reformism in the social sectors stands in considerable contrast to the increasingly bitter reception of the neoliberal economic reforms that dominated the policy agenda in the 1980s and early 1990s.

So is Machiavelli wrong in the case of the social agenda in Latin America? Should we ignore his warning about how difficult change is in the face of so much enthusiasm for it? Opposition to social-sector reform is real and important. At the same time, however, such opposition is on the defensive and its capacity to obstruct change may be overstated. The consensus that something must be done about the social sectors in Latin America has generated an impetus toward reform that will be difficult to forestall. Defenders of the current system have difficulty convincing many that the status quo is preferable to change, and they find little public support for their claims that injustices will be done through reform. The problems attaching to reform of the social sectors in Latin America relate not only to antireformists, but also to the distinct goals and ideological orientations of the reformers and to the inherent difficulty of "second generation reforms." Analysts and reformists need to focus more fully on these latter problems, rather than restricting their concerns to the opposition of distributive coalitions, losers, or entrenched interests. Thus, Machiavelli may not have written the final word in terms of the politics of policy reform in the social sectors.

This chapter raises a series of questions about the politics of social-sector reform. Its intent is to be broad rather than specific and to suggest some hypotheses for future research, while stimulating discussion about how the nature of reform politics is conceptualized. In the following pages, I first explore the social agenda to define its character, look at the impetus behind a changing reform agenda in Latin America, and then turn to the development of consensus about the need to alter current social-sector policies, programs, and delivery systems. The second half of the chapter considers the problems that bedevil reform initiatives and finds that they are rooted in part in fairly traditional interest group politics but also in the agenda-setting and implementation phases of the policy process.

The Social Agenda: Evidence of Poverty and Inequality

The social agenda in Latin America in the mid-1990s was defined by renewed concern about poverty and inequality and their consequences for sustained economic growth and the consolidation of democratic political regimes. This agenda was built on disturbing evidence from the 1980s and 1990s.[8] According to analyses of income, poverty, and social indicators during this period:

- The extent of poverty grew in terms of the number of people affected.
- Urban poverty became more extensive.
- Income inequality increased.
- Investments in the social sectors stagnated or declined.

In a region of the world long noted for the persistence of both poverty and inequality despite considerable evidence of economic development, these trends have encouraged uncertainty about the viability of market-oriented development policies and prospects for the ability of newly democratic political regimes to be responsive to the needs of the majority of their populations.

Considerable evidence speaks to the increase in poverty in the region. According to a World Bank study, 26.5 percent of the population of Latin America and the Caribbean lived below the poverty line in 1980; in 1989, this percentage had risen to 31 percent.[9] At the end of the decade of the 1980s, almost 40 million more people in Latin America and the Caribbean lived in poverty than had done so at its outset. Table 2.1, which provides data on the percentage of households living below the poverty line for individual countries during the 1980s, indicates that poverty was most concentrated in Bolivia, Brazil, the Dominican Republic, Ecuador, El Salvador, Guatemala, Honduras, Mexico, Panama, and Peru; during the decade, its incidence increased most in Brazil, Honduras, Peru, and Venezuela. In addition to increases in the numbers and proportions living in poverty, the identity of those in poverty shifted in important ways. While rural people continued to suffer from a much greater likelihood of poverty, by the end of the decade of the 1980s the majority of the poor were found in the region's cities. Of the 131 million people below the poverty line, some 66 million lived in urban areas.[10]

Available evidence also indicates that increases in poverty were highly correlated with periods of economic recession and the widespread introduction of stabilization and structural-adjustment measures. According to the *Human Development Report*, the per capita GDP of the region was $1,965 (in 1987 U.S. dollars) in 1980, but had

Table 2.1   Poverty and Extreme Poverty in Latin America: The 1980s

Country	Year Survey	Poverty Headcount Index (Percent below $60 poverty line)	Extreme Poverty Headcount Index (Percent below $30 poverty line)
Argentina	1980	3.0	0.2
	1989	6.4	1.6
Bolivia[a]	1986	51.1	22.5
	1989	54.0	23.2
Brazil	1979	34.1	12.2
	1989	40.9	18.7
Chile	1989	10.0	1.5
Colombia[a]	1980	13.0	6.0
	1989	8.0	2.9
Costa Rica	1981	13.4	5.4
	1989	3.4	1.1
Dominican Republic	1989	24.1	4.0
Ecuador	1987	24.2	4.0
El Salvador[a]	1990	41.5	14.9
Guatemala	1986/87	66.4	36.6
	1989	70.4	42.1
Honduras[a]	1986	48.7	21.6
	1989	54.4	22.7
Mexico	1984	16.6	2.5
	1989	17.7	4.5
Panama	1979	27.9	8.4
	1989	31.8	13.2
Paraguay[b]	1983	13.1	3.2
	1990	7.6	0.6
Peru[c]	1983	31.1	3.3
	1990	40.5	10.1
Uruguay[a]	1981	6.2	1.1
	1989	5.3	0.7
Venezuela	1981	4.0	0.7
	1989	12.9	3.1

Region[d]		Percent	Number
	1980	26.5	91,400,000
Urban		16.8	38,200,000
Rural		45.1	53,200,000
	1989	31.0	130,800,000
Urban		22.0	66,000,000
Rural		53.4	64,800,000

Source: George Psacharopoulos et al., *Poverty and Income Distribution in Latin America* (World Bank, 1997), pp. 62, 71.
Notes: a. Urban; b. Asuncion; c. Lima; d. Including Caribbean

declined to $1,793 in 1990. With renewed growth in some countries in the 1990s, the figure increased to $1,931 in 1994, but was still below the 1980 standard (see Table 2.2 for individual country per capita GNP).[11] Income declines were most notable in Argentina, Bolivia,

Haiti, Nicaragua, Peru, and Venezuela, while incomes increased in Brazil, Chile, Costa Rica, and Colombia; such figures mask significant annual fluctuations, however, which were a notable aspect of the decade of the 1980s even in countries that demonstrated income growth overall.[12]

These data also mask disturbing evidence that income inequalities increased in Latin America during the 1980s and 1990s. Table 2.3 indicates that the national income share of the bottom 20 percent of the population was less in Argentina, Bolivia, Brazil, Guatemala, Honduras, Mexico, Panama, Peru, and Venezuela in the late 1980s than it had been at the outset of the decade, while in the same countries the share of income of the top 20 percent increased. In Brazil, Guatemala, Honduras, and Panama, the poorest 20 percent of the population shared less than 3 percent of total income at the end of the decade. According to a World Bank study of poverty and inequality in the region, changes in income inequalities closely mirrored the performance of national economies, with decreasing inequalities following upon growth and increases accompanying recession.[13] Nevertheless, degrees of inequality are not well correlated with overall levels of income, as relatively rich countries such as Brazil, Mexico, Colombia, and Chile had more unequal distributions of income than relatively poor countries such as Ecuador, Paraguay, and Peru.

While Latin American countries are noted for high levels of poverty and inequality relative to overall national income, the picture is less dire in terms of social indicators. Internationally, Latin American countries score high among developing countries in terms of income per capita and basic social indicators. In terms of the Human Development Index (HDI) produced annually by the United Nations Development Programme, the Latin America and Caribbean region lagged only behind industrial countries and East Asia (excluding China) in 1997. Table 4 indicates that life expectancy, infant mortality rate, access to safe water, adult literacy, and school enrollments are generally high and have improved considerably in the region in recent decades. Not shown in this table is the relatively good performance of Latin American countries in terms of narrowing gender gaps in education. Table 2.4 also indicates, however, that some countries have done significantly better than others in terms of social indicators, and the performance of Bolivia, Brazil, Ecuador, Guatemala, and Peru still lags considerably behind other countries.

Advances in social indicators have been achieved despite economic recession and declines in investment in the social sectors in many countries. Per capita social spending in the region declined in real terms by 10 percent from 1982 to 1986 and, while spending grew

Table 2.2   GNP Per Capita in Latin America 1980–1994 (1995 US$)

Country	1980	1981	1982	1983	1984	1985	1986	1987	1988	1989	1990	1991	1992	1993	1994
Argentina	2,890	2,790	2,610	2,810	3,230	3,050	3,420	3,540	3,880	2,950	3,290	3,940	6,130	7,270	8,060
Bolivia	550	600	550	490	460	440	490	610	730	720	700	710	740	760	770
Brazil	2,190	2,090	2,010	1,730	1,630	1,580	1,810	2,060	2,270	2,590	2,790	2,930	2,840	2,930	3,370
Chile	2,160	2,610	2,200	1,790	1,600	1,410	1,410	1,550	1,800	2,060	2,180	2,390	2,850	3,170	3,460
Colombia	1,270	1,360	1,350	1,300	1,290	1,230	1,220	1,240	1,300	1,250	1,230	1,210	1,300	1,390	1,620
Costa Rica	2,030	1,510	1,080	950	1,120	1,270	1,470	1,650	1,680	1,660	1,730	1,810	2,020	2,160	2,380
Dominican Republic	1,160	1,250	1,230	1,150	930	760	760	820	780	870	880	1,000	1,180	1,230	1,320
Ecuador	1,370	1,570	1,490	1,280	1,140	1,150	1,190	1,170	1,180	1,040	980	1,050	1,130	1,200	1,310
El Salvador	790	770	720	710	750	810	850	940	1,000	1,000	1,030	1,090	1,200	1,320	1,480
Guatemala	1,200	1,240	1,160	1,100	1,120	1,150	1,060	1,010	970	960	920	940	1,010	1,100	1,190
Honduras	700	760	710	690	730	790	830	940	980	870	700	600	600	600	580
Mexico	2,640	3,250	2,840	2,280	2,100	2,180	1,980	1,950	1,990	2,210	2,570	2,990	3,440	3,730	4,010
Nicaragua	690	770	780	780	790	760	800	920	830	430	360	280	340	340	330
Panama	1,880	2,030	2,060	2,050	1,800	2,290	2,500	2,560	2,110	1,990	2,040	2,220	2,450	2,600	2,670
Paraguay	1,440	1,740	1,600	1,570	1,420	1,130	980	970	1,080	1,090	1,120	1,250	1,390	1,510	1,570
Peru	1,040	1,290	1,320	1,040	1,010	900	1,030	1,210	1,050	970	1,000	1,310	1,350	1,490	1,890
Uruguay	2,930	3,630	3,190	2,040	1,680	1,500	1,760	2,200	2,500	2,600	2,640	2,910	3,310	3,960	4,650
Venezuela	4,340	4,880	4,810	4,540	4,040	3,750	3,660	3,410	3,440	2,610	2,650	2,700	2,890	2,840	2,760

Source: World Bank, *World Tables* (World Bank, 1995).

Table 2.3   Income Distribution in Latin America: The 1980s

Country	Year	% Share of Income of Bottom 20% of Population	% Share of Income of Top 20% of Population
Argentina (Buenos Aires)	1980	5.3	46.6
	1989	4.2	52.6
Bolivia (Urban)	1986	3.9	56.6
	1989	3.5	57.5
Brazil	1979	2.6	64.4
	1989	2.1	67.5
Chile	1989	3.7	62.9
Colombia (Urban)	1980	2.5	63.0
	1989	3.4	58.3
Costa Rica	1981	3.3	51.4
	1989	4.0	50.8
Dominican Republic	1989	4.2	55.6
Ecuador (Urban)	1987	5.4	50.5
El Salvador (Urban)	1990	4.5	50.0
Guatemala	1986/87	2.7	62.0
	1989	2.2	63.0
Honduras	1986	3.2	59.5
	1989	2.8	63.5
Mexico	1984	4.1	55.9
	1989	3.9	59.3
Panama	1979	3.9	53.4
	1989	2.0	59.8
Paraguay (Asuncion)	1983	4.9	50.9
	1990	5.9	46.1
Peru (Lima)	1983	6.2	49.7
	1990	5.7	50.4
Uruguay (Urban)	1981	4.9	49.3
	1989	5.4	48.3
Venezuela	1981	5.0	48.3
	1989	4.8	49.5

Source: George Psacharopoulos et al., *Poverty and Income Distribution in Latin America* (World Bank, 1997), pp. 137–185.

after that period, at the end of the decade it still remained 6 percent below what it had been in 1980 on a per capita basis.[14] On a country-by-country basis, government expenditures in education declined as a portion of GNP between 1980 and the 1990s in Bolivia, Chile, Costa Rica, the Dominican Republic, Ecuador, El Salvador, Guatemala, and Peru.[15] There is disturbing evidence that investment in education declined more in low-income countries in the region than in lower-middle-income countries, while it increased in upper-middle-income countries.[16] In health, the *Human Development Report* indicates that spending as a percentage of total government expenditures declined over the period in Brazil, Costa Rica, and El Salvador and increased in Argentina, Chile, the Dominican Republic, Panama, and Paraguay.

Table 2.4   Social Indicators in Latin America

Country	Life Expectancy 1994	Infant Mortality per 1,000 live births 1994	Access to Safe Water (%) 1994	Adult Literacy (%) 1994	Gross Enrollment Ratio 1994
Argentina	72.4	2.3	71.0	96.0	77.0
Bolivia	60.1	71.0	66.0	82.5	66.0
Brazil	66.4	45.0	73.0	82.7	72.0
Chile	75.1	13.0		95.0	72.0
Colombia	70.1	26.0	85.0	91.1	70.0
Costa Rica	76.6	13.0	96.0	94.7	68.0
Dominican Republic	70.0	38.0	65.0	81.5	68.0
Ecuador	69.3	47.0	68.0	89.6	72.0
El Salvador	69.3	41.0	69.0	70.9	55.0
Guatemala	65.6	45.0	64.0	55.7	46.0
Honduras	68.4	40.0	87.0	72.0	60.0
Mexico	72.0	32.0	83.0	89.2	66.0
Panama	73.2	24.0	93.0	90.5	70.0
Paraguay	68.8	42.0	42.0	91.9	62.0
Peru	67.4	52.0	72.0	88.3	81.0
Uruguay	72.6	19.0	75.0	97.1	75.0
Venezuela	72.1	22.0	79.0	91.0	68.0

Region	1960 1994	1960 1994	1960 1994	1960 1994	1960 1994
	53.3 69.0	107 38	60 75	72 86	59 70

Source: UNDP, Human Development Report (1997).

For the region as a whole, expenditures on public health amounted to only 1.28 percent of GDP in 1990, well below the standard in industrial economies, below the percentage expended in much more rapidly growing regions of the world such as East and South Asia, and considerably below percentages in sub-Saharan Africa, the Middle East, and Central Europe and Asia.[17]

In a period when total GNP was stagnant or declining in many countries and when government expenditures were being cut drastically, investment data for education and health hide the absolute decline in investment in a broad range of countries. Indeed, by the early 1990s, many ministries of health and education had made no substantial investments in expanded or improved facilities for a decade and were spending almost all of their budgets on personnel.[18] In practice, this often meant health posts and schools fallen into decay, no restocking of medicines or textbooks, no equipment replacement or repairs, and demoralized public-sector employees working two or even three jobs in order to make ends meet. In addition, a variety of perverse incentives for the performance of social-service professionals continued to undermine the quality and quantity of services available.[19] Access to social services continued to be unequally distributed between urban and rural areas, and those with sufficient economic resources continued to flee public services for the private markets in health and education. Investment in the social sector recovered somewhat by the mid-1990s, but the 1980s and early 1990s had left behind a striking social deficit from a "lost decade" (see Table 2.5).

Of course, the social agenda concerns not only income, health, and education. Investments in sewers and potable water and nutrition programs, employment creation, squatter settlement upgrading, land reform, rural roads, environmental protection and conservation, public security, judicial reform, and human-rights protections are also frequently on the list of "what needs to be done" in order to deal with problems of poverty and inequality that bedevil most countries in Latin America. In each of these areas, the numbers paint stark pictures of marginality and vulnerability to disease, abuse, and violence. In addition, pension system reform has achieved a highly visible place on public agendas. Increasing awareness of these quality-of-life issues has broadened the definition of poverty and inequality as social issues have increasingly appeared on the agenda for government action.

Reform Agendas as Moving Targets

In Latin America as elsewhere, public-policy reform agendas evolve and tend to expand over time. At times, policy agendas are altered through the process of putting theory into practice and reflecting on the lessons of practice for theory. Sometimes policy agendas can be explained by an ongoing search for "the solution" to the problematic nature of development, and their expansion can be explained in part by the elusiveness of such a solution. Policy reform agendas also evolve in response to opposition to current priorities in public policy. In still other cases, reform agendas result from a combination of distinct visions of the future that find a common "hook" in a shared set of issues. Current concern with the social agenda in Latin America can be traced back to all four of these dynamics.

The history of the 1980s in Latin America was dominated by the economic-policy agenda that has come be known as the "Washington consensus."[20] This history is largely one of an economic reform agenda that expanded as theory and practice interacted to bring deeper dimensions of a problem to light, emphasizing the difficulty of finding a solution to the problems of economic stability and growth in the region. Mexico's inability to service its foreign debt in

Table 2.5 Public Expenditures in Social Sectors in Latin America (Share of Total Government Expenditures), 1980–1995

Country	Social Security and Welfare		Housing and Community Development		Health		Education	
	1980	1992–1995	1980	1992–1995	1980	1992–1995	1980	1992–1995
Argentina	33.9	45.8	0.3	0.4	1.4	2.8	7.3	9.4
Bolivia		14.6	1.9	0.6	7.1	7.1	24.5	18.5
Brazil	34.6	29.5	0.2	0.5	7.4	5.2	3.8	3.6
Chile	36.6	33.3	4.7	5.6	6.5	12.2	14.7	13.9
Colombia		7.8		1.4		5.4		19.0
Costa Rica	10.3	17.7	2.3	0.4	29.7	20.5	23.7	22.9
Dominican Republic	7.5	4.2	6.1	14.9	9.7	11.3	13.9	9.6
Ecuador		1.9	0.6		11.2			18.4
El Salvador		7.3	1.6	7.8	8.4	8.3	17.9	13.2
Guatemala						10.6		19.0
Honduras								
Mexico	14.7	12.4	4.1	0.6	1.9	1.9	18.2	13.9
Panama	9.3	22.2	3.5	5.5	13.2	20.0	12.8	20.2
Paraguay	19.0	16.2	3.7	0.4	4.5	7.3	11.8	22.1
Peru			0.9		5.3		11.4	
Uruguay		60.6		0.2		5.8		6.5
Venezuela		70.0		2.1		7.6		16.0

Source: UNDP, Human Development Report (1997:186).

1982 precipitated a massive economic crisis that focused the attention of governments throughout the region on problems of debt and inflation. Initial policy priorities centered on stabilization as countries attempted to inhibit inflation, restore fiscal discipline, and restructure foreign debts. In many countries, this meant committing to often draconian conditionalities set by the International Monetary Fund and other international financial institutions. Those searching for the roots of macroeconomic instabilities found a ready culprit in states prone to overspending, overborrowing, and overvaluing.

Academics and policy reformers increasingly agreed that the region's economic crisis was structural and required a new approach to national strategies for development.[21] Thus, the early preoccupation with issues of macroeconomic stability soon expanded to incorporate a major emphasis on liberalization of trade and deregulation of domestic markets. As the agenda moved toward greater concern for structural adjustment, reducing intervention in the economy reinforced a preference among policymakers for a fiscally disciplined state, one that would necessarily reduce the extent to which the public sector contributed toward distortions, rent seeking, and inefficiency in the market.[22] As a result, a decade that began with draconian budget cutting to introduce fiscal discipline continued to evolve in policy terms toward additional measures whose purpose was to restructure the relationship between the economy and the state. Policy preferences for market-oriented development were generally accompanied by a strongly anti-statist ideology among theorists, a new generation of technocrats who had assumed positions of considerable influence and power during the economic crisis, and modernizing private-sector elites.[23]

Indeed, throughout Latin America, the problem of "too much state" in the region's development trajectory was a focus of both policymaking and academic interest.[24] In the dominant discourse among economists, populism and import-substitution had encouraged the creation of a large and interventionist state that was then available for capture by a variety of rent-seeking interests that used their power to demand benefits and protection from the state, leading inevitably to a bankrupt and corrupt public sector and a set of growth-stifling policies that could not be sustained.[25] The remedy for this situation followed logically from the analysis: Cut down on the size, responsibilities, and power of the state and replace its intervention with market-oriented liberalization and deregulation. By mid decade, privatization was high on the list of reforms considered necessary not only to solve a major fiscal crisis, but also to minimize the extent to which government could intervene in the market. The reform of the state, which excited increasing interest as the reformist decade evolved, was initially identified with downsizing, privatization, and minimalism.

By the late 1980s, however, the experience with stabilization and structural-adjustment measures had led some to begin questioning the theory behind anti-statism, and the issue of "too little state" began to influence the reform agenda. This concern was a reflection of increasing awareness among advocates of economic-policy reform that market economies require public sectors with the capacity to manage macroeconomic stability, to design and implement effective regulatory policies, to ensure basic physical and social infrastructure, to maintain public order and the rule of law, and to respond effectively to changing international and domestic conditions. By the early 1990s, references to the reform of the state began to mean more than downsizing and eliminating state intervention in response to fiscal deficits and inefficiencies; it began to be identified with the creation of institutions to buttress the market and to ensure an "enabling environment" for market-oriented development.[26] In the words of Tony Killick, anti-statism was proclaimed a "reaction too far" as international technocrats, policymakers, and academics increasingly referred to the importance of strong and effective states to the evolution of market economies.[27]

In this case, practice clearly interacted with theory to generate renewed interest in defining the role of the state in the process of development. At the level of practice, economic reformers became increasingly convinced of the importance of factors such as legal codes affecting private property and the sanctity of contracts—the experience of developing market economies in Russia and other post-communist states loomed large in this growing conviction—and the role of autonomous central banks to both microeconomic behavior and macroeconomic performance. Views were also shaped by scholarship on the development successes of several East Asian countries that had managed to sustain high rates of growth over long periods of time. Numerous studies probed the way in which the state had facilitated that growth.[28] Similarly, theoretical advances in the fields of institutional economics and economic history raised new questions about paths toward sustained development. The neoliberals who dominated academic and policy debates of the 1980s were challenged by the "new institutionalists" identified with Douglass North and others who argued that the evolution of rules of the game for economic transactions—institutions—was a normal and necessary concomitant of successful economic development.[29] The new institutionalism in economics provided an understanding of the role of

institutions in minimizing transaction costs in markets and the role
of institutional design in minimizing principal-agent problems in
complex organizations.

The need for capable states, not minimalist ones, increasingly
framed reformist discussions and initiatives.[30] By the early 1990s, the
state reform agenda included the kinds of institutional changes that
could contribute to effective macroeconomic management over the
long term—privatization, independent central banks, and autonomous tax boards, for example—and encourage economic growth—
legal reforms to protect private property and contracts, labor code
revisions, and foreign-investment regulatory frameworks, for example.[31] More generally, the decade of the economists, which began
with relatively simple notions of how to right the problems of macroeconomic instability during a deep crisis, developed through a period of greater awareness of the problems created by prior development strategies that relied on extensive state guidance and
intervention, and then further evolved toward a deeper concern with
the nature of the institutions that buttress government policy. The
result was an agenda that increased in scope over the course of a
decade and an expanding list of what needed to be done to ensure
growth.

The policy agenda also expanded because of political developments that increased opposition to economic reform. Beginning in
1978, when Ecuador held elections to end its most recent experience
of military rule, virtually all countries in the region returned to the
democratic fold. Elections increasingly defined the rhythm of public
life, and electoral competition loomed large in political and civic interaction. More broadly, the decade of the 1980s not only brought
economic-policy reform to the top of government agendas, it also
witnessed an extraordinary revitalization of civil society in the region,
much of its activity aimed at restoring and consolidating democratic
political systems. Unions, political parties, neighborhood and identity-
based movements, and church-affiliated organizations became actively
engaged in civic life and public issues; print and broadcast media became increasingly pluralistic and inquisitive at the same time, often
placing politicians and public officials under harsh lights.[32]

The reform agendas championed by democracy advocates were
broad, multifaceted, and at times conflictual. Among the issues that
brought them together, however, was a deep questioning of the right-
ness and efficacy of structural adjustment and an equally emphatic in-
sistence that the state had clear and unavoidable responsibilities to its
citizens—decent social services, protection from the worst effects of
unbridled capitalism, maintenance of law and order, and monitoring

of corruption in both public and private sectors.[33] Indeed, while economic reformers continued to be wary of states that assumed too much responsibility for the quality of life or social welfare, citizens and their organizations were pressing in the opposite direction, demanding that the state do more and do it better in responding to the social needs of the population. Their arguments resonated strongly in a region of the world in which the state had long laid claim to social-sector provisioning.[34]

Demands that the state respond to the social needs of its citizens, particularly during a time of economic recession and hardship brought about by both the crisis and the adjustment process, were not lost on the first generation of democratic politicians, even those who were firmly committed to the economic reform agenda. Initially, the response to such demands tended to come in the guise of short-term actions to meet strong political opposition to stabilization and structural adjustment. In this regard, social-adjustment funds meant to cushion the blow of economic reform through emergency public-works programs, community-based social assistance programs, and other activities were enthusiastically supported by reform politicians as political palliatives to economic policy change.[35] In time, however, the consequences of a decade or more of cutbacks in funding for the social-sector ministries, the persistent demands of citizen groups, unions, and opposition party organizations, as well as the burgeoning of interest in innovative solutions to social-sector delivery problems sparked by the experience of the social-adjustment funds and NGO and community-based experiments, encouraged greater attention to more basic questions of social-sector provisioning and the role of government in assuring such services.[36] Indeed, some politicians began to build their reputations on their capacity to be responsive to citizen demands and to encourage experimentation and innovation in the social sectors.[37]

As with the economic reform agenda, intellectual trends also supported greater attention to the importance of the social sectors to the particular ends of economic and political development. Economists began to reconsider the role of human capital in economic development, a theoretical orientation that had been important in the 1960s but that had received considerably less attention in the 1970s and 1980s. Again sparked by interest in how the East Asian success stories had come about, social scientists drew attention to the extent to which countries such as South Korea, Japan, and Singapore had invested in equity-enhancing economic reforms and welfare-enhancing social service provision, particularly education.[38] Increasing evidence of rapid globalization of trade, technology development, and labor markets added impetus to analyses of the determinants of successful national development within a rapidly changing international context. Human capital in terms of an educated and skilled workforce emerged on many computer screens as an important underpinning of the competitiveness of nations. According to an influential paper by Nancy Birdsall, David Ross, and Richard Sabot, investments in education in particular were strongly correlated with economic growth and poverty alleviation.[39]

Human capital was not a new concept in economics, of course, but the focus on macroeconomic management and the resolution of the crises and recessions of the 1980s had clearly placed concerns about investment in education and health on the back burner and, as we have seen, concerns about their cost on the front burner. The experiences of the social-adjustment funds, which many had regarded primarily as political palliatives to make the medicine of economic-policy reform easier to swallow, provided a set of interesting lessons about innovative solutions to social-sector provisioning for policymakers and analysts concerned about how to address human-capital deficits. They became interested in the extent to which these experiences, which involved a variety of new incentive systems, demand-based competition, and contracting-out mechanisms, could evolve into broader safety nets to address problems of poverty and vulnerability.

While economists were rediscovering human capital and its instrumental role in economic development, political scientists, sociologists, and anthropologists were discovering social capital. Following the publication in 1993 of Robert Putnam's influential book *Making Democracy Work: Civic Traditions in Modern Italy,* the notion of social capital as an underpinning of effective governance gained widespread attention. Social capital, referring to networks of trust and cooperation among citizens, was demonstrated to be the critical ingredient in explaining whether, in the case of Putnam's research, local governments were responsive, efficient, and effective in carrying out their responsibilities. Good government, according to many who were persuaded by the importance of social capital as a concept, originates in the quality of civil societies and in the demand for good government rather than its supply. Social capital could explain why health clinics functioned well and local schools actually delivered quality education, as well as why the post office could be trusted to deliver the mail and how the tax office was able to raise revenue for government programs. Although Putnam's Italian research suggested that whether communities did or did not have enough social capital for effective government was the work of centuries, it was not long before researchers and activists alike were engaged in discussions about the capacity to create social capital.[40]

The intellectual excitement surrounding the concept of social capital spilled over into intense interest among nongovernmental and community organizations in demonstrating the worth of their activities. Its implications as an essential ingredient in the successful development of localities and even nations dovetailed well with emergent civic activism during the 1990s and the claims for participation and mobilization of civil society put forth by democracy advocates. Again, the social-adjustment fund experience provided evidence about the capacity of NGOs and local communities to address basic social problems at local levels. Along with renewed intellectual interest in human capital, the social-capital argument pointed in the direction of increased attention to the quality of government services and their impact on the capacity of countries to develop both economically and democratically. In a similar trend, scholarship on emergent or renewed social movements and the mobilization of civil society around a set of concerns about political voice, democratic responsiveness, and local-level problem solving enhanced the importance of ways in which social-sector policies and programs affected the interaction of state and society.[41]

The agendas of economic and political reformers also coincided with renewed interest in decentralization of government. While there was little new in the arguments presented by economists for decentralizing the functions of government—allocative efficiency and principal–agent solutions had long been held up as benefits of decentralized and locally responsive government—an important change occurred in political assessments of the benefits of decentralization. During the 1960s and 1970s, Latin America had experienced many initiatives to decentralize governments to more regional and local levels, but most had foundered on the unwillingness of politicians, despite their rhetoric, to cede power to more local levels. In the 1990s, however, reformist politicians often emerged as proponents of decentralization, desiring perhaps to shift the fiscal burden of providing social and other services to other levels of government but also demonstrating the legitimacy and effectiveness of democratic government in responding to citizen needs and concerns.[42]

Thus, from a variety of perspectives—growth and human capital, democracy and its consolidation, electoral calculations, social capital and good government, decentralization and legitimacy—many came to identify the social sectors as necessary ingredients for achieving their goals. Their objectives differed, but the social agenda was the hook that brought them together as advocates of change. The policy reform agenda of the 1980s and 1990s was indeed a moving target, but, by the mid-1990s, speaking of "the social agenda" was seen as a recognition of the importance of poverty alleviation, investment in the social sectors, and concern about inequality. The reformist consensus spanned a range of concerns, from those of economists thinking primarily about the underpinnings of growth, to those of politicians worrying about legitimacy as well as elections, to those of social activists demanding responsiveness to deprivation, injustice, and inequality. And, although the poor in Latin America continued to lack a voice in policy debates, these concerns provided a surrogate, advocating the need to address poverty, inequality, and social-welfare issues.[43]

Sources of Opposition

Reformers, confident that the arguments in favor of change were indisputable, nevertheless often anticipated opposition, particularly from those who expected—usually with good reason—loss of power, jobs, and influence. In fact, in recent years, large and powerful teachers' unions stymied or slowed reform initiatives in Mexico, Bolivia, Colombia, Chile, the Dominican Republic, Panama, and Uruguay. In 1997, health workers in Peru called for a national strike in the country's hospitals to protest a health reform initiative. Similarly, doctors went on strike against initiatives to reform the health sector in Venezuela. Teachers and other education workers went on strike and repeatedly protested against policy change in Peru. In Argentina, a major strike of educators was a direct response to reform plans. Powerful unions representing a multitude of sectors protested, marched, and derided privatization and other kinds of reforms to national pension schemes in Uruguay, Brazil, Peru, Ecuador, Argentina, Mexico, Costa Rica, and elsewhere. In many cases, reformers were astute in negotiating away some of the sources of discontent. In other cases, reform initiatives were shelved for the time being, until political change offered additional opportunities for pushing forward with the reform agenda. Opposition to change has been a clear constraint that reformists have had to grapple with.

Public-sector unions, particularly those representing teachers and health workers, have been those most frequently identified for their opposition to reform. These unions are usually the largest and among the most well organized among worker interests in all of Latin America; indeed, ministries of education and health are the largest employers in many countries. Public-sector unions have not welcomed the content of most reform schemes—decentralization, merit examination, productivity-based pay and promotion schemes, accountability to community "stakeholders," and new curricula and job definitions. For them, the reforms have meant constraints on their activities and greater job uncertainty.

Much of the union opposition can be linked to concerns about the impact of change on the power of union leaders and the rent-seeking opportunities that the size and influence of the unions over weak social-sector ministries had encouraged. In fact, in a number of countries the unions had torn personnel management away from ministry control, had used control over jobs to entrench their power and collect rents, and had developed strong ties to political parties based on their ability to deliver votes. Indeed, in the discourse on re- form, union resistance based on a preference for centralization, pa- tronage, and immunity to performance or community demands has been the reaction most frequently decried by the reformers. In many ways, the public-sector unions have been targeted as the enemy of progress and modernization in the social sectors and have been crit- icized for their cynical preference for a broken status quo over the promise of change.[44]

In response to criticism, the unions have protested against injus- tice and the authoritarianism of technocratic elites in capital cities.[45] They have protested against what they see as the antinationalist in- terference of international financial institutions that have been vocal proponents of reform. They have claimed that the spread of market- oriented reforms to the social sectors is inappropriate and unjust. They have charged that the hidden agenda of reformist initiatives is simply to save money, to hit the popular classes yet again with mar- ket-driven systems that disadvantage the poor, and to expose both private and public-sector workers to even greater insecurity and risk. Indeed, against a backdrop of a decade and a half of government policies that spurred unemployment and recession, based on the im- position of austerity, and that were planned and executed by remote and often faceless technocrats in closed executive bureaucracies, public-sector workers and their leaders have had little reason to trust that the proposed reformist schemes would be beneficial to them.

Within the discourse about reform, those who speak of the effi- ciency of new systems and the longer-term professionalization of social-service delivery have not been particularly persuasive to those who are most aware of increasing inequalities and increasing vulner- ability among the region's poor and lower-middle classes. While re- formers have been excited by the prospect of innovative new solu- tions to problems of delivering high-quality social services that can be generated by NGOs and the private sector, those facing the prospect of immediate losses have been much less likely to trust in the capacity of the diverse and unorganized responses of the market to address their short and longer-term concerns. In this regard, the importance of credibility and trust is the other side of the opposition of those with much to lose from social-sector reform.

At the same time, the opposition of those who have much to lose through reform has elicited very little public support. With the exception of a few countries—Costa Rica principal among them—claims of teachers' unions and health care workers have not been widely respected, their images often soiled by their lack of professionalism, the bossism of the unions, and the widespread public dismay at the dismal state of public services. Antireformers have been widely castigated in the press and in public opinion for seeking to protect their privileged and unresponsive positions and have been widely criticized for not delivering the services for which they claim to be responsible. When teachers went on strike in Argentina in 1997, few citizens did much more than criticize them for the poor performance of local schools; when doctors went on strike in Venezuela in 1997, they were met with public disdain and hostility. Public opinion in Bolivia consistently favored an education reform that was opposed by the teachers' union.[46] Moreover, in many countries, decades of bossism, the competing claims of independent unions or the divisive nature of internal reformist initiatives, the expansion of the informal sector, and a decade or more of recession have weakened the power of the union sector generally.[47]

The public-sector unions have been important players in the politics of the reform process, but both reformists and analysts may have overstated their strength. Indeed, many reform initiatives have been adopted despite opposition. The resulting changes have been shaped and reshaped through intense negotiation with workers' unions, but the significance of the reforms has not been fully undermined through this process.[48] In Peru, when unions of education workers went on strike in May, August, and September 1994, and again in July and October 1997, to express discontent with national education reform policies, they actually raised public awareness of the issues and stimulated a national dialogue to promote reform of the system. In regional education reforms in Venezuela, the majority of teachers supported reform, in opposition to their union leadership.[49] In Brazil, health care workers initiated significant reform in the state of Ceará.[50]

Initiatives to introduce pension reforms have been a special case of opposition because they have engaged the generalized hostility of all organized workers. Organized workers in both the public and private sectors, of course, have been the principal beneficiaries of state-sponsored social security systems. While reformists have focused on the evidence that current systems are bankrupt and unsustainable, workers have been far more concerned about their vulnerability in the future if major changes are introduced, particularly privatization of pension schemes. Like their position vis-à-vis the public-sector workers in the case of education and health reform, reformers face a credibility problem when they argue that new systems will provide better social protection in the future because they are more sustainable. There is little experience in Latin America to substantiate this claim, and financial-market volatility continues to feed fears that some of the new systems could be easily undermined or mismanaged. Moreover, new systems that emphasize employee contributions are suspect because of concern that they will marginalize the poorest workers even more than is already the case.[51] In contrast to the gap between public opinion and public-sector union concerns about health and education reforms, the opposition of workers to social security reform has been more broadly supported, precisely because of the lack of trust in government's ability or desire to continue to protect working people.

The credibility problem is particularly severe when reform proposals, such as those to privatize social-security systems or to impose fee-for-service regimes in the health sector or community control in the education sector, confront deeply ingrained value systems. Thus, some kinds of reforms not only raise the specter of vulnerability and loss of protection, they also challenge deeply held beliefs and traditions in Latin America about the role of government and its responsibilities to citizens. While antireformists have spoken loudly about the need for government to guarantee services and protection to citizens, particularly poor ones, these claims have at times been dismissed by reformers as self-serving or populist. In place of populism and paternalism, a number of reform proposals have been explicitly designed to capture the virtues of the marketplace. Of course, many social-protection institutions have origins in the populist and paternalist regimes of the past, but they also have roots in centuries old Catholic social teachings that charge government with providing order, protection, and balance among functional groups in society. Belief systems about the rights and obligations of citizens and states that suffered under the market-oriented reforms of the 1980s and 1990s appear to be reasserting themselves in regard to some of the solutions offered by social-sector reformers. Unfortunately, although those who advocated structural economic reforms frequently acknowledged domestic and foreign private-sector concerns about predictability and durability through institutional innovations designed to demonstrate "credible commitment," social-sector reformers have tended to ignore or dismiss the concerns of organized workers and popular sectors, the "enemies of reform."[52]

Despite obvious and public tension between social-sector reformers and those organizations representing popular-sector workers, the reformers have been quite successful in negotiating agreements and finding space for the introduction of new policy initiatives. Indeed, the number of countries that have successfully introduced fundamental change in the operation of national education and health systems and that have moved aggressively on social security reform is impressive.[53] This is not to deny the importance of resistance to the politics of social-agenda reform, but only to suggest that the tide of reformism has been strong, the opposition has been on the defensive, and the room for maneuver has been greater than our expectations about the dynamics of change have led us to expect.

Sources of Dissensus

Subtle dangers exist in the diverse concerns of the reformers and in the practicalities of moving from reform intentions to reform realities. The particular concerns of economic reformers, reformist politicians, democracy advocates, citizens, and public-sector managers and planners signal distinct priorities and emphases. In embarking upon initiatives to respond to the social agenda, these goals and emphases may play an important role in determining what problems are addressed and how they are addressed.

The Economists

Economic reformers are important members of the new coalition for social-sector reform. Among them are those whose interest derives from renewed appreciation of the role of human capital in the economic destinies of countries. They are eager to see new investment, particularly in education, and structural changes that affect how social services are delivered. A large portion of the economists who advocate social-sector reform, however, have continued to have an overriding concern for the efficiency of social investments and for ways in which change can reduce the fiscal burden of social provisioning. They have, for example, demonstrated that inefficiency, not the level of investment, has been a principal cause of the poor performance of social services in the region.[54] Pension reform has been a high-priority social-sector reform for this group. While a number of innovative solutions to costly pay-as-you-go, state-run pension systems have emerged in the past few years, pension reform has been primarily advocated as a means to address the fiscal crisis of the state rather than as a way to increase the breadth or depth of social safety net protection.[55] Indeed, when the design of pension reform schemes has been left largely in the hands of macroeconomists in finance ministries, the cost of the schemes rather than their social objectives has been the principal concern. In health and education, those concerned with the fiscal and structural limitations of public-sector provisioning have generated proposals for privatization and competition.

Similarly, economic reformers' interest in decentralization has generally been to shift the fiscal burdens for social-sector provisioning downward to more local levels of government.[56] Most proposals for decentralizing social-service delivery systems and devolving responsibilities for the planning and implementation of such services have gone hand in hand with proposals for greater fiscal autonomy of regional and municipal government. Thus, economic reformers expect decentralization to increase efficiency by enhancing fiscal discipline, limiting the role of the (centralized) state, lowering transaction costs in revenue generation, and solving a series of principal–agent problems.

Efficiency is a laudable and important goal. Current evidence suggests the importance of bringing more of it to what are clearly costly and inefficient systems that threaten the fiscal health of governments. But the primacy of efficiency and the management of the fiscal deficit are not necessarily the objectives first sought by reformist politicians, democracy advocates, citizens, or public managers.

The Politicians

Reformist politicians—modernizing elites in the region's older political parties, leaders of new reform-oriented parties, and many elected leaders of local and regional governments that have been ceded greater autonomy and responsibilities in recent years—can be forgiven for being more concerned with effectiveness than with efficiency and the fiscal deficit. Both ideological commitment and electoral calculations have encouraged them to focus on the capacity to deliver the goods in terms of the increased quality and access of services for their constituents. They have been keenly aware of electoral calendars and of the fragility of political careers in more open, participatory, and media-rich democratic settings. Many have become convinced that the old politics of patronage and clientelism cannot ensure electoral success, and they have sought to project modern, "let's get down to work" images in order to stand in contrast to the "dinosaurs," the old party bosses who projected personalism and populist messages but, in a postcrisis world, are no longer able to deliver on their promises.[57] Reformist politicians have become simultaneously aware of the increased power of the media to exploit failure or evidence of corruption and of the increased demands on politicians through civic organizations that have become increasingly autonomous from party politics.

The capacity to deliver—not to solve the fiscal deficit or to be known as a beneficent godfather—has been the implicit promise reformist politicians have made, and it is the legacy by which they believe they will be judged in the future. In part, this concern with effectiveness has led such politicians to support innovation at community and municipal levels among local organizations and nongovernmental organizations and even the private sector, and to be open to rethinking how social services are delivered. Clearly committed to reform, they have been looking for systems and programs that will help them deliver on their electoral promises for more and better services. They are not opposed to encouraging efficiency in this quest, but they will not necessarily agree with the priorities of the economic reformers on the central purpose of change.

The Democrats

Democracy advocates agree with the reformist politicians on the need for effectiveness in social-service provisioning, but they have tended to focus more on the need for responsiveness and participation in these services. Some of these democratic reformers have been deeply engaged in battles within the region's political parties to ensure that the centralizing, boss-driven practices of the past give way to greater awareness of public opinion, greater understanding of public policy and public management, and more attention to popular needs. More frequently, however, democracy advocates have worked with and through local civic organizations whose principal concerns have been to make more effective demands on government and to hold public officials accountable for their actions and inactions, and to bring a much higher degree of local control to service provision. As activists, then, they have sought greater control over government resources, greater participation in decisionmaking, greater autonomy from government, and greater transparency in the operations of government.[58] Many have spent more than a decade denouncing the social costs of adjustment and mobilizing demands for greater responsiveness to citizens. Wary of the old politics of patronage and co-optation, they are equally tired of the centralized imposition of economic reform packages, the consequences of which they deplore and blame on domestic and international technocratic elites who are, they believe, deeply antidemocratic. Economic reformers concerned about the fiscal deficit have not escaped their criticism, nor have reformist politicians, reflecting decades of suspicion about—and, in many cases, experience with—being used and abused by political elites, reformist and otherwise.

The Citizens

As part of the social-agenda consensus, citizens have placed a high priority on social protection and assurance that their needs for such protection will be met into the future. Among the most concerned are those who traditionally have had access to such services, urban workers and the popular sectors more generally. While they may become committed over time to innovative and more efficient and effective ways of delivering social services, they have wanted assurance that government will continue to assume responsibility for providing access to social services, that these services will not be priced beyond the reach of the poor, and that if private-sector providers are involved there will be means of ensuring that they continue to provide accessible and affordable services into the future. Of course, there is little public belief that the old systems are providing useful services, but many citizens have remained skeptical of the promises for improvement, a reflection of the credibility problem referred to earlier in this chapter. Commitment, durability, access, cost—these have been the priorities of large numbers of citizens, and they are priorities that have at times put them at odds with reformers primarily concerned about the cost of social services or with those interested in experimenting with alternative delivery systems involving community groups, NGOs, and the private sector.

The Managers and Planners

Those who champion change from within government are also relevant to the politics of social-sector reform. These reformers, generally found within social-sector ministries and agencies but also within planning ministries and presidential offices, have shared concerns about efficiency, effectiveness, and responsiveness with other reform groups. Their interest in seeing these characteristics embodied in newly designed systems, however, has been focused on the design and delivery of particular social services. Their priorities have been attached to changes in health, or education, or social security, or employment creation, or public sanitation, or urban housing, or some other subsector within the broader agenda. This focus of priorities has been positive for the social agenda because it emphasizes the multidimensionality of human development. It becomes problematic, however, to the extent that it sets up competing claims for resources and action. Tensions about the trade-offs of investing in health or education have been the most obvious way in which such competing claims have created fissures in the social-agenda consensus. Given intense new awareness about the limits of public resources and the need to make important choices about investment priorities, the politics of the budgetary game within the social sectors as well as between the social sectors and other investment categories suggest again that serious differences underlie the broad commitment to the social agenda.

Sources of Frustration

In the future, the politics of sorting out priorities will interact with the more frequently noted kind of politics marked by opposition to change. In addition, social-sector reforms will be deeply affected by the problems inherent in instrumenting second-generation reforms.[59] Indeed, in an insightful analysis of sources of institutional malfunction, Carol Graham and Moisés Naím indicate that public-goods providers, such as those delivering social services, are likely to suffer from a plethora of problems. Among these are the consequences of "chronic congestion" of extensive demand and insufficient resources; low quality in human-resource, regulatory, and technological inputs; overcommitment of resources for personnel reflected in undercommitment for operational needs; capture by interested groups; corruption; politicized personnel management, characterized by high turnover of staff and frequent changes in policy; poorly articulated missions; insufficient competition; and too much interference by government in the on-going delivery of services.[60] These are daunting problems, individually and collectively, and ones that reformers— whether primarily interested in efficiency, effectiveness, responsiveness, or dependability—cannot avoid.

The characteristics of social-sector tasks make reforms particularly difficult to design and implement. They are by definition administratively intense and require ongoing monitoring, supervision, and adjustment, even when contracted out to NGOs or the private sector. The infrastructure of the complex organizations that are required to provide complex services is difficult to construct and subject to a multitude of challenges on a day-to-day basis. Services can eventually be well delivered and appreciated by clients, but they are rarely perfectly provided nor is high-quality service easily sustained over time. These characteristics have led organization specialists in advanced industrial countries to stress the importance of the "learning organization" and to focus on ways in which self-monitoring and quality control can be incorporated into service delivery design so that sustainability can be more easily achieved.[61]

In this sense, organization specialists have identified the enemy to be creeping bureaucratization, tendencies toward insensitivity to client needs and demands, loss of focus on quality, and the potential for decreased professionalism over time. This is quite different from the focus on antireformists as the enemy in much of the discussion of Latin America's social services. The distinction is related to the difference between the issues that plague policymaking and those that bedevil implementation, but analysts tend to focus much more attention on the former and assume that the latter problems will take care of themselves in time. This assumption is probably false.

The challenge is to create administrative systems that work reasonably well; design human-resource systems that incorporate appropriate incentives for worker productivity and mechanisms that call forth norms of commitment, service, professionalism, and teamwork; invent organizational structures that are routinized yet flexible enough to respond to a variety of circumstances; and introduce mechanisms that promote positive community or client participation and orientation.

These are not factors that can be put in place easily nor can it be assumed that once designed, such systems, norms, structures, and mechanisms will function well or be sustained without constant attention. Numerous organizations, actors, and levels of government are generally involved in any effort to introduce change in the social sectors. In their popular decentralized versions, such changes draw deeply on technical and administrative skills of local governments that have rarely had the capacity to manage even very limited responsibilities. The kinds of changes required generally emerge piecemeal and over considerable time, as learn-by-doing and iterative approaches are often needed to assess alternative implementation practices. Moreover, the benefits of changes in organizational design, human-resource training and management, and altered rules of the game in these sectors do not usually produce clear results in the short term.

Even when the private sector, community organizations, or NGOs are charged with delivering social services, implementation problems

are inevitable. While community organizations and NGOs in particular benefit from the greater flexibility that small scale allows them,
they must not only face difficult problems of financial sustainability,
they are also prey to organizational choices that lead to inefficiency,
low-quality service, and tensions resulting from community involvement. Equally, private-sector services face widespread problems of
quality control, management of extensive demand, and administrative burdens attaching to the delivery of complex services. The discipline of the market and the vigilance of beneficiaries may make
such problems more readily detectable but no less avoidable. Problems of organizational design and human-resource management are,
of course, most intense in the public sector, in part because of scale,
but also because governments usually cannot design organizations
and systems from scratch nor do they often have the luxury of being
able to select their clients. Most reforms in public-sector ministries
must begin with the realities of demoralized and poorly incentivized
workers and large, badly organized, politically weak, and heavily bu-
reaucratized organizations.[62]

Efforts to overcome such problems have, in fact, encouraged extraordinary innovation among those committed to the provision of
more and better services in the social sectors. A wide variety of models for resolving organizational and human-resource challenges have
been developed, and the current period is notable for the interest in
and communication about such innovations.[63] Those currently being
experimented with and communicated about are striking for their diversity and originality.[64] A new teacher incentive program in Colombia; education vouchers in Chile, Colombia, and Guatemala; greater
school autonomy in El Salvador, Nicaragua, and Minas Gerais in
Brazil; bilingual education in Bolivia; enhanced consumer choice in
health in Chile and Colombia; decentralized health provision in
Colombia, Mexico, and Venezuela; privatization linked to a new pension scheme in Bolivia—these are among the innovations that are offering lessons about change in the region.

From another perspective, those searching for a "solution" to the
ongoing problems of delivering good-quality services efficiently, effectively, responsively, and dependably may find the array of possibilities daunting. Multiple models exist, and, as yet, there is little experience or research to suggest which among them is appropriate to
which kinds of contexts. The models themselves offer a rich menu of
innovative ideas, but reformers do not have a template that corre-
sponds to the model of stabilization or structural adjustment
adopted by macroeconomic reformers; they are thus deprived of clear

models about what to do about what kinds of problems.[65] Indeed, there is no single solution to the problem of providing high-quality and dependable social-sector services, but rather a need for ongoing learning, innovation, and experimentation. Particularly for the public sector, this is a difficult proposition to accept; experimentation can lead to loss of momentum, credibility, and support if it does not deliver clear improvements and contribute to stable expectations about future services. For NGOs and private-sector providers, the risks of innovation include the possibility of financial unsustainability, forcing social demands back onto already overextended public sectors.

The political economy of social-sector reform may have focused far too little on the challenge of embedding reform firmly within the norms, systems, and structures of the organizations that are assigned responsibilities for carrying out service delivery over the long term. The inherent problems of second-generation reforms are not insurmountable, but they are inherently threatening to the aims of reformers. They appear not only as issues of design and incentives, but also as bureaucratic resistance, sabotage, and implementation leakage, and as the failure to mobilize and sustain political and bureaucratic support for change. As such, these problems deserve greater attention in the analysis of the political economy of reform in the social sectors.

Conclusion

In an analysis of the politics of economic reform in Venezuela under the administration of Carlos Andrés Pérez (1989–1993), Moisés Naím refers to the problem of paper tigers and minotaurs.

> From the perspective of policymakers, introducing large-scale societal changes through deliberate policy reforms is akin to walking through a constantly shifting maze filled with menacing beasts. When confronted, some of these monsters turn out to be harmless—paper tigers—while others are deadly minotaurs. Whereas paper tigers are often only a distraction, minotaurs force governments to look for ways to avoid the risky and costly confrontations with them or even to exit the policy reform maze altogether.[66]

The problem, as Naím explains, is that reformers have few clues about how to identify whether the beast is a paper tiger or a minotaur.[67]

Paper tigers and minotaurs, as they emerge in the politics of economic reform, may not find perfect parallels in social-sector reform.

In this arena, anti-reformers—where analysts and reformers alike anticipate minotaurs—cannot be dismissed as paper tigers. Nevertheless, although the opposition of those who are likely to lose through change continues to be real and threatening, it may be a less threatening beast than analysts and reformers have anticipated. At the same time, and to extend the analogy, the fiercest beasts may be those that only purr softly in the background, hiding extensive capacity to slow or disfigure reform. The more-threatening minotaurs, then, may be dissensus within the reform coalition and the problematic nature of second-generation reforms.

Eventually, the problems created by dissensus among reformers and the difficulties of organizational design and human-resource management may be recognized as very real minotaurs. If, as suggested above, the tide of reform is very strong and the opposition weaker and more vulnerable than anticipated, the much less dramatic reality of agreeing upon objectives and designing systems that work well over extended periods of time will no doubt become the subject of greater attention, analysis, and criticism. Currently, however, analysts continue to focus on the enemy of antireformism while reformers focus their energy on getting something up and running. As a consequence, neither the academics nor the practitioners have given sufficient attention to the need for solutions that are sensitive to the ongoing need for learning and change, for monitoring and adjustment, and for credibility and dependability.

This suggests that expertise in organizational design and management is needed as well as attention to organizational and bureaucratic politics. While Machiavelli was not wrong to alert reformers to the destructive potential of antireformers and the lukewarm character of enthusiasm for change, he may have signaled the easy problems to deal with when considering the social sectors. The more powerful enemy of reform in the longer term may be the inability to deliver on the promises of the reformers. We can well ask whether he, or we, are asking the right questions about the politics of reform.

Notes

1. Max Lerner, Introduction to Niccoló Machiavelli, *The Prince and the Discourses* (New York: The Modern Library, 1950), p. xxvi.

2. For examples, see Robert Holt and Terry Roe, "The Political Economy of Reform: Egypt in the 1980s," in Robert H. Bates and Anne O. Krueger, eds., *Political and Economic Interactions in Economic Policy Reform* (Cambridge, Mass.: Basil Blackwell, 1993); Robert Bates and Paul Collier, "The Politics and Economics of Policy Reform in Zambia," op. cit.; Stephan

Haggard and Robert R. Kaufman, eds., *The Politics of Economic Adjustment* (Princeton, N.J.: Princeton University Press, 1992); Joan Nelson, ed., *Economic Crisis and Policy Choice: The Politics of Adjustment in the Third World* (Princeton, N.J.: Princeton University Press, 1990); The World Bank, *World Development Report* (New York: Oxford University Press, 1997), chap. 9; and Dani Rodrik, "Understanding Economic Policy Reform," *Journal of Economic Literature* 34, no. 1 (1996). For an overview of the literature on the political economy of reform, see Barbara Geddes, "The Politics of Economic Liberalization," *Latin American Research Review* 30, no. 2 (1995) and Mariano Tommasi and Andrés Velasco, "Where Are We in the Political Economy of Reform?," *Policy Reform*, vol. 1 (1996).

3. See Inter-American Development Bank (IDB hereafter), *Economic and Social Progress in Latin America* (Washington, D.C.: Johns Hopkins University Press, 1996), for a description of the range of problems and inefficiencies affecting the social sectors in Latin America. See also IDB/United Nations Development Programme (UNDP hereafter), *Social Reform and Poverty: Toward a Comprehensive Agenda for Development* (Washington, D.C. and New York: IDB/UNDP, 1993), for a description of the social agenda.

4. This argument is strongly presented in IDB, *Economic and Social Progress*.

5. Many of these models can be traced to social-adjustment programs and to NGO and community-level efforts to provide services that the state increasingly failed to provide during the economic crisis of the 1980s.

6. The extensive notice taken of a "success story" in the delivery of public health services in northeast Brazil, analyzed by Judith Tendler, *Good Government in the Tropics* (Baltimore: Johns Hopkins University Press, 1997), is a case in point.

7. Genero Arriagada and Carol Graham, "Chile: Sustaining Adjustment During Democratic Transition," in Stephan Haggard and Steven B. Webb, eds., *Voting for Reform: Democracy, Political Liberalization, and Economic Adjustment* (New York: Oxford University Press/World Bank, 1994), report on the widely studied experience of targeting social-welfare expenditures and services in Chile. Bolivia and Costa Rica have likewise attracted international attention for their social-adjustment programs (see Carol Graham, "The Politics of Protecting the Poor During Adjustment: Bolivia's Emergency Social Fund," *World Development* 20, no. 9 [1992], and Joan Nelson, "Poverty, Equity, and the Politics of Adjustment," in Stephan Haggard and Robert R. Kaufman, eds., *The Politics of Economic Adjustment* [Princeton, N.J.: Princeton University Press, 1992]).

8. Good studies of poverty and inequality in Latin America and the Caribbean are found in Nora Lustig, ed., *Coping with Austerity: Poverty and Inequality in Latin America* (Washington, D.C.: Brookings Institution, 1995); George Psacharopoulos, Samuel Morley, Ariel Fiszbein, Haeduck Lee, and Bill Wood, *Poverty and Income Distribution in Latin America: The Story of the 1980s* (Washington, D.C.: World Bank, 1997); Eliana Cardoso and Ann Helwege, *Latin America's Economy: Diversity, Trends, and Conflicts* (Cambridge: MIT Press, 1992); Samuel Morley, *Poverty and Inequality in Latin America* (Baltimore: Johns Hopkins University Press, 1995); and Richard Tardinico and Rafael Menjívar Larín, eds., *Global Restructuring, Employment, and Social Inequality in Urban Latin America* (Miami: The North-South Center Press, 1997). For comparative data with other regions of the world, see World Bank, *World Development Report* (1997) and UNDP, *Human Development Report* (New York: Oxford University Press, 1997).

9. Based on a poverty line set at $60/month/person, 1987 $U.S. (PPP, purchasing power parity). See Psacharopoulos et al., *Poverty and Income*, p. 71.

10. The probability of being poor, however, remained twice as likely in rural areas as in urban settings. Psacharopoulos et al., *Poverty and Income*, p. x.

11. UNDP, *Human Development Report* (1997), p. 224; see also Cardoso and Helwege, *Latin America's Economy*, chap. 9.

12. Psacharopoulos et al., *Poverty and Income*, p. 24.

13. Ibid., p. 116.

14. IDB, *Economic and Social Progress*, p. 47. See also Cardoso and Helwege, *Latin America's Economy*, p. 227, which documents declines in central-government spending on health and education (as a percentage of total government spending) in every country in the region between 1979 and 1985, with the exceptions of Honduras, Panama, and Peru.

15. IDB, *Economic and Social Progress*, p. 332.

16. Ibid., p. 331.

17. Ibid., p. 336.

18. See Merilee S. Grindle, *Challenging the State: Crisis and Innovation in Latin America and Africa* (New York: Cambridge University Press, 1996), chaps. 2 and 6.

19. See IDB, *Economic and Social Progress*.

20. See John Williamson, Introduction to John Williamson, ed., *Latin American Adjustment: How Much Has Happened?* (Washington, D.C.: Institute for International Economics, 1990).

21. A useful discussion of this evolving agenda of what needed to be done is found in Joan Nelson and collaborators, *Fragile Coalitions: The Politics of Economic Adjustment* (New Brunswick, N.J.: Transaction Books, 1989). See also Colin A. Bradford, ed., *Redefining the State in Latin America* (Paris: Organization for Economic Cooperation and Development, 1994).

22. Achieving fiscal discipline meant drastically cutting public spending as a proportion of GDP by reducing subsidies, allowing public-sector salaries to decline relative to the cost of living, cutting back on the number of public-sector employees, reducing ministerial budgets to a minimum, and eliminating investment budgets. Among the hardest hit by the initial budget- and personnel-cutting measures were social-sector ministries of health and education, as well as those providing for rural development and agriculture. This reflected in part the substantial portion of national budgets claimed by such personnel-intensive ministries, but also the relative weakness of these ministries in terms of budgetary politics.

23. See Grindle, *Challenging the State*, chap. 5; John Williamson, ed., *The Political Economy of Policy Reform* (Washington, D.C.: Institute for International Economics, 1994); Miguel Angel Centeno, *Democracy Within Reason: Technocratic Revolution in Mexico* (University Park, Pa.: Pennsylvania State University Press, 1994); Jorge Dominguez, ed., *Technopols: Freeing Politics and Markets in Latin America in the 1990s* (University Park, Pa.: Pennsylvania State University Press); James Malloy, "Policy Analysis, Public Policy and Regime Structure in Latin America," *Governance: An International Journal of Public Policy and Administration* 2, no. 3 (1989); and Catherine Conaghan and James M. Malloy, *Unsettling Statecraft: Democracy and Neoliberalism in the Central Andes* (Pittsburgh, Pa.: University of Pittsburgh Press, 1994).

24. In an epigram that sums up a decade and a half of concern about the state, João Guilherme Merquior ("A Panoramic View of the Rebirth of

Liberalism," *World Development* 20, no. 8 [1993]: 1265) wrote about his native Brazil, "We have simultaneously too much state and too little state."

25. See, for example, Rudiger Dornbusch and Sebastian Edwards, *The Macroeconomics of Populism in Latin America* (Chicago: University of Chicago Press, 1991). Much analysis during this period, particularly that of economists attempting to explain the relationship between politics and economics, conformed closely to the influential model of the origin of irrational public policy put forth by Robert Bates in his *Markets and States in Tropical Africa* (Berkeley: University of California Press, 1981).

26. The "rehabilitation" of the state as an important actor in the process of development was signaled in mainstream thinking about development in the 1991 *World Development Report*, which included a chapter on the state and its role in economic development. By 1997, the topic of the state merited a full volume of the *World Development Report*.

27. Tony Killick, *A Reaction Too Far: Economic Theory and the Role of the State in Developing Countries* (London: Overseas Development Institute, 1989). See also Bradford, *Redefining the State*, for several "revisionist" views on the role of the state, and IDB/UNDP, *Social Reform*.

28. See Alice Amsden, *Asia's Next Giant: South Korea and Late Industrialization* (New York: Oxford University Press, 1989); Robert Wade, *Governing the Market: Economic Theory and the Role of Government in East Asian Industrialization* (Princeton, N.J.: Princeton University Press, 1990); World Bank, *The East Asian Miracle: Economic Growth and Public Policy* (New York: Oxford University Press, 1993); Hilton L. Root, *Small Countries, Big Lessons: Governance and the Rise of East Asia* (Hong Kong: Oxford University Press, 1996); and Peter Evans, *Embedded Autonomy: States and Industrial Transformation* (Princeton, N.J.: Princeton University Press, 1995).

29. See especially Douglass North, *Institutions, Institutional Change, and Economic Performance* (New York: Cambridge University Press, 1990).

30. See Grindle, *Challenging the State*; Moisés Naím, *Latin America's Journey to the Market: From Macroeconomic Shocks to Institutional Therapy*, ICEG Occasional Paper 62 (San Francisco: International Center for Economic Growth, ICS Press, 1995); and World Bank, *World Development Report* (1997).

31. This revisionism about the state did not mean a return to an earlier perspective that encouraged extensive intervention in the market and state guidance of economic development, but rather a greater awareness that states could have positive consequences for growth as well as negative ones.

32. On the new social movements and democratization in Latin America, see Guillermo O'Donnell, Philippe C. Schmitter, and Laurence Whitehead, eds., *Transitions from Authoritarian Rule: Latin America* (Baltimore: Johns Hopkins University Press, 1986).

33. See, for example, Bradford, *Redefining the State*.

34. In Latin America, nineteen constitutions identify health and education as basic rights and commit government to their provision. IDB, *Economic and Social Progress*, p. 246.

35. In their important book, *Adjustment with a Human Face* (Giovanni Andrea Cornia, Richard Jolly, and Frances Stewart, eds., *Adjustment with a Human Face*, 2 vols. [New York: Oxford University Press, 1987]), Cornia, Jolly, and Stewart helped spark interest in social adjustment funds. These are discussed in Graham, "The Politics"; Arriagada and Graham, "Chile: Sustaining Adjustment"; and Alan Angell and Carol Graham, "Can Social Sector

Reform Make Adjustment Sustainable and Equitable? Lessons from Chile and Venezuela," *Journal of Latin American Studies* 27, part I (1995).

36. IDB, *Economic and Social Progress.*

37. Examples of such politicians would include Tasso Jereissati and Ciro Gomes in Brazil, whose reform initiatives are reported and analyzed in Tendler, *Good Government,* Gonzalo Sánchez de Lozada in Bolivia, Enrique Salas Romer in Venezuela, and César Gaviria in Colombia. Carlos Salinas in Mexico promoted his image as a social reformer through attention focused on PRONASOL, introduced as a social-adjustment program. See IDB/UNDP, *Social Reform* for a variety of statements about the importance of social-sector reforms from high-level politicians in Latin America.

38. See, for example, World Bank, *The East Asian Miracle.*

39. See Nancy Birdsall, David Ross, and Richard Sabot, "Inequality and Growth Reconsidered: Lessons from East Asia," *World Bank Economic Review* 9, no. 3. (1995); see also Angell and Graham, "Can Social Sector Reform"; J. Benhabib and M. Spiegel, "The Role of Human Capital in Economic Development: Evidence from Cross-National Aggregate Data," *Journal of Monetary Economics* (1994); and L. Law, *Human Capital, Physical Capital, and Growth in the Southeast Asian Countries* (Stanford, Calif.: Stanford University Press, 1995).

40. See Robert Putnam, *Making Democracy Work: Civic Traditions in Modern Italy* (Princeton, N.J.: Princeton University Press, 1993). Following the publication of his Italian research, Putnam initiated the Saguaro Project at Harvard University to explore the ways in which social capital might be created in the United States.

41. See Susan Eckstein, ed., *Power and Popular Protest: Latin American Social Movements* (Berkeley: University of California Press, 1989); Arturo Escobar and Sonia E. Alvarez, eds., *The Making of Social Movements in Latin America: Identity, Strategy, and Democracy* (Boulder, Colo.: Westview Press, 1992); and Anthony Bebbington and Graham Thiele, *Non-Governmental Organizations and the State in Latin America: Rethinking Roles in Sustained Agricultural Development* (London: Routledge, 1993).

42. See Merilee S. Grindle, *Audacious Reform: The Politics of Institutional Invention* (Baltimore: Johns Hopkins University Press, 2000).

43. The idea of surrogate voices for the poor is discussed in Nelson, "Poverty, Equity."

44. See IDB, *Economic and Social Progress;* and Victoria Murrillo, "Latin American Unions and the Reform of Social Service Delivery Systems: Institutional Constraints and Policy Choice" (Inter-American Development Bank, Office of the Chief Economist, 1996); and Kurt Weyland, "How Much Political Power Do Economic Forces Have? Conflicts Over Social Insurance Reform in Brazil," *Journal of Public Policy* 16, no. 1 (1996).

45. For a critique of the policymaking pursued by technocratic reformers, see Malloy, "Policy Analysis."

46. See Manuel Contreras, "Génesis, Formulación, Implementación y Avance de la Reforma Educativa en Bolivia" (paper prepared for a conference on governability and human development, La Paz, Bolivia, 13 February 1996), 14–15.

47. See Giovanni Arrighi, "Workers of the World at Century's End," *Review: Fernand Braudel Center* 19, no. 3 (1996); and Victoria Lawson, "Workforce Fragmentation in Latin America and its Empirical Manifestations in Ecuador," *World Development* 18, no. 5 (1990); Kevin Middlebrook, *The Paradox*

of Revolution: Labor, the State, and Authoritarianism in Mexico (Baltimore: Johns Hopkins University Press, 1995); Murrillo, "Latin American Unions."

48. On strategies for reformers to overcome sources of opposition, see Carol Graham and Moisés Naím, "The Political Economy of Institutional Reform," in Nancy Birdsall, Carol Graham, and Richard Sabot, eds., *Beyond Trade-offs: Market Reforms and Equitable Growth in Latin America* (Washington, D.C.: Brookings Institution/IDB, 1999), pp. 11–16; Tendler, *Good Government;* and Nelson, "Poverty, Equity."

49. Juan Carlos Navarro, "Implementing Social Reform: Lessons from the Venezuelan Experience," *Social Policy Reform in Latin America,* Working Paper Series no. 230 (Washington, D.C.: Latin American Program, Woodrow Wilson International Center for Scholars, 1997).

50. Tendler, *Good Government.*

51. See Tardanico and Menjívar Larín, *Global Restructuring* and Carmelo Mesa-Lago, *Changing Social Security in Latin America: Toward Alleviating the Social Costs of Economic Reform* (Boulder, Colo.: Lynne Rienner, 1994).

52. On the issue of credibility, see Persson and Tabellini, *Monetary and Fiscal Policy.*

53. IDB, *Economic and Social Progress,* pp. 220–221, compares reforms in Chile, Peru, Colombia, Argentina, Uruguay, and Mexico. See also Mesa-Lago, *Changing Social Security.*

54. This is a principal argument made in IDB, *Economic and Social Progress,* part III, chap. 2. This publication demonstrates that expenditures per pupil in education as a percentage of GDP are quite good by international standards.

55. See ibid., chap. 7.

56. See Andrew R. Nickson, *Local Government in Latin America* (Boulder, Colo.: Lynne Rienner, 1995).

57. See Tendler, *Good Government.*

58. See, for examples, Joe Foweraker and Ann L. Craig, eds., *Popular Movements and Political Change in Mexico* (Boulder, Colo.: Lynne Rienner, 1990); and Ann Hornsby, *Pushing for Democracy in Colombia: Non-Profit Challenges to Dependence on the State* (Ph.D. diss., Department of Sociology, Harvard University, 1991).

59. Second-generation reforms are those that require ongoing institutional commitment and administration. See Naím, "Latin America's Journey"; Grindle, *Challenging the State,* chap. 6; Graham and Naím, "The Political Economy"; and Navarro, "Implementing Social Reform."

60. Graham and Naím, "The Political Economy," pp. 6–11.

61. See Chris Argyris and Donald Schon, *Organizational Learning: A Theory of Action Perspective* (Reading, Mass.: Addison-Wesley, 1978); and *Organizational Learning II: Theory, Method, and Practice* (Reading, Mass.: Addison-Wesley, 1996); and David Osborne and Ted Gaebler, *Reinventing Government: How the Entrepreneurial Spirit is Transforming the Public Sector, from Schoolhouse to Statehouse, City Hall to the Pentagon* (Reading, Mass.: Addison-Wesley, 1992).

62. See Navarro, "Implementing Social Reform."

63. See, in particular, K. Subbarao, Aniruddha Bonnerjee, Jeanine Braithwaite, Soniya Carvalho, Kene Ezemenari, Carol Graham, and Alan Thompson, *Safety Net Programs and Poverty Reduction: Lessons from Cross-Country Experience* (Washington, D.C.: World Bank, 1997).

64. IDB, *Economic and Social Progress,* includes important new ways of conceptualizing service delivery and social security reforms.

65. This point is made by Joan Nelson, in the next chapter in this book. She argues that there is little consensus on what needs to be done in providing effective social services and that the lack of a clear set of options impedes debate and consensus building.

66. Moisés Naím, *Paper Tigers and Minotaurs: The Politics of Venezuela's Economic Reforms* (Washington, D.C.: Carnegie Endowment, 1993), p. 13.

67. Ibid., p. 14.

3

Reforming Social Sector Governance: A Political Perspective

Joan M. Nelson

As recently as the early 1990s, fundamental social sector reforms were not on the agenda of governments in most developing, semi-industrialized, and post-Communist countries. Today, these reforms are among the top priorities in many Latin American and Central East European nations, and are growing in priority almost everywhere.[1] The surge of attention reflects a remarkable convergence of three broad perspectives:[2]

- A recognition that social sector reforms are imperative to consolidate and to reap the benefits from the painful economic adjustment measures that dominated government agendas in the 1980s and early 1990s
- A new or renewed emphasis on poverty reduction
- A desire to consolidate democratic openings

Despite these powerful motivations, major reforms in health and education almost everywhere have been slow, modest, and subject to erosion or reversal. Basic systemic changes in pension systems have proved somewhat easier and have been adopted in roughly a dozen countries in Latin America and the post-Communist world in the 1990s. In many other countries, though, pension systems have been extraordinarily difficult to change in more than marginal ways.

New Zealand's experience might serve as a parable for this chapter's theme. From the mid-1980s, New Zealand responded to an intensifying economic crisis with a sweeping array of macroeconomic and sectoral reforms. A few years into this ongoing process, in the early 1990s, radical changes were extended to the health care delivery system. The process of reform in health was similar to that used earlier for tightened macroeconomic management, the overhaul of central fiscal institutions, and a range of sectoral reforms. Despite New Zealand's firmly democratic tradition, the approach was top-down, rapid, and nonconsultative. The reforms were designed and put in place by a series of commissions and boards, with the Department (later the Ministry) of Health largely sidelined, and with little consultation (despite a great deal of protest) from health workers. Nor was public opinion addressed: Polls indicated that 75 percent of the voters opposed the changes.

What is striking is that while the broad design of New Zealand's market-oriented reforms were sustained over four administrations spanning Labour, Conservative, and coalition party control, the health reforms proved fragile. Within a very few years, parts of the original reform plan were modified (user fees) or abandoned (the effort to define core services) in response to public pressure and technical and administrative difficulties. Then, in late 1996, national elections were held under a new electoral system based on proportional representation. As a result of the vote, the National Party (which had introduced the health reforms several years earlier) entered into difficult coalition negotiations with New Zealand First. The two parties reached an agreement that generally endorsed and continued the broader principles of economic policy and an array of institutional reforms that had been put in place over the previous decade. But the major features of the health sector reforms, including privatization of hospitals, were reversed. Radical, rapid, top-down reform worked in many respects in New Zealand, but not in the health sector.

As the tale of New Zealand suggests, problems of social-sector reforms are not confined to developing countries, nor to the post-Communist world: Virtually every industrialized democracy is struggling with similar issues. Why are systemic reforms in social sectors so particularly difficult? Effective strategies and tactics for better social-sector governance require an understanding of the features that inhibit changes in the direction of greater efficiency and improved governance.

Obstacles to Social-Sector Reforms

To a large degree, problems of social-sector reforms appear also in other areas requiring extensive institutional and organizational changes. It may be useful to think about a spectrum of types of reforms, arrayed according to several characteristics:

1. The degree to which changes are guided by a clear model, template, or vision supported by a strong technical consensus
2. The number and variety of actors who must collaborate in order to design and implement major changes
3. The length of time needed to implement reforms, due to technical requirements (for instance, a long series of sequential steps), even if there were no political delays
4. The kinds and amounts of detailed information required to fine-tune and implement each successive stage of the reform, and the extent to which mechanisms already exist for collecting that information
5. The evident costs of postponing action

At one end of the spectrum are certain macroeconomic reforms, especially those centered on price changes such as devaluation or interest rate adjustments. In inflationary contexts, these measures are guided by a clear technical consensus. They can be put into effect by a handful of high economic officials (with the backing of top political authority), and they take effect extremely rapidly. They require certain basic economic indicators, which are available in all but the least-sophisticated countries. Postponing action has extremely high costs, affecting much of the population immediately and directly.

Somewhere toward the center of the spectrum are reforms entailing more organizational restructuring and legal changes, such as financial-sector reforms. Broad principles of financial-sector reform are fairly well established, but there is considerable room for debate and adjustment of precise design to specific country circumstances. A wider range of government and private-sector actors must collaborate on the reforms, and they are likely to take some months or years to put into effect. Such reforms also require considerable detailed information; mechanisms to collect and analyze that data often need to be created or upgraded. Postponing reforms implies direct and clear costs for some groups but only indirect and/or delayed and often unrecognized costs for many others.

Toward the far end of the spectrum are systemic reforms in education and health services. Clearly, multiple models are available, influenced by very different national and regional traditions and histories. More important, there is only limited consensus among technical specialists regarding basic principles of reform. Experts argue bitterly over the merits of, say, single-payer health care systems or charter schools. They agree only to a minor extent on the principles that should guide the degree and design of privatization or decentralization.

Even after initial agreement is reached on a course of action, implementing that course is extremely complex. Both ministries and legislatures at national, state, and local levels are usually involved. Reforms intended to increase efficiency and save money in the long run may nonetheless have high up-front costs. Not only the ministry of finance but often subnational financial authorities must concur. Social-sector reforms require years to implement. Even under Pinochet's authoritarian rule, Chile's education reforms took a decade to put in place. A great deal of detailed information is required to fine-tune design of successive steps. Much of that information is only available when new arrangements are made for gathering it. All of these complications are reinforced by the fact that, despite widespread dissatisfaction with the status quo, there are no evident and compelling costs of postponing action.

These characteristics—no blueprint, long timetable, many actors, dense information requirements, low apparent costs of delay—affect the politics of social-sector reforms. If many actors must cooperate to put a reform into effect, any one of them can weaken or stop the reform. In other words, there are many potential veto actors. Moreover, the large number of actors increases transaction and enforcement costs. If implementation takes many years, there are many potential veto opportunities. The long timetable also means that the benefits of the reforms often do not become apparent to users for some time. If they suffer costs in the interim, they will oppose reforms. In any event, it may be hard to mobilize proreform coalitions to counter opposition from vested interests. Information needs also affect the course of reform. Lack of information may stall action; new information may alter perceptions and reopen debates. The reform process is not linear (decision followed by implementation), but iterative.

Several additional characteristics of social sectors further complicate major systemic change.

Entitlement psychology is an obvious impediment to social-sector reforms. Entitlements are benefits that are guaranteed by law or even by a country's constitution; they are viewed not as privileges but as rights. Pensions often carry an additional moral claim: Workers and pensioners believe (often erroneously) that they have paid in full or overpaid during their working lives for the pensions they receive after retiring. In the post-communist world, older workers believe their pensions (and other benefits) have been paid for by a lifetime of working for low state wages.

Quite a different obstacle to reform is posed in many cases by the influence of service providers, reflecting strong organization, high social status, or both. Medical doctors and university rectors often can use social status and connections to divert or dilute reforms. In a great many countries, teachers and health workers are the two largest single categories of wage workers; they are often strongly unionized. (However, it matters whether there are one or many unions, how they are linked to political parties, and how they relate to the key ministries.) It is worth noting that service providers often resist reforms not only because change is disruptive and may threaten their incomes, but also because they see the reforms as a threat to professional standards and broad public interests.

While the political influence of health and education service providers is well recognized, a somewhat different point also warrants consideration. In much greater degree than in most other mainly public services, the quality of output in health and education depends on the motivation and initiative of the service providers themselves. What happens in the classroom between teacher and student, or in the clinic between healthworker and patient, largely determines the effectiveness of schooling or health care. Most other public services where large numbers of workers deal directly with the public—for example, the post office or customs service—involve much less intensive and sustained interaction with clients, and the interactions are much more routinized. In part for this reason, it is hard to monitor and measure health and particularly education workers' effort and performance fairly. Principal-agent oversight problems are acute. Therefore, the effects of reforms on morale and incentives are particularly important.

Users of social services are also stakeholders, but their interests tend to be narrow and intermittent or temporary or divided. Most of the public are direct or indirect beneficiaries of health and education services and therefore strongly interested in access, quality, and cost—but usually only at particular times and with a narrow focus. In many countries, parents of school children form associations, but those associations focus on the individual school. Parents' organizations that seek to alter education policy (including budgets) are comparatively rare, as are citizens' associations focused on health care. An instructive exception is organizations of the permanently ill or disabled (mainly in wealthy countries). For these clients, social services address needs that are both central to their lives and permanent. Similarly, pensions are a topic of absolutely central and sustained concern to pensioners. Their associations have become formidable lobbies not only in wealthy nations, but also in Argentina, Uruguay, and to a lesser extent in Poland, Hungary, and other developing and post-Communist countries with aging populations.

When broader public interest is aroused, public priorities often run counter to those of technical experts advocating reform. In most countries there is strong demand for expanded curative facilities and little interest in public health measures. Most people are more impressed with a vigorous school building program than with organizational changes to improve supervision or to introduce national examinations as a way to assess schools' and teachers' performance.

Where reforms emphasize better access and quality of service for the poor, an additional problem is likely to arise: competition between the middle strata and the poor. In most developing countries, the wealthy rely on private (often foreign) health and education facilities. In much of Latin America, Africa, and South Asia, many of the poorest have limited access to health and education, partly because so many live in rural areas. In contrast, the public-school system (including the universities) is often the main avenue of social mobility for the middle strata, and public hospitals or facilities linked with publicly subsidized social security systems are the main sources of their medical care. Moreover, in many countries the middle strata lost most, relative to earlier incomes, from the hard times of the 1980s. Lower quality of life results not only from shrunken real incomes but also from deteriorated public services and the spreading practice of under-the-table payments for those services. Therefore, social-service reforms that entail major resource shifts from middle to poorer groups may be strongly resisted, despite the equity arguments for such shifts.

Because the obstacles to change are so formidable, many reform efforts evade rather than confront the core problems of institutional change.

• Some programs, often quite successful in their own terms, focus on aspects of education or health that fall outside the concerns of major vested interests and/or add new program elements rather than attempting to restructure old ones. For example, a number of highly successful preschool education programs have been launched in Latin America.

• "Social safety net" programs and Social Funds, popular since the late 1980s, are another approach that evades the more difficult challenges of institutional reform. Such programs are usually set up outside of mainline ministries; much of their success is due to more flexible procedures plus utilization of local nongovernmental organizations. Often they are explicitly temporary (like the Bolivian Emergency Social Program). Sometimes they are used as the direct instruments of particular political leaders or parties: Examples include the social fund and school building program within the Ministry of the Presidency in Peru in the mid-1990s, and (less clearly) the Program of National Solidarity in Mexico. Not all such programs are partisan, and many have been quite successful in accomplishing specific goals. But, they leave untouched the problems of the mainline services.

• While there are many persuasive reasons for partial decentralization and privatization, it seems likely that the current enthusiasm for those approaches is also driven by despair with the rigidity of traditional social service bureaucracies and their political entanglements. There is now a growing consensus that even well-designed decentralization and privatization measures will not work well unless they are matched with redirected and much more efficient roles for central administration. In the end, the formidable problems of reforming the old-line ministries cannot be evaded.

While many attempted reforms have been aborted or only partly implemented, or evade the core problem of institutional changes at the center, there have been important instances of radical change. Chile offers probably the most dramatic examples: Education, health, and pension systems have all been drastically re-structured. The basic outlines of these changes took place during the Pinochet era. They are being closely studied for both positive and negative technical lessons, within and beyond Latin America. Systemic reforms, though, pose far greater political hurdles for democratic regimes. More recently, Mexico has carried through substantial decentralization and related reforms in education, including reshaping the roles of the national ministry. Argentina, Bolivia, Colombia, Mexico, Peru, and Uruguay have adopted major pension reforms, and others are in the process of doing so. Colombia adopted sweeping reforms in health care finance and delivery in 1993. Argentina and Mexico are trying to implement major, though somewhat less radical, changes in the health care sector. There are also impressive instances of reform (often on a pilot basis) at the state or provincial level: for instance, primary health services in the state of Ceará, Brazil; a promising pilot program restructuring primary education in the state of Mérida, Venezuela; basic education reforms in the state of Minas Gerais, Brazil. In most of these cases, successes and shortcomings are still unfolding. For this discussion, the important point is that major changes were introduced and, thus far, have been sustained.

In short, major institutional reforms in social services are extremely difficult, but they do happen. What circumstances and tactics bring them about?

Factors and Tactics Facilitating Social-Sector Reforms

The specific circumstances and the process of reform vary from country to country. Certain themes, though, emerge in most reform stories. Among these themes are the emergence of new advocates of reform, weakened resistance among vested interests, growing receptivity to new ideas, and, with respect to pension reforms, the key role of a new paradigm or model.

New Advocates of Reform

This chapter noted at the outset that social-sector reforms lay at or beyond the periphery of structural-adjustment efforts in the 1980s, but in the 1990s they have been incorporated into the agenda of reoriented economic strategies and structures. Growing recognition of links between successful market-oriented economic strategies and more efficient and effective social services has created new and powerful advocates for social-sector reforms.

The broadest links relate to the need to consolidate fiscal reforms in the context of democratic pressures. Several Latin American countries have for some time provided basic education, health services, and pension coverage to most of their citizens, but these systems have been eroded by economic and demographic pressures. In other countries, much of the population never had adequate access to basic social services and security. Elected governments are now confronted with growing pressures for improved and expanded services. At the same time, technicians and politicians are more convinced than in the past of the importance of macroeconomic stability and, therefore, the need for prudent budget, monetary, and exchange rate policies. They must find ways to respond to pressures for better basic services within these constraints.

This balancing act neither permits nor requires cuts in overall spending on social sectors. Indeed, most far-reaching reforms in pension, health, and education systems have sizable up-front costs. Rather than squeezing social-sector outlays as a whole, medium-term fiscal considerations call for sharply increasing the efficiency and effectiveness of the services and transfers. Where privileged groups have been receiving extraordinarily generous benefits—for instance, high pensions at low retirement ages for civil servants in Brazil, or free higher education for the sons and daughters of social elites— these benefits may indeed need to be cut. But the broad imperative of balancing fiscal and democratic consolidation requires systemic reforms, not overall budget cuts.

High payroll taxes are a second, more specific link between evolving market strategies and social-sector reforms. In some countries, pension and health care systems are financed in large part from social security contributions levied on employers and employees. Often these and other payroll taxes add 50 percent or more to the basic wage bill and distort and discourage investment and job creation.

A third connection focuses on the quality of labor. The now defunct import substitution strategies imposed the costs of low-quality labor on consumers, who had no alternative sources for the goods they wanted. In contrast, open-market development strategies put a premium on efficient and flexible labor. Healthy and well-educated workers become much more valuable once liberalization opens the doors to imports and creates the need to compete for markets at home and abroad.

Savings constitute a fourth link between economic strategy and social-sector reform. Partly privatized pension systems, where workers' contributions are channeled into individual savings accounts invested in securities, may provide a rapidly growing pool of savings and investment to boost economic growth.

These links between social-sector reforms and the consolidation of market-oriented changes in economic policies and structure have created strong new advocates of social-sector reforms. Most obvious and central among these new actors are ministries of finance (and, depending on the specific organizations in different governments, other high-level officials responsible for the performance of the economy as a whole). In a long list of countries in and beyond Latin America, ministers of finance or central economic teams have taken the lead in pressing for basic reforms in pensions, health care finance (and often delivery), and sometimes education.

The connections between fiscal consolidation, effective open-market strategies, and social-sector reforms have also begun to draw progressive business leaders into the debates and political struggles for reform. The more specific tie between pension reforms modeled to some degree on the Chilean system and the creation of an increased pool of private savings has attracted considerable interest from domestic and foreign insurance and financial firms.

Nongovernmental, nonprofit organizations have long been advocates for more and better education, health, and social services. Over the past decade they have become much stronger, more numerous, and more vocal. Some among them have also changed their outlook: Convinced that increased resources alone will not bring the desired results, they have begun to advocate and pioneer new ways to finance and deliver better services.

Once certain types of social-sector reforms have been adopted, they may rapidly create additional new stakeholders. Thus, for instance, pension reforms in Argentina, Colombia, Mexico, Uruguay, Hungary, and Poland permit workers in middle age brackets to remain with the long-established pay-as-you-go system or to allocate part of their social security contributions to individual accounts, where the funds will be invested in securities by a private management firm of their choice. Unexpectedly large numbers of workers have opted for the new system, because they believe this will provide more adequate pensions. In Colombia, health system reforms have given roughly eight million poor people subsidized access to health care, thus creating a large new set of stakeholders. Reforms in education often provide parents with improved opportunities to have some influence on their children's schooling, creating a third kind of new stakeholder.[3] In these examples, potential new beneficiaries played little or no active role in promoting adoption of the reforms but would probably resist attempts to reverse or severely dilute those reforms after they are in place.

Defused Resistance to Social-Sector Reforms

The fact that major social-sector reforms have in fact been put in place in a fair number of cases reflects not only new proponents and stakeholders, but also unexpected weaknesses or loopholes in the organized opposition to such reforms.

For instance, pensioners' resistance to social security reforms often turns out to be manageable. Most pensioners are concerned to protect the value of their own pensions. Pension reforms of the kind being adopted in many Latin American (and other) countries in the 1990s generally affect existing pensions mainly through new provisions for indexing. While pensioners obviously want as advantageous an indexing formula as possible, they also stand to gain from establishing a fixed formula rather than depending on annual or periodic ad hoc adjustments, which permit tough finance ministers to persuade legislatures to enact de facto cuts in times of budget crises. Pension reforms may also threaten current pensioners to the extent that new contributions are diverted to individual accounts, leaving the old pay-as-you-go system underfunded. For that reason most reforms have included guarantees to existing pensioners that any shortfall in social security revenues will be covered, if necessary, from the general budget. Once reassured as regards these issues, in many countries pensioners have taken surprisingly little role in opposing pension reforms, though there have been exceptions (as in Uruguay).

Service providers' unions also are not always effective opponents of social-sector reforms. Often doctors and other health care workers are organized in a multiplicity of associations and unions, dividing their force. Sometimes they are slow to grasp the implications of complex reform proposals, as in the case of the Colombian health sector reforms of late 1993. Sometimes they view specific reforms as marginal to their interests. This appears to be the case with respect to efforts to introduce competition among union-managed health care services in Argentina. (As noted below, unions in general fiercely opposed this reform, but health workers' and doctors' organizations played almost no role.)

Pension systems do not have large numbers of service providers similar to teachers or health workers, and therefore reformers do not face opposition from that quarter, although social security institutes (with strong financial and political links to labor unions, politicians, and political parties) often are formidable obstacles.

Labor unions in general (as distinct from organizations of social service providers) often hold solidaristic values and principles that lead them to oppose reforms designed to encourage greater self-reliance and fuller use of private market mechanisms in pensions, health care, and education. However, really strong union opposition (other than from service providers) is likely to reflect specific financial interests. In Argentina, most unions bitterly oppose the introduction of consumer choice and competition among union-run health services, because workers' social security contributions for health traditionally are channeled directly to each union and comprise by far their largest source of revenues. In contrast, a number of Argentine unions reversed their initial opposition to pension reform when they realized that they could themselves manage (and profit from) pension funds. Similarly, in Hungary, the major post-Communist labor federation ardently opposed both pension and health care reforms. The federation effectively controlled the governing boards of the autonomous Pension and Health Insurance Funds through which social security contributions were channeled. Major reforms were certain to weaken or destroy their control.[4]

Growing Receptivity to New Ideas

In sum, changed structure and circumstances have created new proponents of social sector reforms, while old opponents sometimes are less formidable than is generally assumed. Moreover, protracted economic crisis has stretched receptivity to new ideas. Many stakeholders initially viewed the fiscal pressures starting in the 1980s as temporary:

Their instinct was to wait until things "returned to normal." Only after more than a decade, during which it became increasingly clear that the "golden age" would not return, did they begin to accept the idea that major changes were inevitable. Education and health practitioners and specialists traditionally have also tended to be fairly parochial, familiar mainly or solely with their own nation's traditions or with those of a former colonial or dominant power. The mid- and late 1990s have seen much greater interest in alternative models and the rapid growth of transnational networks among specialists (facilitated by new communications technology).[5] Heightened efforts by the World Bank and the regional development banks in social-service sectors also help to spread information and analysis of experiences in different countries.

With regard to pensions, a new paradigm lay ready at hand as more and more governments resolved to seriously address long-standing weaknesses in national systems. In 1981, Chile replaced its old pay-as-you-go system with a mandatory system of fully funded, individual accounts invested largely in securities and managed by private, competitive firms. By the late 1980s, the system was attracting worldwide interest. From 1994, the World Bank strongly encouraged reforms that incorporated ideas from the Chilean model, though it did not press for full and direct imitation.[6] In many middle-income and wealthy countries with well-established social security systems, specialists had long recognized accumulating problems and the specter of unsustainability, but reform debate and action focused on marginal changes to the existing systems. The emergence of the Chilean model offered a radical alternative and galvanized debate. Almost no country adopted reforms directly modeled on the Chilean experience, but the alternative model and its substantial technical backing provided a way to move beyond old debates regarding, for instance, raising the age of retirement. Moreover, the attraction of individual accounts for younger workers created a benefit to balance against the costs to workers of other elements of pension reform.

In health and education, in contrast, no clear-cut single model stood as an alternative to existing systems. Instead, there were (and are) a multiplicity of approaches and models, each with admirers and critics. Models that have drawn reformers' interest include, for instance, the Canadian single-payer system and various versions of U.S.-style health maintenance organizations and German health care arrangements; school voucher systems and charter schools; decentralization of both health and education authority; and privatization of different components of education and health finance and delivery. Specialists increasingly agree on certain basic principles: for instance, the desirability of separating funding from delivery of health services and the importance of introducing a degree of competition among providers of health and education services. However, precisely how these principles should be applied in specific cases remains hotly debated. In part reflecting the complexity of the sectors themselves, approaches to reform tend to be fragmented and are seldom integrated into a unified vision for a sector as a whole. Increased receptivity to new ideas helps to promote specific changes, but multiple models do not seem to galvanize broad systemic reform as effectively as the focused Chilean challenge to traditional pay-as-you-go pension systems.

The Political Process of Social Sector Reforms

New actors and increased receptivity to new ideas promote social-sector reforms, and divided or uncertain opposition leaves room for negotiation, persuasion, and compromise in a growing number of countries. However, as latecomers on the structural-adjustment agenda, social-service reforms are likely to unfold in a quite different political climate than initial macroeconomic measures. If early stabilization measures were reasonably successful, then widespread public perceptions of acute crisis are likely to have faded. In some countries, of course, such perceptions never were widespread. In others, poorly designed or irresolute stabilization measures may have had only limited effect, leaving most groups disillusioned with what are labeled "reform programs." In any of these scenarios, what Lezcek Balcerowicz, architect of Poland's initial reforms, labeled the period of "extraordinary politics" will have passed. Interest groups, legislatures, and the general public are likely to be much more resistant to autocratic styles of executive leadership that impose measures designed by technocrats with minimal consultation. Social-service reforms will usually have to be designed, launched, and implemented in the context of "politics as usual," even if the impetus and rationale for reform comes from perception of a deep-rooted structural crisis.

Pension reforms in Argentina illustrate the point. The pay-as-you-go system had been plagued with growing deficits as early as the 1960s, and the crisis had deepened in the next two decades as a result of the aging population, high replacement rates, lax entitlement provisions, and widespread evasion of high payroll taxes. In June 1992, fourteen months after Cavallo's radical Convertibility Plan to stabilize the economy was launched, the Menem government proposed radical pension reforms largely modeled on the Chilean system. The governing Justicialista Party, still dominated by Peronist and trade union influences, had supported the crisis measures to halt hyper-inflation and restart the economy. By mid-1992, however, the legislators were in no mood to wave through these additional measures. Most were deeply suspicious of the pension proposals. Some may also have welcomed the opportunity to reassert legislative power after a period of overwhelming executive dominance.[7] The initial government proposal was withdrawn; a less radical revision was submitted to Congress in August 1992. Factionalism splintered the strong Justicialista majority in Congress, and the pension law passed both houses only after thirteen months of bitter argument. Congress forced many major revisions, including some the government felt were not sustainable. Several specific features were later eliminated by decree or by new laws passed in mid-1995 under pressure of the ripple effects of the Mexican crisis.

In other countries pension reforms introduced as part of late-stage structural-adjustment agendas also required extensive debate and compromise. In Hungary and Poland, much of the discussion and negotiation took place before the bills were submitted to the legislatures. In Hungary the process was particularly striking, since the government commanded a super-majority in Parliament but chose to build consensus over an extended period rather than force through the pension package.

Systemic reforms in health and education are still more likely to require long periods of consultation, consensus building, and compromise. As noted earlier, multiple models and splintered technical opinions structure debate regarding health and education less productively than the two competitive paradigms that dominate debate regarding pension reforms. Moreover, effective reforms in social services demand the acceptance and cooperation of a wider array of groups and organizations at national and local levels than does pension reform. Once enacted, pension reforms can be implemented within a few months; in contrast, reforms in education and health are likely to require a long series of steps or phases, providing multiple opportunities for opponents to slow, divert, or derail the effort. These characteristics of social-services reform point toward a most-probable scenario of step-by-step, piecemeal, learn-by-doing reform rather than the introduction of a comprehensive grand scheme.

Implications of the Special Features of Social Sectors for Reformers

This discussion has focused on the tactics and processes of reform, rather than the substance. Stringent austerity and stabilization measures are virtually always imposed in a rapid, top-down, technocratic manner and probably have to be. The tactics and approaches used by reformers like Menem, Fujimori, de la Madrid, and Salinas (and, in Eastern Europe, Balcerowicz, Klaus, Bokros, and Chubais) have drawn criticism from many observers concerned with democratic processes and democratic consolidation, whether or not the critics were in broad agreement with the economic content of the reforms. Critics of autocratic economic reforms are likely to welcome the conclusion that in social sectors, at least, the intrinsic character of the sectors themselves probably requires a more gradual, participatory approach.

Although the gradual, consultative approach is more attractive for those uncomfortable with top-down tactics, it poses its own problems and dilemmas.

Which are the appropriate groups and organizations for consultation and participation? And how can they most constructively participate? In both education and health, service providers are usually the best-organized stakeholders, but they are often grouped in multiple, rival associations, each of which may or may not represent its members well. Within both sectors certain groups (some categories of doctors; university rectors) exercise much more influence than others (nonmedical health workers; elementary school teachers). Some stakeholders' groups are almost sure to be so rigidly opposed to changes that they must be sidelined (or split) if any progress is to be made.

Other groups may not recognize their stake in reforms or may not be organized in ways that facilitate consultation. Many are not aware of some of the basic facts affecting their interests. There is now growing interest in educating and mobilizing silent stakeholders. In Latin America there are several wide-ranging programs, national and cross-national, to draw the media, businesspeople, churches, and other groups with some concern for the public interest into debate on social-sector reforms.[8] In Hungary a prominent economist and a reputable survey analysis center teamed up to conduct a survey of attitudes regarding a range of social-sector reforms. Respondents were asked their views on specific issues, then provided with basic information on the costs to the average taxpayer of a range of options, and again asked their preferences. Many respondents shifted their replies significantly.[9] Clearly a good deal more resources and imagination need to be directed to this kind of public-interest education and mobilization. What internal groups are available for the task? What are the appropriate roles of external public and private agencies?

If piecemeal reforms are virtually inevitable (especially for social services, in contrast to monetary transfers such as child allowances or pensions), should much effort be devoted to trying to promote consensus on a larger vision (not a blueprint) to provide a framework for step-by-step measures? How wasteful are uncoordinated or even conflicting initiatives? Are specific reforms in aspects of a system likely to inadvertently cut off avenues of later change, or greatly raise the costs thereof? Or is that an exaggerated concern or residue of "central-planning" thinking?

Can piecemeal reforms capture some of the benefits of bundling? Significant shifts of resources in favor of the poor are politically very difficult in many countries, unless they are combined with real benefits for middle strata. Can such pairings be engineered on a piecemeal basis?

What are the implications of the special character of social-sector reforms for the roles of international financial and development institutions and for bilateral-aid agencies? External agencies can make major contributions to internal debate, by providing information about experience elsewhere in the world, and by pointing out interactions between proposed social-sector reforms and broader economic stability and growth. Because there are no (or only very general) models for education and health-sector reforms that command technical consensus and because top-down approaches are less feasible and promising in these compared to some other areas of reform, external pressure and conditionality should be used only sparingly. For what specific kinds of social-reform goals and measures is conditionality appropriate? And under what circumstances?

Are there real risks in the current drive to dramatically increase external financial assistance for social sectors? The World Bank, the Inter-American Development Bank, and other multilateral development organizations have already sharply raised the share of their programs directed to social sectors, and plan to continue the trend. Does increased funding for social sectors itself constitute a disincentive for painful reforms? Despite the appeal of providing aid for education, health, and other social programs, in many countries much of this aid is likely to be ineffective or diverted by corruption, in the absence of major systemic reforms. The entire thrust of this chapter has been to argue that such reforms are likely to be very slow. It may well be that while conditionality should be used sparingly, the principle of stringent aid selectivity—that is, of providing support only in response to demonstrated commitment to reform—is at least as important, and perhaps more important, in social sectors than in other fields.

Notes

1. By "fundamental social-sector reforms" I mean major changes in the organization, management, financing, and incentive structures of pension

and other social transfer systems, and of basic social services like health care delivery and education.

2. Pension and health finance and delivery reforms are also urgent issues in many wealthy democracies, but the driving motivations are somewhat different.

3. For an extensive discussion of the "new stakeholders' approach" to promoting reforms, see Carol Graham, *Private Markets for Public Goods: Raising the Stakes in Economic Reform* (Washington, D.C.: Brookings Institution, 1998).

4. Under the new Hungarian government elected in spring 1998, the Pension and Health Insurance Funds have been stripped of their autonomy. It remains to be seen whether this will affect the post-Communist union federation stance toward health reforms currently under debate.

5. See Stephen P. Heyneman, "International Educational Cooperation in the Next Century" (paper prepared for presentation to the International Commission on Education for the Twenty-First Century, Paris, 9 February 1995). Also, Stephen P. Heyneman, "America's Most Precious Export," *The American School Board Journal* 182, no. 3 (March 1995), especially pp. 24–25.

6. See World Bank, *Averting the Old-Age Crisis* (Washington, D.C.: 1994).

7. Juan Carlos Torre, *El proceso políti*

4

From Safety Nets to Social Sector Reform: Lessons from the Developing Countries for the Transition Economies[1]

Carol Graham

Few topics have received as much discussion in transition economies as have the social costs of market-oriented reforms.[2] Yet the empirical evidence upon which the debate is based is far from complete. This is in part due to the difficulty of comparing poverty lines across countries: Poverty has both absolute and relative dimensions and is quite different in Zambia than it is in Poland, for example. It is also difficult to distinguish the effects of prolonged economic crisis on the poor from those of difficult but necessary macroeconomic adjustments. Furthermore, the truly poor and vulnerable tend to have a weak political voice and therefore little influence on the debate about social costs. Not surprisingly, the numerous attempts to implement safety net measures during economic adjustment in both developing and transition economies have had varied results.[3] This experience has led to an evolution of thinking about social-welfare issues during transition, which has implications not only for the design of safety net measures in the short term, but also for the reform of social-sector institutions over the longer term.[4]

During the first wave of adjustment programs in the early 1980s, most attention was focused on developing the appropriate mix of policies to achieve stabilization and structural reform; little attention was paid to the issue of social costs. This changed by the mid-1980s. First, a consensus gradually developed on the appropriate policy mix: the reduction of fiscal deficits, the elimination of price controls and trade restrictions, the introduction of realistic and unified exchange rate regimes and positive real interest rates, and a shift to reliance on the private sector rather than the state to run most productive enterprises. As this consensus became clear, policymakers could begin to focus attention on social-welfare issues.[5] Second, by the mid-1980s, as the results of adjustment policies became clear, a broad debate began about their social costs. Concerns about these costs were heightened by the publication of a highly critical study by UNICEF in 1987.[6] Initially, this debate focused solely on the social costs of adjustment policies and resulted in numerous efforts to develop safety net measures within the multilateral development banks.

By the late 1980s, the debate was altered once again by evidence from country experience. It became increasingly clear that the poor fared far worse in the countries that failed to adjust than in those that adjusted in a timely manner. The contrasting examples of Chile and Peru are illustrative. During the adjustment crisis in the early 1980s in Chile, the poor were effectively protected from declines in social welfare through targeted employment and nutrition policies. With the subsequent resumption of growth in the late 1980s and early 1990s, poverty decreased substantially, falling from approximately 45 percent of the population in 1986 to 28 percent in 1994. In contrast, in Peru, during a prolonged period of "postponed" adjustment from 1985 to 1990 that resulted in hyperinflation and economic collapse, per capita consumption fell 50 percent on average. It fell even further for the poorest two deciles: over 60 percent. Poverty rates rose from 17.3 percent in 1985 to 54.7 percent in 1990.[7] In Africa, meanwhile, the few countries that successfully adjusted also had better records on the poverty reduction front than did nonadjusters.[8]

Adjustment is a necessary but not a sufficient condition for poverty reduction, however, and there are still many unanswered questions. The first of these is the relationship between poverty and inequality. The evidence is not convincing, although some recent work clearly suggests that poverty increases with inequality.[9] Another important area increasingly recognized as critical to poverty reduction, but where we have very little empirical evidence, is that of institutional reform.[10] Nevertheless, it is very difficult, in the absence of growth, to either reduce inequality or to implement institutional reform. While some countries that adjust (such as Bolivia) grow more slowly than others (such as Peru) due to differences in resource endowments, institutional structure, and other factors, overall, adjusters outperform nonadjusters on the growth and poverty reduction front.

There are two reasons why nonadjusters perform poorly on the poverty reduction front. First of all, crosscountry evidence demonstrates a clear relationship between growth and poverty: Poverty declines during periods of growth and, alternatively, increases during periods of recession.[11] While adjustment has short-term costs, its ultimate objective is to achieve sustainable growth. Thus, countries that adjust successfully also tend to reduce poverty. Beyond the issue of adjustment, empirical evidence suggests that countries that maintain market-oriented macropolicies, and in particular liberalized trade regimes, over time grow much faster than those that do not, regardless of initial conditions.[12] Second, while adjustment has costs for certain sectors, it does provide a coherent policy framework in which one can identify and protect vulnerable groups. In contrast, it is very difficult to protect poor and vulnerable groups in a haphazard policy framework, where macroeconomic distortions and high inflation erode real income levels and provide numerous opportunities for rent-seeking. The poorest tend to be the least able to protect themselves from the costs of inflation, while the wealthy are better positioned to pursue strategies such as sending assets abroad. At the same time, the poor are less able than wealthier groups to use economic distortions for personal profit, such as through speculating on exchange rate differentials.

With the implementation of adjustment programs in many countries, the debate has shifted somewhat, from an emphasis on short-term safety nets to one on appropriate macroeconomic policies coupled with longer-term investments in health and education. Recent research exploring the long-contested relationship between inequality and growth has found that investment in longer-term social welfare policies, education in particular, has positive effects on growth and therefore poverty reduction.[13] The effects on growth of transfers—a category that includes safety nets—are mixed and seem to depend on the nature of the transfers and how they are allocated.[14] This should come as no surprise, as the ability of safety nets to reach the truly poor and vulnerable depends to a large extent on the political context and on the administrative capacity in particular country contexts. This does not diminish the important role that safety nets can play as transition tools but does emphasize the importance of evaluating investments in safety nets in the broader context of social policy. From both political and administrative standpoints, it is much easier to set up short-term safety net programs than it is to implement reforms of the public-sector institutions that deliver basic services. At least in Latin America and Africa, this, combined with concern about the immediate costs of adjustment, may have resulted in too much emphasis on safety nets at the expense of attention to the institutions that provide basic social services.

A brief review of selected experiences with safety net policies helps explain the changing nature of the debate on the social costs of adjustment. These experiences also provide relevant lessons for the transition economies, many of which have made far less progress either in implementing effective safety nets or in reforming social-welfare institutions than have countries in other regions.

Safety Nets: Lessons from Experience

The cross-regional record of safety nets is mixed. In some cases, safety net programs have been able to reach the poor and vulnerable and contribute to the political sustainability of economic reform at the same time. Yet in other cases, they have merely been short-term palliatives to stave off the political opposition of vocal groups and have had little impact on either poverty reduction or the longer-term political sustainability of reform.[15] There are two reasons for this mixed record. First of all, the overall policy framework is critical. Safety nets cannot serve as poverty reduction tools—or even provide effective social-welfare protection—in the absence of policies to generate sustainable growth in the long run. Safety nets are short-term mechanisms that can play an important role during transition periods. The benefits they provide, however, such as short-term employment and income support, cannot substitute for macroeconomic reform and sustainable growth, on the one hand, and for basic social-welfare policies, such as primary health and education, on the other. And safety nets must complement rather than contradict the general direction of the macroeconomic reform program: They should not generate fiscal deficits or create labor market distortions.[16] In practice, safety nets have not always been implemented according to these principles.

The second reason for the mixed record of safety nets is that their implementation is not free of political constraints, and there are distinct tradeoffs between directing benefits to the politically vocal versus the truly needy. The conventional wisdom, and usual practice, is that the poor have a weak political voice, and governments in the process of implementing reform and facing intense political opposition have few incentives to focus safety net benefits on the poorest. In addition, the poorest are often not as directly affected by adjustment measures as are slightly better-off urban consumers. Thus, governments tend to respond to this political tradeoff by focusing most of the benefits of compensation efforts during reform on vocal rather than needy groups. Yet it is not necessarily cost-effective, from either a political or poverty reduction perspective, to concentrate all benefits on vocal opponents of reform, as they are unlikely to be as well-off as they were prior to reform, regardless of the level of compensation. In contrast, reaching groups previously marginalized from public benefits is likely to have greater political as well as poverty reduction effects. This is more likely to occur if benefits are distributed in a manner that incorporates the participation of beneficiaries, thereby increasing their political voice as well as their economic potential. This is best demonstrated by the experiences of many countries with demand-based social funds.[17] Such a dynamic is not always possible: There are political contexts where governments must expend a fair amount of resources in order to placate the opposition of vocal and organized opponents of reform, or reforms will be politically unviable and face reversal, an outcome that tends to be far worse for the poor.

There are positive examples of countries that have implemented extensive macroeconomic reforms that generate growth and in which safety nets are an important part of the reform process. The models for successful safety nets differ. The contrasting examples of Chile and Bolivia, for example, demonstrate how the choice of a safety net program reflects different political and institutional contexts. In Chile, reform was implemented under an authoritarian regime and in a highly developed institutional framework. The government was able to rely on a preexisting and extensive network of mother and child nutrition programs and target them to the poorest sectors. A series of public-works employment programs was also targeted to the poorest by keeping the wage level well below the minimum. Public social services were restructured to benefit the poor, and private alternatives were introduced for those who could afford them. While per capita social expenditure decreased during the crisis years, it increased for the poorest deciles.[18] These safety nets were critical to protecting the welfare of the poor during deep recession. Unemployment, for example, peaked at almost 30 percent of the workforce in 1982. Yet welfare indicators such as infant mortality not only continued to improve, but accelerated in their rate of improvement during the crisis years. Chile's record was possible because of its extensive, preexisting social-welfare system and its relatively efficient public-sector institutions. Political context also played a role: A democratic government might face greater obstacles to reorienting social-welfare expenditures to the poorest at the expense of the middle sectors than the Pinochet regime did. Yet it is important to note that the targeted approach has been maintained and even extended since the transition to democracy in Chile.[19]

Bolivia, in contrast to Chile, had much higher levels of poverty and far less developed institutions. The government implemented the Emergency Social Fund (ESF), a demand-based social fund (the first of its kind) that relied on proposals from beneficiaries to allocate projects, and on local governments, NGOs, and the local private sector to implement them. While the ESF was not able to target the poorest sectors, as they were the least able to present viable project proposals, the program was able to reach large numbers of poor at a critical time (one million people out of a population of seven million benefited from ESF projects). At the same time, the ESF provided important impetus to local organizational and institutional capacity. Since the completion of macroeconomic reforms, the ESF's successor, the Social Investment Fund (SIF), relies on the same basic principles but focuses specifically on health and education benefits rather than on short-term employment, and incorporates collaboration with the line ministries into its operations.[20] This is an attempt to overcome one of the primary drawbacks of social funds: Although operating outside the realm of the mainstream public sector is precisely what makes social funds flexible and rapid, it also signifies that they do not contribute to reform of the public sector.

Both the Chilean experience with targeted social policies and Bolivia's experience with the incorporation of beneficiary participation have helped to shape the debate on safety nets as well as social-welfare policy more generally. The Chilean experience emphasizes the importance of targeting safety net efforts (and social policies) to the truly needy in order to provide effective protection. The Bolivian experience, meanwhile, demonstrates the importance of participation by the poor and by local institutions in order to enhance the sustainability of poverty reduction efforts.

There is also a plethora of examples of countries that have failed to implement comprehensive reform and where safety net policies have neither led to sustainable poverty reduction efforts nor reached needy groups. One such experience was the DIRE program in Senegal, a country that has postponed important structural reforms for over a decade. The DIRE, a credit program designed to help laid-off civil service workers and unemployed university graduates during adjustment, channeled interest-free loans to these groups, without incorporating need criteria or project viability into the allocation of loans. Not only did the resulting projects have an extremely high failure rate (32 percent), but over three million dollars were lost or "filtered" through the public bureaucracy. This is hardly an efficient manner to allocate resources in one of the poorest countries in Africa, nor did it contribute to sustainable reform. The DIRE's failure was due to poor design as well as to political objectives that superseded those of poverty reduction. In addition, and perhaps most important, because the program was not part of a government commitment to a comprehensive macroeconomic reform effort, it was not sustainable in either economic or political terms.

While safety net efforts in adjusting countries have a mixed record, the experience provides some important lessons, both for future safety net policy and for social-welfare policy more generally.

The effectiveness of targeted social safety net benefits has high-lighted the extent to which the allocation of basic social services such as health and education is skewed toward better-off groups in many countries, and the need for better targeting of social-welfare benefits in general. Social expenditures have to be at a realistic level, and in many countries in Latin America these expenditures fell well below desirable levels during the debt crisis. Nonetheless, the allocation of expenditures is as critical as overall amounts, if not more so. In Brazil, for example, only 18 percent of the poorest income groups—who account for over 40 percent of the population—are covered by social security, and they receive only 3 percent of social security benefits. In Venezuela, over 50 percent of the education budget is spent on higher education.[21] Chile, in contrast, provides a good example of how social expenditures can be made far more effective in reducing poverty when they are targeted. With the transition to a democratic regime in 1990, the targeted approach of the military government was maintained while social expenditure was increased at a rate of almost 10 percent per year. Because the demand of upper- and middle-income groups for social services is now in the private sector, government increases were able to disproportionately benefit the poor. Poverty has fallen markedly: from 45 percent in 1986, to 40 percent in 1990, to 28 percent in 1994. It is projected to fall to 17 percent by the year 2000 if the economy maintains its current trajectory of 6 percent annual growth.[22] Bolivia, meanwhile, provides an important example of how the incorporation of beneficiary participation can lead to more sustainable poverty reduction efforts and, in particular, enhance local institutional and organizational capacity. In Bolivia, the demand-based approach is now being extended to reforms in the education sector, in addition to the Social Investment Fund's cooperation with the ministries.

In many other countries, social expenditure remains skewed to wealthier groups. Public focus on the social costs of reform and on short-term safety net measures, particularly in the absence of progress on the macroeconomic-reform front, can divert attention from necessary reforms in the mainstream social sectors. Precisely because many safety net programs are implemented outside the mainstream public-institutional framework, they avoid addressing difficult problems within it. This underscores the importance of safety nets being implemented in a broader context of macroeconomic reform. When safety net measures are implemented effectively and introduce key principles such as targeting of the poorest and the incorporation of beneficiary participation, they can provide impetus—as well as some guiding principles—for the broader process of social-sector reform.

The Next Stage:
The Politics of Reforming Social-Sector Institutions

While there are clearly political tradeoffs involved in the implementation of safety nets, the politics of implementing permanent reforms of the institutions that deliver public services are even more complex. Reform of such institutions requires more implementation capacity than does macroeconomic reform or the implementation of safety net measures and entails very different political dynamics. The providers of public services tend to be politically powerful and highly organized, while the users, although numerous, tend to be diffuse and poorly organized. It is no surprise that most governments, already faced with the political challenges of macroeconomic reform, postpone or avoid more difficult reforms of public institutions, particularly when the implementation of visible safety net policies can address public concern about social-welfare issues, at least in the short term. Yet in most countries that complete adjustment programs, it becomes evident that in the long run, for growth to be sustainable, there are no alternatives to reform, or complete restructuring, of the social sectors. In much of Latin America, for example, public attention has shifted from the costs of adjustment measures to concern about the quality and quantity of basic public services, particularly health and education.

Despite these difficulties, it is possible to make progress in reforming social-sector institutions, and to do so under democratic rule. In Latin America, Chile is the country that has made the most progress in implementing structural reforms of the social sectors, and it did so under authoritarian rule. Chile also had a preauthoritarian legacy of relatively efficient public-sector institutions and a qualified civil service.[23] Yet the reforms have been maintained and even extended since the 1990 transition to democracy. Since then, a number of other countries in Latin America—and a few in Africa—have implemented Chile-style reforms under democratic rule. Progress has been most visible in the social security arena in Latin America, but there have also been some reforms in the health and education sectors, which tend to be even more complex and more difficult to reform than social security.[24] The policy framework—rapid and extensive macroeconomic reform—has been critical to the political viability of these reforms. Extensive economic change provides governments with unique *political* opportunities to implement additional reforms in the social-welfare arena, since the changes undermine established interest groups that frequently monopolize public services at the expense of the poor.[25] Slow or stalled economic reform, in contrast, allows such groups greater political opportunities to maintain their privileged positions.

In addition to the political opportunities provided by reform, expectations of the state are already very weak in much of the developing world, which also makes it easier for governments to introduce change. Poor management over time, coupled with the fiscal constraints imposed by the economic crisis and debt problems of the 1980s, resulted in a deterioration of the quality and coverage of basic public services in most countries. Upper- and middle-income groups with the means to do so have shifted to private systems, leaving the poor and lower-middle-income groups as the primary users of public services. This reduces the potential opposition to reforming public systems, yet at the same time highlights the importance of social-service reform for poverty reduction. In countries where the public sector is particularly weak, extensive institutional restructuring, as well as reallocation of expenditures, may be necessary.

Integral to the sustainability of such reform efforts is altering the political balance so that the beneficiaries of reform have a stronger voice in the political debate. Many of the successful reform efforts have included explicit or implicit efforts to create new stakeholders in reformed systems. Chile's education reform, for example, which introduced choice between public schools and publicly subsidized private schools, created substantial numbers of new stakeholders in the private education system. Zambia's health reform, by devolving responsibility for management and resources to local-level actors, has similarly created new stakeholders who have proven to be capable of resisting central-level efforts to reverse the reform process. The Peruvian government is attempting to build support for the privatization process by selling off a portion of public company shares through a citizen participation program, which allows low-income investors to buy shares in installments at low interest.[26] The Bolivian government is planning a similar scheme, which will distribute 50 percent of the proceeds from privatized companies to all adult Bolivians as shares in a new private-pension scheme.

While these are positive trends, there is a great deal of room for progress. East Asia's investments in basic education early on, coupled with sound macroeconomic management over time, are now paying off with higher sustained growth and lower levels of poverty than in other regions.[27] Latin America's progress on the macroreform front in recent years has been impressive. It is only now turning to the social-investment side of the equation, and results will take time. Chile, which began its process of reform in both these arenas much earlier than the other countries in the region, is now seeing results in terms of both growth and poverty reduction. Other countries will follow suit, but only as they complete both sides of this policy equation. Thus, social-sector reforms will be critical. Most countries in Africa, meanwhile, have yet to implement the macroeconomic reforms that can make social-sector reforms economically and politically possible.

Lessons for the Transition Economies

The record of safety nets and social-policy reform in the developing world is relevant for the transition economies, although the contexts are quite different. First, the macrotransformations in the transition economies are necessarily far more extensive than the adjustments in developing countries are. In many cases entire workforces must be deindustrialized. Existing social-welfare systems, many of which are run through public enterprises rather than the central government, are fiscally unsustainable and are not designed to cope with poverty and unemployment resulting from the transition to the market. This obviously makes it more difficult to provide effective safety nets. One potential approach for safety net policies in such a context is to concentrate specific programs on pockets of high unemployment, where social funds or public works could alleviate negative welfare effects, and at the same time to target the universal system of social-welfare benefits, such as monetary allowances, to particularly vulnerable groups, such as children in large families. Under the current structure, these benefits are universally provided, but due to fiscal constraints their real value is marginal and eroding further. Targeting these benefits to vulnerable groups would allow governments to raise their levels enough to reduce poverty without adding to the fiscal burden.

Second, the politics of the process are more complex in the transition economies: Expectations of the state are higher, reform has stalled in many cases, and the concerns of some politically influential groups, such as pensioners, dominate the public debate while very little attention is paid to the situation of needier and more vulnerable groups, such as the children of the working poor. The public debate on social welfare in the transition economies has mistakenly focused on two issues—the plight of pensioners and the pace of reform—while excluding several equally critical ones. Pensioners have fared worse than the average in some countries (most notably the countries of the former Soviet Union) and better than the average in others (the Eastern European countries). Not all pensioners are vulnerable; it is elderly pensioners living alone who are most at-risk. In contrast, children in large families, most of whom have at least one parent working, are the group that is most likely to be poor in all the transition economies.[28]

The debate about rapid versus gradual reform has focused on the high social costs purportedly associated with rapid reform. Yet in the countries that pursued rapid reform and were able to implement it fully—Poland, Czechoslovakia, Estonia, Latvia, and Albania—inflation was brought down quickly, and growth has begun to recover, which will have consequent effects on poverty reduction.[29] In large part reflecting the extent to which production under central planning did not reflect genuine consumer demand, output declined markedly in the initial reform stages in these countries. Gradual reformers have merely postponed inevitable declines and now lag far behind the faster reformers in terms of recovering growth. In addition, contrary to common assumptions, gradualists have not fared better in the political arena: More of them have been voted out of office than have their radical counterparts.[30]

The debate has focused on social-sector reform in few countries. And even in the strongest performing radical reformers, such as Poland and Czechoslovakia, attempts at social-sector reforms, such as pension reform, have stalled due to political opposition. Only Estonia, which for several years had the most promarket government of the transition economies, has moved ahead with pension reform. Yet progress in this arena is critical. No other region has experienced as great a deterioration of basic social-welfare indicators, such as infant mortality and life expectancy, as the transition economies.[31] In addition, due to demographic as well as economic changes, existing systems are simply not sustainable from a fiscal standpoint. Pension systems in particular, which account for the bulk of social expenditure in most transition economies, are likely to present the most immediate financial crises in the absence of social-security reform. Pension spending as percent of GDP ranges from 5–6 percent in Russia and the Baltics to 12 percent in Poland and Hungary.[32]

The debate over social-sector reforms in the transition economies resembles the stalled debates over social-welfare reform in the OECD countries. Yet the social-welfare and financial situations in the transition economies are far more fragile. A Catch-22 type of scenario is also in play: The maintenance of current social-welfare systems in many countries is part of the explanation for stalled reforms. Under the enterprise-based social-benefits system, if workers become unemployed, they lose access to social-welfare benefits. This is one of the principal reasons that managers are reluctant to lay off redundant workers, keeping them on the payroll even if they do not work or get paid, so that they can maintain access to critical benefits such as health and education services.[33]

While it is evident that social systems in transition economies need reform, there is no clear example in the region to which countries can turn. Recently even the highly successful Czech prime minister, Vaclev Klaus, faced an electoral setback over the social-sector reform issue. As he lost his majority in Parliament by a narrow margin, he now needs to make extensive efforts to build a new coalition of support for his reform agenda.[34] Some OECD countries, such as Italy, have attempted to implement social security reform, yet because the reform was watered down due to union opposition, it is likely to be far less effective in either providing better pensions or reducing the government's implicit debt. Other countries, including the United States and France, are debating the issue, with little progress to date. The rapid reformers in the transition economies should look to Latin America, not to the OECD countries, for examples. Chile is by far the world's leader in the social security reform arena, with its complete switch to an individual-contribution-based system that is credited with substantially increasing that country's savings capacity.[35] Now other countries, such as Peru, Colombia, and Argentina, provide hybrid models to examine. Rapid reformers also should capitalize on the political context: It is much easier to implement far-reaching change at a time when the overall policy framework is in flux and interest groups have yet to establish clear positions (as in the Latin American examples), than in a status quo policy framework like that of the OECD countries.

Two final tactical points are worthy of note. The first is the need to alter the political balance through strategies that create new stakes in the process of reform. Czechoslovakia, with its voucher privatization strategy, provides a prime example of such a strategy. While many observers criticize the measure from an economic-efficiency standpoint, virtually all observers concur that the program was key to building widespread support for the privatization process, thus making it irreversible. In contrast, in Russia, voucher privatization was poorly implemented, allowing insider traders to dominate the process and monopolize the benefits, further delegitimizing the process of reform in the public mind. Chile's social security reform was based on the concept of creating new stakeholders in the private system. Explaining and selling the reform to potential participants was key to its success, even in an authoritarian context.[36]

This points to the second critical tactical component of reform: government communication. Effective government communication has been key to the success of macroeconomic and sectoral reforms in a variety of contexts.[37] It is particularly critical in the transition economies, where public anxiety about the social costs of reform is high and understanding of the market process and of the potential benefits of social-welfare reforms is very low.[38] The misguided debate on poverty in the transition economies noted above is a case in point. An effective government communications policy, to explain and sell reforms to the public, will be key to any successful social-sector reform effort in these countries. For example, if the public understood that the tradeoff from increasing expenditures on pensions might well be a reduction in immunizations for children, the debate over social-sector reform might be more conducive to reform.

Conclusion

There is no clear recipe or model for successful social-sector reform in the transition economies. There are valuable experiences in the developing world, and in particular in Latin America, with both safety net policies and with social-sector reform, that are far more relevant for the transition economies than are the experiences of the OECD countries. Several conditions necessary for effective safety nets and for social-welfare policy emerge from these experiences. First, in the absence of a sound macroeconomic policy framework, no social-welfare reform is likely to succeed. Second, social expenditures targeted at the poorest sectors are far more effective from a poverty reduction standpoint. Third, there are major political obstacles to reallocating expenditures to the poorest, but a context of rapid and far-reaching macroeconomic reform provides governments with political opportunities for doing so. Political opposition can in part be overcome with strategies that involve the beneficiaries in the process of reform, thereby creating new stakeholders. Finally, effective government communication with the public will be critical to any reform effort.

Notes

1. Copyright 1999 by the National Academy of Sciences. Courtesy of the National Academy Press, Washington, D.C.
2. The term "transition economies" here refers to those countries in transition from state-led central planning to market-oriented economies.
3. For detail on the experiences of several countries, see Carol Graham, *Safety Nets, Politics, and the Poor: Transitions to Market Economies* (Washington, D.C.: Brookings Institution, 1994).

4. This chapter focuses only on social-sector reform in the context of economic transition and will not attempt a full-scale discussion of theories of institutional change. One of the most influential and comprehensive studies of institutional change is Douglass North, *Institutions, Institutional Change, and Economic Performance* (Cambridge: Cambridge University Press, 1990).

5. For a description of the so-called "Washington Consensus" policies, see John Williamson, ed., *The Political Economy of Policy Reform* (Washington, D.C.: Institute for International Economics, 1994).

6. See Giovanni Andrea Cornia, Richard Jolly, and Francis Stewart, eds. *Adjustment with a Human Face*, 2 vols. (New York: Oxford University Press, 1987).

7. Poverty figures for Peru are for Lima only and would be much higher if data for rural areas were available. For the case of Chile, see Mario Marcel and Andres Solimano, "The Distribution of Income and Economic Adjustment," in Barry Bosworth, Rudiger Dornbusch, and Raul Laban, eds., *The Chilean Economy* (Washington, D.C.: Brookings Institution, 1994). For the case of Peru, see Paul Glewwe and Gillette Hall, "Poverty, Inequality, and Living Standards During Unorthodox Adjustment," *Economic Development and Cultural Change* 42, (1994): 689–717.

8. Data for Africa is extremely limited, due both to unavailability of household level data and to the small number of successful adjusters. See Lionel Demery and Lyn Squire, "Poverty in Africa: The Emerging Picture" (Washington, D.C.: World Bank, 1995, mimeograph). For general cross-country evidence, see Michael Bruno, Martin Ravallion, and Lyn Squire, "Equity and Growth in Developing Countries: Old and New Perspectives on the Policy Issues," *Policy Research Working Paper,* no. 1563 (Washington, D.C.: World Bank, January 1996).

9. See Nancy Birdsall and Juan Luis Londoño, "Asset Inequality Does Matter" (paper presented to the American Economics Association Annual Meetings, New Orleans, 4–6 January 1997.

10. See Carol Graham and Moisés Naím, "The Political Economy of Institutional Reform," in Nancy Birdsall, Carol Graham, and Richard Sabot, eds., *Beyond Tradeoffs: Market Reforms and Equitable Growth in Latin America* (Washington, D.C.: Inter-American Development Bank: Brookings Institution Press, 1998).

11. A number of studies have established this relationship. For an overview, see Bruno et al., "Equity and Growth." For Latin America, see Samuel A. Morley, *Poverty and Inequality in Latin America* (Baltimore: Johns Hopkins University Press, 1995).

12. See Jeffrey Sachs and Andrew Warner, "Economic Reform and the Process of Global Integration," *Brookings Paper on Economic Activity*, vol. 1, (1995), pp. 1–96.

13. See Nancy Birdsall, David Ross, and Richard Sabot, "Inequality and Growth Reconsidered: Lessons from East Asia," *World Bank Economic Review* 9, no. 3 (1995).

14. Ronald Benabou, "Inequality and Growth," *NBER Macroeconomics Annual* (forthcoming).

15. For a review of several countries' experience, see Graham, *Safety Nets.*

16. Wages paid in employment programs, for example, must be below the market minimum so that they do not serve as disincentives for searching for alternative employment in the private sector.

17. See Graham, *Safety Nets.*
18. See Ibid., chap. 2.
19. For detail, see Genero Arriagada and Carol Graham, "Chile: Sustaining Adjustment During Democratic Transition," in Stephan Haggard and Steven B. Webb, eds., *Voting for Reform: Democracy, Political Liberalization, and Economic Adjustment* (New York: Oxford University Press/World Bank, 1994).
20. For detail on the ESF, see Carol Graham, "The Politics of Protecting the Poor During Adjustment: Bolivia's Emergency Social Fund," *World Development* 20, no. 9 (September 1992).
21. For detail see Nancy Birdsall and Estelle James, "Efficiency and Equity in Social Spending: Why Governments Misbehave," *WPS* 274 (Washington, D.C.: World Bank, May 1990); and Alan Angell and Carol Graham, "Can Social Sector Reform Make Adjustment Sustainable and Equitable? Lessons from Chile and Venezuela," *Journal of Latin American Studies* 27, part 1, (1995).
22. See Kevin Cowlan and Jose de Gregori, "Distribución y Pobreza en Chile: Estamos Mal? Ha Habido Progreso? Hemos Retrocedido?" (paper presented to Ministry of Finance/Inter-American Development Bank Workshop on Inequality and Growth, Santiago, 12–13 July 1996).
23. East Asia also provides several examples of efficient and well-targeted social expenditures, in particular investments in basic education. See Birdsall, Ross, and Sabot, "Inequality and Growth." Yet because the East Asian countries were neither democracies nor undergoing major economic adjustments at the time that their social-welfare frameworks were established, their experiences are less relevant to the transition economies. Indeed, most East Asian countries have not had to dramatically reform their social-welfare systems; rather, they were initially set up in an efficient manner in the context of good macroeconomic policies. Pension systems, for example, were not established in most countries until it was clear that they were affordable from a fiscal standpoint. This is in sharp contrast to the experience of most Latin American or transition economies.
24. Argentina, Bolivia, Columbia, and Peru have all implemented major social security reforms. A major health sector reform is underway in Argentina, and Peru is beginning such a process. In Africa, among other countries, Zambia has implemented a far-reaching health sector reform.
25. For detail on these political dynamics and the implementation of social safety net policies, see Graham, *Safety Nets.* For empirical evidence demonstrating how wealthier urban consumers disproportionately benefit from public utilities in Peru, see B. Adrianzen and G. Graham, "The High Costs of Being Poor," *Archives of Environmental Health* 28 (June 1974): 312–315. The allocation of public health and education services is often similarly skewed towards wealthier groups. For detail see Angell and Graham, "Can Social Sector Reform."
26. For detail on these programs, see Carol Graham, "Macroeconomic and Sectoral Reforms in Zambia: A Stakeholders' Approach?" (Brookings Institution, May 1996, mimeograph); Carol Graham, "Popular Capitalism Makes Headway in Peru," *Wall Street Journal,* 19 April 1996.
27. Birdsall, Ross, and Sabot, "Inequality and Growth."
28. See Branko Milanovic, *Poverty and Inequality in the Transition* (Washington, D.C.: World Bank, forthcoming); and Jeanine Braithwaite, "The Old and New Poor in Russia" (Washington, D.C.: Poverty and Social Policy Department, World Bank, January 1995, mimeograph).

29. Russia attempted radical reform, but the reformers were ousted from the government before the reforms took hold. See Anders Aslund, Peter Boone, and Simon Johnson, "Why Stabilize: Lessons from Post-Communist Countries," *Brookings Papers on Economic Activity*, no. 1 (1996).

30. Ibid. Radical reformers have lost elections primarily in situations where pro-reform forces were less united than the former Communists. And even where this has been the case, as in Poland and Estonia, reforms have not been reversed.

31. Some of the decline may reflect the extent to which pretransition statistics were not reliable. I am grateful to Dr. George Graham of Johns Hopkins University for raising this point.

32. These figures are for 1992. See "Old and Unaffordable," *The Economist*, 30 April 1994. The implicit debt of Ukraine's pension system, for example, is 214 percent of GDP. Among OECD countries, only Italy's debt, at 242 percent, is higher. Hungary's is 172 percent, Japan's is 144 percent, and the United States' is 89 percent. See Kane, "Notes on the Ukrainian Pensions System."

33. See Brian Pinto, Marek Belka, and Stefan Krajewski, "The Microeconomics of Transformation in Poland: A Survey of State Enterprise Responses" (Washington, D.C.: World Bank, June 1992, mimeograph).

34. Social-welfare reform (health and pension) was a major issue in the parliamentary elections in June of 1996. While Klaus's party received a higher percentage of the vote than it did in 1992 (44 percent versus 42 percent), it received fewer parliamentary seats, which went to the Christian Democrats in three industrialized regions. See "Czech Republic: Surprise," *The Economist*, 8 June 1996.

35. Private-sector saving in Chile increased from nearly zero in 1979–81 to an average of 17.1 percent of GDP in 1990–92. See Giancarlo Corsetti and Klaus Schmidt-Hebbel, "Pension Reform and Growth," *Policy Research Working Paper*, no. 1471 (Washington, D.C.: World Bank, June 1995).

36. Author's interviews with Jose Pinera, Minister of Labor and Social Security at the time the reform was implemented; Washington, D.C. and Santiago, June–July 1996.

37. For examples, see Graham, *Safety Nets*.

38. For a detailed description of this dynamic in one transition economy, see Carol Graham, "Strategies for Enhancing the Political Sustainability of Reform in Ukraine," *PSP Discussion Papers*, no. 50 (Washington, D.C.: World Bank, January 1995).

5

Safety Nets and Service Delivery: What Are Social Funds Really Telling Us?[1]

Judith Tendler

Social Funds (SFs) have drawn widespread enthusiasm and support from the international development community in recent years. They are said to reduce poverty and unemployment and to bring services and small works projects to myriad poor communities in a way that is decentralized, demand-driven, participatory, low in cost, and fast-disbursing. In Latin America alone, the World Bank, the Inter-American Development Bank (IDB), and the European Community have expended more than US$2 billion on eighteen social funds since the late 1980s—the IDB leading with US$1.3 billion. There is no sign of slackening, and proposals for SFs have even figured prominently in recent donor reform packages for the crisis-afflicted Asian economies. Strangely enough, however, the numerous studies of SFs carried out or funded by the donors themselves provide more grounds for skepticism than for enthusiasm. This chapter explores this conundrum and suggests a way out.

Donors view the SFs as a breakthrough in providing poor communities in developing countries, mainly in rural areas, with works projects and some services. Roughly one-third of the funds goes to economic infrastructure; another third to education and health, nutrition, and population activities; and another third to miscellaneous activities like microfinance, training, and environmental interventions.[2] The SFs, with their more independent project agencies or units and their "demand-driven" features,[3] are described as "an imaginative effort to make government actions and resources more beneficial to the poor." They are said to show "considerable potential as instruments of collaborative partnership between public-private community sectors for sustainable service delivery. . . . " They are reported to succeed, often, "in targeting the poor and in providing

87

basic services more cheaply and speedily than public sector agencies that have traditionally been charged with these functions."[4]

This chapter, drawing mainly on evidence about SFs provided by donor evaluations, raises questions about the presumed greater desirability of SFs as an alternative to traditional government supply, or reformed versions of it. My fieldwork on four SFs in northeast Brazil, as reported elsewhere, reinforced this interpretation of the evidence.[5] Through the lens of the SF projects, this chapter also seeks to contribute to the broader debates around issues of decentralization, partial privatization, and other attempts to improve the quality of public service delivery in developing countries. The acclaimed strengths of SFs, after all, are variations on a more general set of arguments about the problems of overcentralized and "supply-driven" public service provision, and about the superiority of more decentralized and demand-driven approaches.

With some exceptions, the donor community has interpreted the SF experience through a rather ill-fitting template, which categorizes it as demand-driven, decentralized, partially privatized, and therefore "good." In certain ways, for example, SFs represent the *opposite* of real decentralization. They are run by central-government agencies, either newly created or newly empowered by their association with international donors and with strong support from the country's president. In the majority of cases, moreover, they do not devolve power and responsibilities to local governments. When they do, this is usually not part of a larger reform of intergovernmental transfers and other decentralizing measures, and sometimes even works at cross-purposes to such reforms. To the extent that SFs do try to reduce the size (though not power) of the "central" part of their operation, they may be more accurately described as "deconcentrated" rather than as "decentralized."

Without the template through which SFs are usually viewed, the experience could yield some interesting evidence on which to build a less limiting view of opportunities for reform. This chapter encourages the development community to expand its thinking beyond SF-type models to ways of improving government performance that may not be as new and different but that have shown no more defects than the SFs.

What follows is not meant to be a thorough review of the SF experience or of the arguments for and against SFs. For this, the reader can turn to several comprehensive donor-funded reviews of the evidence and a handful of other excellent studies of SFs by social scientists, all referred to in the endnotes. The arguments that follow also do *not* constitute a brief against SFs or demand-driven approaches in general, or in favor of supply-driven approaches. I will argue not that SFs are performing poorly, but that the donors' own evidence does not demonstrate that they are clearly superior to other approaches to improving government services in a sustained way. I therefore question the large amounts of funding dedicated to them and the importance attributed to them as a new approach to delivering services and reducing poverty.

Social Funds and Their Strengths

Since the late 1980s, the two largest donors have spent roughly US$2.6 billion on SFs—US$1.3 billion by the IDB on eighteen social funds in sixteen countries of Latin America, US$1.3 billion by the World Bank in thirty-four countries (mainly in Latin America and Africa), and roughly that same amount by the European donors combined.[6] Social Funds started in Latin America, according to the lore, as a temporary antidote to the adverse impact of structural-adjustment programs on the poor in various countries.[7] The Latin American experience came to be the reference point for SF promotion elsewhere. Originally, SFs were meant to provide quick employment through public-works projects and emergency social services in rural areas, partly in lieu of the increasingly faltering presence of fiscally strapped line ministries. Some were designed explicitly to compensate for layoffs caused by downsizing of the public sector and its parastatals.

After three or four years, donors judged the SFs to be so effective at temporary relief, and so appealing as an alternative model of public-sector service delivery, that they provided follow-on funding to several SFs and elevated some to more permanent status. They also came to see the SFs not just as a temporary measure for hard times, but also as an attractive model—decentralized, partially privatized, and demand-driven—for the delivery of some services and small works projects, particularly to the poor and in rural areas.

Though SFs vary widely across countries, they tend to have the following common components: (1) grant funds are made available to communities or municipal councils who choose among a menu of possible projects (a well, health center, school, grain mill, road repair, etc.); (2) project design and construction are decentralized and partially privatized, involving local actors—private firms, NGOs, or local governments; (3) community groups make contact with and contract the design or construction firm or equipment supplier, monitor project execution, and/or take responsibility subsequently for operations and maintenance; and (4) a local contribution is often required, roughly 10 to 15 percent of project costs.

In addition to their emphasis on the virtues of these demand-driven and decentralized features, donor evaluations portray the SF success in terms of characteristics that are just the opposite of the typical government agency—namely, rapid rates of disbursement,[8] flexibility, low overhead due to "lean" administration, and low unit costs for projects like schools, health posts, road repairs, and other standardizable works.[9] As depicted in the numerous documents on social funds, the organizational features considered key to these achievements are: (1) they are run by semi-autonomous units or agencies operating outside line agencies, sometimes newly created and often close to the office of the country's president; (2) they work outside civil service regulations, particularly with respect to the setting of salaries and hiring and firing; (3) their managers are often recruited from the outside and have experience with management in the private sector, while many of their staff members represent the best of the public sector, lured to the SFs by the higher salaries; (4) they have succeeded in operating *outside* government procurement regulations and simplifying procurement in a way that has sped up the execution of small works projects; and, as a result, (5) they use design standards that are not overdimensioned and hence are more appropriate for rural areas. Other contributing factors are said to be the use of private contractors and the competition they must face; the involvement of beneficiary communities in project execution through contributions of management time, labor, and cash; and the high dedication of project staff "in comparison to their inefficient counterparts in government public works departments."[10]

The Problem and How to Solve It

Underlying these acclaimed features of SF design is a broader set of arguments about the problematic nature of the traditional organization of government programs—namely, that they are overly centralized, inflexible, and supply-driven; their costs are high, mostly for personnel; and their pace of work is encumbered and slow. These arguments, based mainly on recent literature in economics and political science, suggest that more decentralized, demand-driven, and partially privatized provision reduces many of the undesirable aspects of traditional government provisioning. Because the arguments about decentralization are by now quite familiar and have attained the status of self-evident truths, they are summarized only briefly here.

The problematic nature of much of government service provision is said to arise from its position not just as a monopoly, but one that is unregulated. In this sense, government's problem is similar to that of any other monopoly, private as well as public: It is over-centralized and inflexible and suffers from low responsiveness to consumer preferences and other inefficiencies that go unpunished by competitive pressures. Decentralization is thought to reduce these problems, partly by introducing competitive pressures or surrogates for them. It locates service provision more locally and also brings in new providers from outside government—most importantly, firms and nonprofit organizations. Operating at more local levels, firms and NGOs are expected to be more flexible than government and more capable of creating locally tailored solutions; NGOs in particular will be more committed to working with the poor than government. For these pressures and incentives to bear fruit, it should be noted, decentralizing programs need not necessarily be *formally* demand-driven.

For decades, donor monitoring and evaluation reports have bemoaned the problems associated with overly centralized government—excessive standardization, overdimensioning of projects, and unnecessarily high unit costs. The sorry results of these failings include, particularly, faulty operations and maintenance (O&M) and the shortage of financing for recurrent costs and other operational support. It is exactly these kinds of problems that led to the current preoccupation of the development community with "sustainability" and "ownership." In that decentralization transfers the process of project choice and design closer to where users live, this is expected to lead to lower costs and more customized results. Providers will be more vulnerable to pressures from users, and a good part of the responsibility for O&M can be handed over to the users themselves.

Today, these linked arguments for decentralized and demand-driven service delivery seem to make obvious sense. At the same time, they also represent a refreshing departure from previous thinking about planning and government organization. They deny, often only implicitly, the importance of economies of scale and of standardization and specialization, particularly in the provision of small-scale and local-level infrastructure and services to the poor. The arguments suggest that planning, design, and execution by agencies with functional expertise and responsibilities simply do not work under a wide variety of circumstances. This is because something gets in the way that prevents the traditional economies of scale and standardization from materializing.

The demand-driven approach, in contrast, starts the process of project design and implementation not with decisions by planners but with choice by the user—namely, "the community." Government's role is not to be the sole designer and provider of the well or power hookup or other project, but to lead a *process* by which it offers an array of options from which people can choose. The community's choice, in turn, does not simply trigger provision of the project by a specialized agency or the SF itself. Rather, the tasks of design, construction, and equipment purchase can now be carried out as well, and at the community's behest, by private firms, nongovernment organizations, or municipal governments.[11]

For the logic of decentralization to work properly, user choice is key. Users must have good information about their rights and options; they must be informed of the procedures for gaining access to service providers, for registering their preferences or dissatisfactions, and, in the case of SFs, must know how to design projects and present them for funding. For this reason, many SFs include public information campaigns. It is not only the donors who have drawn attention to the importance of providing information to users. The last decade's literature on transactions costs has devoted much greater attention to the issue. This includes, in particular, the concern about the "information asymmetries" that are so common in the transactions between intended project beneficiaries and their providers.

Acclaim and Evidence

The numerous studies of SFs carried out or funded by development institutions usually start and end on an enthusiastic note.[12] But certain findings reported in the middle—sometimes in sections related to "problems" or "issues"—provide serious grounds for skepticism. Even two quite critical papers on social funds have drawn for their supporting evidence on these very same donor documents, or on research funded by the donors.[13]

Social Funds started with the purpose of creating temporary employment for the poor and thereby reducing poverty through small, decentralized works projects in rural areas. With the seeming success early on in Latin America, the donors came to see Social Funds more broadly as a good model for permanently serving poor rural communities—not only with works projects, including the building of schools and health clinics, but also with a variety of other services like day care centers and microfinance programs. Through the years, the donors have tended to place more emphasis on the claim about service delivery than that about employment creation and poverty reduction; nevertheless, SFs still appear as important instruments in the donor arsenal of "safety net" policies for the poor. The findings of my own fieldwork, as reported elsewhere, also relate more to the claims about SFs as an alternative way of organizing service delivery than to their strength as safety nets.[14] Unfortunately, there has been more systematic and quantitative empirical research into the claims about employment creation and poverty reduction than into the alleged superior performance of SFs as a model of public administration.

In what follows, the evidence for each of the two claims is discussed separately—poverty reduction and employment creation, as distinct from the new model of organizing services and works projects. The evidence is drawn mainly from four recent multicountry reviews of the SF experience by the Inter-American Development Bank, the World Bank, and UNICEF, in addition to some studies by outside researchers.[15]

Reducing Unemployment and Poverty

With respect to the claims about employment creation, the SF reviews reveal that these programs have "created relatively few jobs" and reached only a small fraction of the labor force (in the Latin American case, less than 1 percent at best).[16] They devoted only 30 percent of their expenditures to labor costs, a rather low share for programs dedicated to employment creation.[17] Jobs provided by the SFs were temporary, of low quality, and provided no training. Most of the better jobs went to skilled laborers brought in from elsewhere by outside contractors; 42 percent of labor expenditures in the Nicaraguan SF, for example, were for skilled labor.[18] Several employment creation programs that antedated the SFs created significantly more jobs, employed a more significant share of the labor force,[19] and elicited significantly greater budgetary resources from their respective governments. In comparison to the demand-driven SFs, these programs were supply-driven and mainly not funded by donors (at least initially).

Wages paid by Social Funds, although often set at the legal minimum, were nevertheless typically lower than subsistence, and sometimes significantly so.[20] The wage in the Nicaraguan SF, for example, represented 57 percent of a basic family food basket. Granted, wages are often set this low in employment-creating programs so as not to draw labor away from private-sector employers and to keep the nonpoor from applying for these jobs. At the same time, however, the lower-than-subsistence level plus the temporariness of the jobs adds up to a weak instrument for a more sustained reduction of poverty and unemployment. In the same vein, the voluntary labor often required of communities for SF projects, although meant to serve the goal of reducing costs and eliciting "ownership" of the project, represents a regressive tax on the poor.[21]

With respect to poverty reduction, the donor evaluations do not bear out the claim that Social Funds do well in reaching the poor. Either the available data do not permit such judgments, the studies report,[22] or the data show, at best, quite mixed results. Higher per capita SF expenditures often go to better-off communities or provinces than to the poorer or the poorest.[23] Even in the "star" Bolivian SF, the richest of five income areas received two-and-a-half times as much SF funding per capita as the poorest five ($25 versus $10).[24] This mistargeting happens partly because the better-off communities are better organized, better educated, and have greater access to local decisionmakers, and are therefore more capable of taking advantage of the demand-driven structure.[25] Other kinds of programs, different from SFs and typically more supply-driven, seem to have had more identifiable impacts in reducing poverty—programs like food stamps, food commodity programs, or school feeding programs.[26] The message is clear, the IDB evaluators conclude: if these funds have had an impact on poverty, this impact has not resulted from employment creation and income generation for the poor.[27]

In conclusion, Social Funds have "created relatively few jobs and generated little additional income for the poor,"[28] even though many of them included income and employment generation among their stated objectives. They were not "effective safety nets in any significant scale," and many countries therefore did not have "an effective mechanism to protect the poor from output, employment, and price risks."[29] This was true despite the fact that all Latin American countries with SFs gave them a "high profile and a central role in the campaign to reduce poverty."[30] Clearly, these findings are disappointing.

To the credit of the donors, their published evaluations have owned up to some of these results, albeit without at the same time losing enthusiasm for the SFs as a model. First, they say that "fundamental fiscal and institutional reforms" at the macro level are so much more determining of changes in poverty and unemployment that one cannot really expect that much from such a limited programmatic intervention.[31] (It is not clear why that conclusion was not foreseen when donors were promoting SFs from temporary to permanent status, on the grounds of their desirability as a model for reaching poor communities.)

Second, the donors argue that even if Social Funds have not made the inroads on poverty and unemployment that were originally hoped for, they have turned out to be on firmer ground as a model for service delivery.[32] Social Funds "help to improve the living conditions of the poor," the IDB reports, by being "efficient providers of social and economic infrastructure" (p. 72). In this sense they "are a response to a permanent problem"—namely, that "Latin American governments, as presently constituted, have few agencies through which to channel resources and services to the poor," and that, as a result, the benefits of most government programs "go to better-off communities" (p. 64). The SFs, in contrast, "have shown an impressive ability to deliver social infrastructure to the poor in a relatively efficient and transparent manner" (p. 4). The World Bank, similarly, concludes that SFs are an "effective instrument" for emergency assistance and have proven to have "significant potential for community development for the *sustainable* delivery of services to the poor" (italics mine).[33] In this way, they have contributed to important "asset building" in rural areas—schools, health clinics, power hookups, road repairs or construction, the sinking of wells for drinking water. Even some of the more-critical outside commentators on SF weaknesses in alleviating unemployment and poverty have taken this position. Social Funds "appear to have been successful in building water and sanitation systems, schools and health posts in underserved areas with relatively high concentrations of the poor;"[34] they are "better at creating assets" than at targeting;[35] and they have "resulted in an invaluable increase in the level of services to many previously marginalised poor. . . . "[36] Is this depiction accurate?

Social Funds as an Alternative

Upon closer examination, the evidence of the donor evaluations for the claim about SFs as a desirable model of service delivery seems weak. More seriously, the SF problems flagged in the donor evaluations appear to represent the flip side of their acclaimed strengths. This suggests an inherent difficulty in remedying the problems, which take the following forms.

Social Funds versus the comparators. Except for various eyewitness reports from the evaluators and repeated assertions about the superiority of SFs in creating much activity in the countryside, there have been almost no attempts to systematically select comparator programs in traditional ministries against which to judge SF performance as a model. (This, of course, is partly a methodological problem of comparing apples and oranges.) One interesting exception is an attempt by the World Bank to measure the performance of its SF projects in relation to the more traditional supply-driven programs it funds. Surprisingly, however, no clear superiority emerges for SFs from this comparison, even though the evaluation still concludes on a positive note about the SF as a model.[37] The IDB evaluators, also concluding positively, reported that the evidence they reviewed was not sufficient to form a judgment as to whether SFs have actually made a difference in the availability of basic economic and social services in the various communities where they operate.[38] In addition, they found that the most successful and innovative of the SFs were those conceived *without* donor input and financing (Chile, Costa Rica, and Guatemala) and were different from the typical SF in important ways.[39] (This is discussed in more detail below.)

Relations with line ministries. The donor evaluations express considerable concern about the wisdom of investing so much energy and resources in creating new structures outside government instead of more directly supporting reform of existing government institutions. The World Bank review warned that SFs "should not take attention away from—or work counter to— . . . fundamental fiscal or institutional reforms . . . that address poverty systemically."[40] Cautionary examples were that of Egypt, where the central government explicitly cut back allocations to local governments because of the expected "inflows from the Social Fund"; and Honduras, where allocations for the ministries of education and health declined at the same time that local governments began receiving more funds as a result of the SF there.[41]

A variation on this problem, related to the grant-funded nature of the SFs, was the "unfair" competition SFs presented to other government agencies. While these latter agencies were providing *loan* financing to municipalities or communities for similar projects, SFs were offering more attractive grant funding; this sometimes happened, moreover, at the same time that the non-SF agencies, urged by donors themselves, were trying to make the difficult transition from providing grant to loan financing to communities for appropriate projects. When able to choose between grant and loan financing, of course, the communities or municipalities understandably preferred the free funding of the SFs; sometimes, SFs even funded applications that existing agencies had rejected for loan funding on technical or other grounds. The World Bank gives examples of two such cases, one in Senegal and the other in Bolivia.[42] I also heard complaints of this nature in Brazil from modernizing mayors who had introduced new loan-funded programs and received only complaints from their constituents, who pointed to the "free" funds from the SF.

The IDB evaluators dubbed the tendency to create Social Funds, rather than attack problems directly, as "funditis."[43] For example, the IDB reported that if the ministries of health and education in various countries had not been subject to the budget constraints of fiscal austerity programs, a good part of the replacement and upgrading of schools and health posts would normally have been undertaken by these ministries, rather than by SFs.[44] The evaluators worried that the SFs would become "shadow governments." They warned that SFs "should not replace the public sector in tasks that are the government's inherent responsibility . . . , " and that this could "undermine ongoing public-sector reforms and institution building programs." Noting that most SFs were not subject to ordinary government legislation with respect to salaries and procurement—one of the acclaimed *strengths* of SFs emphasized in the donor studies—the evaluators cautioned that the goal should be "to improve the laws and regulations under which the line ministries work," rather than to get around them. Similar concerns were expressed by outside researchers.[45]

Donors and outside critics seem to agree, then, that Social Funds can jeopardize the larger task of reform of the public sector, or at least distract attention from it. The particular problems they point to, ironically, are grounded in the same mode of operations that is said to account for the SFs' acclaimed strengths. None of the evaluations face this particular conundrum, expressing confidence that the problems can be fixed.

Sustainability. Both major donors gave distinctly low marks to the Social Funds for "sustainability" and "ownership."[46] There were frequent reports of health clinics without refrigerators for vaccines, school buildings without textbooks, wells that were not maintained. More generally, the evaluators admitted to finding little evidence regarding sustainability and ownership, and in this sense were not able to back up the claim that SFs are a better alternative that merits permanent funding. Where they did find evidence, it was mixed.

The World Bank evaluators could find no data on the extent to which SF projects were being operated and maintained.[47] An approach that aims for user "ownership" of operations and maintenance (O&M) or pressuring of local entities into providing it, the evaluators noted, often requires different technical design, at least for economic infrastructure. But a large number of the SFs were found to have been designed without issues of sustainability in mind.[48] It was "not clear" if communities even knew what the O&M costs and responsibilities would be, according to the evaluators, before they chose their project. And only a small percentage of the SFs turned out to have actually required community contributions, even though the SF projects presented for approval to the World Bank board of directors (the "appraisal reports") always included an estimate for upfront contributions from communities. Little follow-up information on such contributions was available.[49]

Social Funds financed many activities—such as schools, clinics, water—that would need sustained support from line ministries or other agencies of government, once completed. However, either no formal arrangements were made, or arrangements that *were* made were not respected.[50] In many cases, no operating funds came through for staff and maintenance, particularly for schools and health.[51] In theory, and at least for some types of projects, this should not be a serious problem. The decentralized and demand-driven features of the SF are believed to lead inexorably to ownership by communities of the new projects, and they will therefore take responsibility for operations and maintenance themselves, or they will pressure local governments successfully to do so. As noted above, however, little of this has happened in practice, or, at the least, little evidence has been gathered to support this claim.

If, as the evaluators report, neither the donors nor the recipients created these programs with sustainability in mind, then it is not fair to judge the programs by that criterion. But the donors themselves have made strong claims for these programs as successful, on the grounds of community involvement. Indeed, they have hailed the SFs as models of sustainable service delivery, as attested to by the quotes cited above.

Another observation about sustainability relates to the effectiveness of Social Funds in reaching wide swaths of the rural poor. Much has been made of the low unit costs involved in SF construction of buildings and other works in comparison to those of existing government agencies. Presumably, this would make it possible to reach larger numbers of communities more cost-effectively with the same amount of funding as existing government agencies. The donor evaluators reported various cases, however, in which new schools and health centers were constructed when rehabilitation of existing structures was more appropriate.[52] This is not unusual for various types of government programs, so it is certainly not peculiar to SFs. But the focus on low unit costs begs this question because it assumes that new construction—as opposed to less costly rehabilitation in this example—was needed in the first place.

With respect to sustainability and ownership at a more macro level, finally, both the IDB and the World Bank lament the fact that most SF programs, ten years after they were started, continue to be dependent for most of their financing on outside donors.[53] After noting that most Latin American governments with SFs have financed less than 20 percent of their SF operations, the IDB evaluators warn that "[d]onors cannot claim that the funds are successful and sustainable" until countries make a greater contribution. "[D]onors cannot be expected to provide 80–90 percent of the cost of fund operations indefinitely."[54]

At least with respect to the findings on sustainability and ownership, in sum, the Social Funds do not seem to do much better than the older programs on which they were supposed to improve.

Nongovernmental organizations in the new space. At various points, the donor evaluations noted, sometimes with puzzlement, that NGOs were either not present in the program area or were associated with disappointing results when they were.[55] NGOs turned out to account for no more than 15 percent of expenditures by most Latin American SFs.[56] Reddy's review for UNICEF noted that "[f]avouritism in the disbursal of contracts to NGOs" was a "serious issue" in various countries, as was the "proliferation" of NGOs "of dubious grassroots credentials" as a result of the new availability of SF funding.[57] The IDB review reported that the "recurrent-cost problem" was most acute in the case of NGOs; a study of the Bolivian SF, for example, showed NGOs to be disproportionately represented among the projects that were *least* likely to be sustained.[58] The World Bank found that nongovernmental, religious, and other grassroots organizations were found *not* to operate in the poorest regions because of their location in cities and towns, in and close to which they seemed to concentrate their work.[59] With respect to the microfinance components now gaining popularity in the SFs, moreover, the World Bank evaluators found that NGOs had not shown an ability to incorporate best-practice lessons learned from the microfinance experience around the world.[60]

These scattered reports, though perhaps not conclusive, do raise questions as to whether NGOs are present enough, or well enough suited, to play the role required of them for the decentralized and demand-driven model to work. It may be, moreover, that the time, funding, and attention needed to get them up to speed would be substantial.

Community choice and rapid disbursement. In the donor portrayals, the SF approach combines flexible and unencumbered disbursement with a demand-driven style. These features, however, are often at loggerheads with each other. For example, some SF managers expressed a distaste for, and therefore sometimes discouraged, genuine processes of community decisionmaking. These processes, they said, "slowed down" the rates of disbursement so prized by these managers and their donors.[61] Other managers actually liked the eligibility criteria which, even though slowing down disbursement, gave them some kind of protection against political interference.[62] The researchers comparing SFs with earlier supply-driven programs, moreover, found that the latter actually disbursed *more* rapidly than the SFs. Their explanation for the SFs' slower disbursement also pointed to the demand-driven design: if taken seriously and at its best, it resulted in a time-consuming process of organizing and decisionmaking by communities or municipal councils. Although these reports reveal the somewhat contradictory nature of the evidence on fast versus slow disbursement, they are consistent in pointing to the problematic tradeoff—inherent in the demand-driven model—between quick disbursement and the expression of user voice.

The requirement that communities organize for purposes of "ownership" seemed to take a particular toll on poorer communities. They are more isolated from the promotional visits of government agents, NGOs, and firms, and they are handicapped by the requirement that they prepare and present an acceptable project.[63] Even when the project agency painstakingly mapped poverty and deficiencies of social services in the region served by SFs—considered one of their important achievements—this could not counteract the comparative advantage of better-off communities *within* the "poor-designated" municipalities or sub-regions in the competition for funds.[64] In the education projects of the Mexican SF, for example, the program's requirement that a community have an effectively functioning solidarity school committee before seeking funding was said to explain why fewer per capita funds went to poor indigenous communities as compared to others.[65]

In itself, the evidence presented above does not necessarily add up to an indictment of SFs. It does, however, reveal some disappointing results and serious contradictions within the model. These kinds of problems, after all, are not the teething problems of a new approach. They have cropped up for some time in donor evaluations of programs other than SFs, and prior to them. Indeed, they have for some time gained the status of boilerplate in the narratives written by project supervision missions and evaluation consultants returning from the field. For as long as large donors have been financing roads and other infrastructure in developing countries, for example, supervision reports have lamented the lack of maintenance and the failure to generate or allocate funds for operations and maintenance. But these kinds of problems are exactly what the incentives and pressures of the SF approach were supposed to reduce—at least for programs serving poor communities in rural areas with a variety of works projects and services.

Given this evidence and the unsettling questions it raises, the Social Funds seem to have emerged remarkably unscathed. The World Bank evaluation concludes that the SFs "*probably* surpass other sector portfolios in the cost and speed of service delivery, success in reaching the poor, and extent to which they respond to community initiatives" (italics mine).[66] It is surely difficult to draw any such conclusion, however, given the evidence laid out above. The most one can say is that SFs and SF-like programs have not proven to be consistently and sustainedly better than the more traditional supply-driven programs or the reformed versions of them. This does not amount to an indictment of SFs, but it certainly is a far cry from the enthusiastic support they have been accorded by donors.

The Fixes

Why do the owners of these negative findings continue to be so enthusiastic? Is this simply a question of choosing to view the glass as half full rather than half empty? I suggest that the difference between the two views lies elsewhere. The donors see the SFs' shortcomings as eminently fixable, as requiring the fine-tuning of an otherwise preferable model of public service delivery. I see the problems, however, as inherent in the SF model itself—particularly when operating in rural areas and serving poorer populations—exactly the situations to which the model is thought to be eminently suited. In addition, the proposed fixes would have the SFs improve their operation in ways that would make them more like the traditional agencies from which they are supposed to differ so markedly.

Although the fixes prescribed by the donors seem perfectly reasonable, that is, they also require just what the SF model is trying to get away from—additional presence, effort, and resources from an agency of central government. A representative sampling of the most common fixes appearing in the donor reports includes more monitoring and supervision, more transparent and objective selection criteria for projects, more training, more public information campaigns about project choices available to communities, more tolerance by project managers for "participation," more poor-targeted selection criteria, more "demand orientation" and community participation in helping communities to choose their projects, and, that old chestnut, more coordination with line agencies and their sectoral programs.[67]

These remedies, if taken seriously, would require substantially more time, personnel, resources (for travel, vehicles, and per diems), and more presence in the countryside by the program agency—an agency of the central government. The remedies would surely increase the SFs' low overheads and reduce their strong disbursement rates—the model's pride and joy. They would move these programs back in a supply-driven direction, rather than closer to the demand-driven model's vision of citizen demand-making, partially privatized provision, and more active government at the local level. The strength of the demand-driven model, after all, is supposed to be its reliance on *local* forces to solve such problems. It is these forces that, in substituting for the presence and planning of more centralized agencies, are supposed to bring down costs, improve quality, please users, and elicit ownership arrangements for upkeep and financing. Even if one assumes that the fixes could be carried out effectively, moreover, this could well require as much effort as reforming a traditional supply-driven agency, or improving the capacity of a set of local governments, or even reducing the problem of lack of ownership by rewarding local tax-collecting efforts.

Putting together the findings with the fixes, in sum, seems to get the donors into something of a bind. A striking example is donor concerns about the difficulty SFs have in working with line ministries or following their sectoral priorities. The IDB evaluators warn that SFs should not operate "outside the planning process" but instead should "teach line ministries to be more responsive to local needs and build more efficiently."[68] To build schools and health clinics outside a "functional allocation" of the line ministries for this purpose, the evaluators say, leads to outcomes like the construction of new schools and clinics, as noted above, where rehabilitation of old ones would have been sufficient. They condemn such outcomes as "a failure of the planning process."[69]

This is a surprising conclusion about a model whose strength is said to lie in having communities rather than bureaucrats decide what they are to receive. Sector planning and execution by central-government agencies, after all, has been defined as the *problem*, not the solution. Without perhaps meaning to, then, the critiques and the suggestions of these donor evaluators seem to undermine the very model of which they approve: they identify shortcomings above which demand-driven programs were supposed to rise, and they recommend fixes that smack of supply-driven sectoral planning.

What's wrong here? The model itself? Or the fixes? This bind may be actually of the donors' own making. A close reading of the evaluations themselves provides some clues for getting out of the bind.

Conclusion: Getting Out of the Fix

As portrayed in the donor evaluations, some of the stories about better Social Funds or better-performing aspects of them appear to contain possible lessons about how to reform existing government agencies, in contrast to the SF agency or unit itself. This material, however, has not been sufficiently mined to draw any firm conclusions, although it raises intriguing questions that merit further exploration. One example is the Chilean FOSIS noted above, which worked more closely with line agencies than the typical SF. Another is the Peruvian fund FONCODES, which has started evolving toward more coordination with the line agencies on works projects. FONCODES will finance only those works-project proposals that are in accordance with sectoral policies and norms and for which operating revenues are guaranteed.[70]

The Chilean FOSIS is not only among the more successful of the Social Funds. It is also notable for, among other things, the ways it differs from the typical SF model or experience: (1) created by the Chilean government in 1990, it started with only 20 percent donor funding, in contrast to the 80–95 percent range of most other SFs, and by 1997 it had no more than 11 percent donor funding; (2) it now raises 40 percent of its funding not from a guaranteed allocation of the national budget but by competing for service agreements offered to it by regional governments with newly acquired federal-revenue transfers; (3) national procurement laws are observed rather than waived; (4) staff are paid the same salaries as in the line ministries, rather than the higher salaries that characterize most SFs; and (5) much of its founding management and staff were professionals who came from the NGO sector that emerged during the Pinochet period, who share a strong commitment to poverty concerns and a long history of experience in this area. (This last trait contrasts, by the way, to the emphasis of the SF studies on private-sector, or private-sector-like management.)

Finally, the Chilean FOSIS is more integrated into the line ministries than almost all the SFs. It is directly dependent on the Ministry of Planning and Coordination rather than standing outside the line agencies. Ministry support has been key in setting up of a network of regional FOSIS offices, and FOSIS works through collaborative agreements with various other line agencies.[71] An outside research study comparing FOSIS with the Venezuelan SF, by Angell and Graham (1995), cited this unusual integration of the Chilean SF with the line ministries as an explanation for why it was more successful.[72]

The unusual success of the Chilean Social Funds raises questions about the model's assumed key features—the waiving of procurement regulations, the paying of higher salaries, the importance of private-sector-like management, the "disentanglement" of the stand-alone SF unit from traditional bureaucracy, and the resulting rapid rates of disbursement. With respect to rapid disbursement, for example, the IDB evaluators report that the pressures for rapid disbursement tend to conflict with the very interaction with line ministries that was so important to the performance of cases like Chile's FOSIS.[73] The Chilean case, in short, begs for an explanation as to why and how procurement regulations, civil service salaries and regulations, and close involvement with line ministries were *not* a problem. Though many would respond that Chile is a special case or that Chile is doing everything right, this is to dismiss the opportunity to learn the more generic lessons that such a case, when combined with others, has to offer.

Another intriguing item of interest requiring further exploration is that both the IDB and World Bank evaluators note a certain pattern of performance with respect to some types of projects as against others. They found that sustainability was more likely in education and health than in two other important project types—economic infrastructure (roads and road repairs, irrigation, water, etc.), and microfinance.[74] In contrast to these other sectors, they said in explanation, the education and health components tended to have line ministry involvement in the approval of projects and to be more compatible with broader policy in these sectors.[75] Indeed, because many of the task managers for the SF projects at the donor agencies actually came from education and health ministries, this made them "more sensitive to and knowledgeable about" issues of sustainability when project proposals came up in these particular sectors.[76]

Both the World Bank and IDB evaluators attributed the greater likelihood of sustainability in education and health types to the greater standardizability of design in these sectors. Standardization made it possible to create project prototypes that, with computer-generated designs, have been helpful in establishing costs and designs.[77] One wonders if the greater possibility of creating a standardized language and procedures for dealing with project design and approval might have laid the groundwork for an easier relationship between the SFs and the line ministries in the education and health sectors as opposed to the others. Whether or not this interpretation is accurate, it is not clear how to reconcile the positive role of standardizability alleged here with the *negative* traits of standardization as portrayed by the same donors in their critique of the supply-driven model.

Exploring these kinds of findings further might reveal more about how to improve traditional line ministries and other agencies than about the desirability of a demand-driven model run by a semiautonomous government unit. At this point, however, the donor evaluations themselves do not provide us with enough information to understand lessons of this nature. Focusing on the SF experience itself and trying to fit the findings within the confines of the current claims about SFs, the donor evaluations do not seem to scan the experience broadly enough for clues about improving government performance in general. One of the more important lessons to be learned from the SF experience may be that it contains lessons about possible pathways to reform in line ministries and other agencies, and about providing succor to reform advocates within their ranks.

The donors, in sum, do not seem to have made a convincing case for the superiority of Social Funds as a model of service delivery and asset creation, let alone for reducing unemployment or poverty, notwithstanding their assertions to the contrary. The focus on the demand-driven logic and on other traits of the SF model, moreover, has distracted attention from the lessons to be learned about reform of traditional government agencies, as well as other matters like strengthening local government. In addition, the conceptual dichotomy between demand-driven and decentralized as "good," versus supply-driven and centralized as "bad," probably obscures more than it illuminates. Trimming our expectations of SFs down to size is not to say that traditional supply-driven agencies are necessarily better. Rather, if SF experiences *and* those of the traditional line agencies could be looked at with a more open and curious mind, it is quite possible that more constructive lessons could be drawn from both.

Notes

1. This chapter is based on a longer monograph prepared for the Division of Management Governance and Development of the United Nations Development Programme. See Judith Tendler (with the assistance of Rodrigo Serrano), *The Rise of Social Funds: What Are They a Model Of?*, Department of Urban Studies and Planning, Massachusetts Institute of Technology, monograph for the United Nations Development Programme

(UNDP), draft January 1999. I thank the following institutions for supporting the research and/or writing: the United Nations Development Programme, the Massachusetts Institute of Technology, the Latin American Program of the Woodrow Wilson Center, and the state governments of Ceará and Maranhão. None of these institutions is responsible for or necessarily agrees with the analysis and opinions reported here.

I am particularly grateful to Mick Moore for discussing these ideas with me at length, and for providing me with excellent feedback on an earlier draft. Anu Joshi provided valuable editing and substantive comments.

2. "Portfolio Improvement Program Review of the Social Funds Portfolio," The Working Group for the Social Funds Portfolio Review, headed by Ishrat Husain (PREM) (forthcoming as World Bank Technical Paper) (Washington, D.C.: World Bank, May 1997), p. 5.

3. Not all SFs are explicitly demand-driven. A recent World Bank review reported that between 10 percent and 40 percent of the SFs use demand-driven mechanisms. ("Portfolio Improvement Program, p. 24). The narratives about SFs and their strengths nevertheless often describe them as "participatory," if not demand-driven.

4. The first quote is from Margaret Goodman et al., *Social Investment Funds in Latin America: Past Performance and Future Role,* Evaluation Office, Social Programs and Sustainable Development Department (Washington, D.C.: IDB, March 1997), p. 71, and the second from World Bank, "Portfolio Improvement Program," p. vi.

5. Tendler, *Rise of Social Funds.* This monograph goes beyond this chapter to explore certain dynamics of SFs at the field level: how communities decide on one project option over another; how partial privatization actually works—namely, how the newly included private-sector suppliers operate in complementarity with public bodies; how the political opportunities opened up by highly distributive programs like SFs influence, together with corresponding political costs, the shape of these programs and their outcomes; and how the bureaucratic challenge of rationing the "excess" demand coming from myriad communities clamoring for projects influences program outcomes.

6. World Bank data for end-fiscal-year 1996 (World Bank, "Portfolio Improvement Program," p. vi); IDB data reported in March 1997 in IDB, *Social Investment Funds,* p. 10, table 2.1.

7. Nora Lustig, in *Coping with Austerity: Poverty and Inequality in Latin America* (Washington, D.C.: Brookings Institution, 1995) and "The Safety Nets Which Are Not Safety Nets: Social Investment Funds in Latin America," draft (Washington, D.C.: 31 October 1997), quite persuasively contests this statement, which has been frequently repeated in donor documents. With respect to the Latin American SFs, at least, she shows that donor-funded SF projects were actually under way before the structural-adjustment programs began to show any hint of adverse effects on the poor.

8. The evidence on quick disbursement is actually somewhat mixed, as reported by Frances Stewart and Willem van der Geest, "Adjustment and Social Funds: Political Panacea or Effective Poverty Reduction?," in Frances Stewart, *Adjustment and Poverty* (London: Routledge, 1995), chap. 5, pp. 108–137); the World Bank study of three social funds in Latin America—Thomas Wiens and Maurizio Guadagni, *Designing Rules for Demand-Driven Rural Investment Funds: The Latin American Experience,* World Bank Technical

Paper no. 407 (Washington, D.C.: May 1998), p. xvii; and in the complaints of project-agency managers about the way community decisionmaking "slows down" the rate of disbursement. The World Bank report attributes the slow disbursement to delays by the central government in providing counterpart funding to the projects. Stewart and van der Geest ("Adjustment and Social Funds") attribute the problem to the demand-driven structure itself, which results in a time-consuming process of community- and municipal-level organizing and decisionmaking. They also point to the concern of project agencies about "clientelism" and political meddling in project selection and location, which causes agency managers to impose criteria and requirements that slow things down. Their concern about reducing delay is at odds with the World Bank study, "Portfolio Improvement Program," which suggests that *more* time and attention be paid to imposing project criteria that assure better participation and inclusion of the poor.

9. For example, the World Bank—K. Subbarao, et al., *Safety Net Programs and Poverty Reduction: Lessons from Cross-Country Experience* (Washington, D.C.: World Bank, 1997), p. 104—reports savings of 30–40 percent in school construction in Mexico's SF, PRONASOL; and savings of up to 35 percent in Mexico's Mendoza Provincial Program for Basic Social Infrastructure (MENPROSF). (PRONASOL is one of the SFs initiated without donor assistance, and to which the Mexican government has committed more funds than all of the Latin American SFs combined.) Some SFs, it should be pointed out, do not include their own overheads in reporting unit costs; for Peru, see Norbert R. Schady, "Seeking Votes: The Political Economy of Expenditures by the Peruvian Social Fund (FONCODES), 1991–1995" (Princeton University and the World Bank, 1998) p. 5.

The World Bank itself also spends less on SFs for project preparation and supervision than on other projects run through existing ministries or agencies in education and health, economic infrastructure, and targeted or participatory poverty projects. The cost of World Bank input into the SF projects varied from 39 percent to 85 percent of equivalent costs for comparator projects. (World Bank, Portfolio Improvement Program, p. 42, and calculated from data in Table 6, p. 43). These lower costs, however, do not seem to be related to the SF model in itself, but to the fact that the World Bank does not make disbursements on SF loans contingent on "policy conditionality," which can slow down disbursements on these other projects substantially. World Bank, "Portfolio Improvement Program," p. 42, and note 55.

10. Subbarao et al., *Safety Net Programs,* pp. 105–106.

11. The bad rap acquired by standardization in the hands of government actually goes well beyond the mainstream development community. It is the centerpiece of a recent historical analysis of the ills of government by the political scientist James Scott. Scott points to the inevitable "need" to standardize as *the* central root of government's mistreatment of citizens throughout history. In so doing, of course, he goes substantially beyond the donors' critiques of developing-country governments. Indeed, Scott and others writing in this vein would probably even treat donor proposals about improving government through decentralization with equal skepticism. (Other studies that take a negative stance similar to Scott's with respect to government interventions in developing countries, including donor-assisted ones, have appeared in development anthropology, particularly but not exclusively among the post-modern anthropologists.)

12. The study written for UNICEF—Sanjay Reddy, *Social Funds in Developing Countries: Recent Experiences and Lessons*, UNICEF Staff Working Papers, Evaluation, Policy, and Planning Series no. EPP-EVL-98–002 (New York: June 1998)—is the least sanguine in this sense.

13. Lustig, *Coping with Austerity* and "The Safety Nets"; Stewart and van der Geest, "Adjustment and Social Funds."

14. Tendler, *The Rise of Social Funds.*

15. (1) World Bank, "Portfolio Improvement Program"; (2) Goodman, *Social Investment Funds*, and Dagmar Raczynski, "Chile: Fondos de Solidaridad de Inversión Social (FOSIS), Informe de la Consultora, Evaluation Office, EVO (June 1996)," in *Social Investment Funds in Latin America: Past Performance and Future Role,* A Joint Project Between the Evaluation Office and the Social Programs and Sustainable Development Department (Washington, D.C.: June 1997), chap. 2; (3) a chapter on SFs in Subbarao et al., *Safety Net Programs;* and (4) a review by Sanjay Reddy for UNICEF, *Social Funds.* All four studies, together with a more recent one on three SFs in Latin America (Wiens and Guadagni, *Designing Rules*) are thoughtful and candid attempts to review the SF experience. To the extent that half of the Latin American SFs are funded by both the World Bank and the IDB (9 out of 18), there is a significant overlap in the experiences on which they both report.

16. Goodman, *Social Investment Funds,* p. 71. Lustig reports that even the best known, oldest, and most highly praised Latin American SF, the Bolivian Social Emergency Fund (started in 1986), employed roughly only 6–8 percent of workers in the two lowest income deciles. The Honduran Fund employed only 7 percent of the unemployed (1990–1995), the Peruvian fund, 2.7 percent (1991–1995), and the El Salvador fund, 2.5 percent (starting in 1990). (For the Guatemalan fund, no data on employment generation were even gathered.) Data are from Lustig ("The Safety Nets," pp. 4–5), citing as sources the World Bank ("Portfolio Improvement Program") for Bolivia; and IDB-funded studies by Cisneros (1996) for El Salvador and Guatemala, and Moncada (1996) for Honduras.

17. Goodman, *Social Investment Funds,* p. 71. In a study of the employment-creating works programs in various developing countries funded out of U.S. agricultural surpluses, John W. Thomas in "Food for Work: An Analysis of Current Experience and Recommendations for Future Performance," Development Discussion Paper no. 213 (Cambridge: Harvard Institute for International Development, Harvard University, 1986), p. 26, reports an average 52 percent of total expenditures on labor, with a maximum of 77 percent. Joachim von Braun, Tesfaye Teken, and Patrick Webb in "Labor-Intensive Public Works for Food Security in Africa: Past Experience and Future Potential," *International Labour Review* 131, no. 1 (1992):19–34, stipulate at least 60 percent for labor expenditures as desirable for African programs. Studies of the Maharashtra Employment Guarantee Scheme in India—E. Costa, "An Assessment of the Flows and Benefits Generated by Public Investment in the Employment Guarantee Scheme of Maharashtra," Working Paper no. 12 (Geneva: International Labour Organisation/World Employment Programme, 1978); E. H. D'Silva, "Effectiveness of Rural Public Works in Labour-Surplus Economies: Case of the Maharashtra Employment Guarantee Scheme," Cornell International Agricultural Monograph no. 97 (Ithaca: Cornell University, 1983)—considered to be among the best in the world—show how labor intensity varies with the kind of project, water projects

using the largest percentage (80 percent) and road projects the lowest (55 percent). More recently, the Maharashtra Scheme has required that at least 60 percent of total costs be spent on unskilled labor. Anil B. Deolalikar and Raghav Gaiha, "What Determines Female Participation in Rural Public Works? The Case of India's Employment Guarantee Scheme" (University of Washington and the University of Delhi, April 1996).

18. Goodman, *Social Investment Funds,* pp. 22, 71. The evaluators also note that estimates of SF job creation are often overestimated, because of the large amount of temporary employment that usually lasts only a few months (p. 22).

19. In reporting these findings, Stewart and van den Geest ("Adjustment and Social Funds") note that these unimpressive outcomes for benefits are partly a result of the fact that governments in SF countries committed more resources to these non-donor-funded programs than they did to the SFs. But even if SF countries had committed more resources, they say their calculations show that the SFs would still have reached only a smaller share of the unemployed in the lower deciles because of their greater difficulty in targeting (p. 126).

20. Goodman, *Social Investment Funds,* pp. 22–23.

21. Ibid.

22. For example, the IDB review of SFs found that, for all but one of the countries (Peru), it was not possible to determine the extent to which those employed by SFs were poor. (In Peru, an unrelated survey from the ongoing World Bank Living Standards Measurement Project had included a question about employment in the SF; 36 percent of the SF jobs went to the extremely poor, and 57 percent to the poor. Ibid., p. 32.)

In most cases, the evaluators found it impossible to determine whether poverty had been reduced or income increased in the regions served by SFs; or, even when such changes were detected, it was not possible to determine whether they were attributable to the program. Ibid., p. 15. The IDB study noted that baseline data are not available for employment and income in the regions served by SFs, making the estimate of changes in poverty and income not possible. (Data have been collected in several cases, however, on the employment and income generated by the projects themselves, their benefits, and surveys of project beneficiaries.)

"[W]e have no way of comparing," a World Bank study concludes, "how well DRIFs target poverty compared with other programs." Wiens and Guadagni, *Designing Rules,* p. xvi. (DRIFs are a subspecies of SFs called Demand-Driven Investment Funds that, according to this classification, support mainly productive infrastructure and natural resource management.) The study reports on three DRIFs in Latin America—in Mexico, Colombia, and Brazil—the latter being the same programs looked at in Tendler, *The Rise of Social Funds.*)

23. As reported by the World Bank, "Portfolio Improvement Program," p. 18; Wiens and Guadagni, *Designing Rules,* p. xv; Goodman, *Social Investment Funds;* Lustig, *Coping with Austerity* and "The Safety Nets"; and Stewart and van der Geest, "Adjustment and Social Funds." In its study of four countries with SFs (Bolivia, Egypt, Sri Lanka, and Zambia), the World Bank study found that, "the higher the poverty headcount index of the province, the lower was the actual per capita Social Fund expenditure it received; or the actual expenditures lagged behind allocations in the areas with the highest

poverty index while they far exceeded allocations in areas with low poverty indices." Subbarao et al., *Safety Net Programs,* as cited in World Bank, "Portfolio Improvement Program," p. 18.

For the 1990–1992 period with respect to Mexico's PRONASOL, Cornelius et al. reports that middle-income states received more funds per capita than poor states (as measured in terms of indices of poverty and underdevelopment). Wayne A. Cornelius, Ann L. Craig, and Jonathan Fox, *Transforming State-Society Relations in Mexico: The National Solidarity Strategy* (San Diego: Center for U.S.-Mexican Studies, University of California, 1994), pp. 22–23. Carol Graham, in "Mexico's Solidarity Program in Comparative Context: Demand-Based Poverty Alleviation Programs in Latin America, Africa, and Eastern Europe," in Cornelius et al., *Transforming State-Society* (1994), chap. 15, pp. 309–328, reports that, more generally, none of the poverty alleviation programs in Latin America, Africa, or Europe have been particularly successful in targeting the poorest members of the population. The IDB study points out that even using its own calculations, it is very difficult to determine targeting from the data, which does not distinguish between rich and poor within municipalities or between some administrative units and higher-level ones from which the data were drawn.

Some of the studies show that whereas the SFs did not reach the poorest communities, they often reached communities that, though poor, were not among the poorest. The IDB study found that the poorest-decile municipalities received less than the others, but that the non-poorest poor received more than the best-off. A study of the Peruvian SF FONCODES (Schady, "Seeking Votes"), found that poorer communities actually get *more* SF funding per capita.

These somewhat conflicting results have to do in part with inadequacies of the data, commented on by most authors of these studies; they also relate to the different politics at particular moments in different countries. President Fujimori of Peru clearly relied on a strategy of reform that alienated urban and middle-class sectors, and he vigorously and explicitly courted the rural poor through FONCODES to compensate. Kenneth M. Roberts, "Neoliberalism and the Transformation of Populism in Latin America: The Peruvian Case," *World Politics* 48, no. 1 (1996): 82–116.

Complicating these outcomes even further, the intensity of political courtship through SFs varies from one period to the next, depending not just on the electoral cycle, but on many variables like the strength of each opposition party at a particular moment and how much of a challenge it represents, on whether the elections are midterm or not, on the balance struck between rewarding loyalists, punishing the opposition, or courting fence-sitters. Schady, "Seeking Votes"; Cornelius et al., *Transforming State-Society;* Theda Skocpol and Kenneth Finegold, "State Capacity and Economic Intervention in the Early New Deal," *Political Science Quarterly* 97, no. 2 (1982): 255–327; and Carol Graham and Cheikh Kane, "Opportunistic Government or Sustaining Reform? Electoral Trends and Public-Expenditure Patterns in Peru, 1990–1995," *Latin American Research Review* 33, no. 1 (1998): 67–104.

24. Lustig, "The Safety Nets," p. 5, citing K. Subbarao et al., *Safety Net Programs.*

25. K. Subbarao et al., *Safety Net Programs;* Goodman, *Social Investment Funds.* Based on studies of the Bolivian and Honduran SFs, Stewart and van der Geest ("Adjustment and Social Funds") reported that poorer communities

present fewer proposals for funding than richer communities (p. 128). Similar results were found for India by Raghav Gaiha, "Do Anti-Poverty Programmes Reach the Rural Poor in India?" (New Delhi: Faculty of Management Studies, University of Delhi, May 1998).

26. In a review of the Latin American SFs, Lustig (*Coping With Austerity*, p. 31) noted that they "compare unfavorably" with these programs (she is considering only the direct-transfer aspects of SFs in the comparison). Lustig, a researcher at the Brookings Institution at the time of her study, drew on various SF evaluation studies by the donors.

27. Goodman, *Social Investment Funds*, pp. 22.

28. Ibid., p. 71.

29. Lustig ("The Safety Nets," pp. 2–4 and *Coping With Austerity*) and Stewart and van der Geest ("Adjustment and Social Funds") arrive at similar conclusions, in a study including African as well as Latin American countries.

30. Goodman, *Social Investment Funds*. The citation (p. 16) comes from a December 1996 version of this report, as cited in World Bank, "Portfolio Improvement Program," p. 47, note 58.

31. World Bank, "Portfolio Improvement Program," p. 47.

32. These arguments can be found in various donor documents. See, in particular, Subbarao et al., *Safety Net Programs*, pp. 93–116; World Bank, "Portfolio Improvement Program."

33. World Bank, "Portfolio Improvement Program," p. 47.

34. Lustig, "The Safety Nets," p. 6, and *Coping With Austerity*.

35. Stewart and van der Geest, "Adjustment and Social Funds."

36. Alan Angell and Carol Graham, "Can Social Sector Reform Make Adjustment Sustainable and Equitable? Lessons from Chile and Venezuela," *Journal of Latin American Studies* 27, no. 1 (February 1995): 202–203.

37. World Bank, "Portfolio Improvement Program." The evaluators also pointed to the inability to truly compare the demand-driven SFs to other programs, due to the lack of or poor quality of the data, the classic apples-and-oranges problem of such a comparison, and the limitations of their data and methodology. The sample size was small (ranging from eight to sixty-nine); they did not compare SFs to non-Bank-funded programs (as Stewart and van der Geest did); and they were not able to separate out, on the SF side, the sectoral piece of the SF program that corresponded to the comparator project in a functional ministry—health, education, water, roads, etc. (They also did not rank the kinds of impacts of unemployment and poverty reported above.)

38. Goodman, *Social Investment Funds*, p. 68. The study notes that this is because of the reliance on follow-up beneficiary questionnaires for these evaluations, and the lack of baseline data prior to funding. The report does mention, however, that the impact evaluations are a valuable source of information on whether projects are operating, and whether selection and construction were satisfactory.

39. Ibid., pp. 6, 46, 73. The evaluators attributed this finding to the "inflexibility" of the donors and their "rules and limitations," which inhibited the ability of local officials to experiment with innovative solutions. One interesting example of this donor "inflexibility" related to the use of private contractors for works projects. In trying to serve the poverty-reducing goals of the SFs, donors typically emphasized works projects that trained and employed local people, even when private contractors preferred bringing in

their own workers from outside, particularly for skilled work, and complained that hiring unskilled laborers locally would compromise their efficiency. In focus group meetings convened by the IDB, however, mayors and community representatives expressed more concern for project quality than for local employment, and therefore preferred that contractors use their own skilled labor. With respect to "inflexibility," then, the IDB evaluators were making the same critique of the donors that the latter had been making of line ministries.

40. World Bank, "Portfolio Improvement Program," p. 47.

41. Ibid., p. 47, note 59.

42. In Bolivia, a municipal development bank (FNDR) financed water and sanitation systems through lending, while the SF financed these same investments on a grant basis. In Senegal, a Municipal and Housing Development project provided credit through a municipal credit fund for financing income-generating projects; at the same time, these municipalities could receive free funding from the SF (an AGETIP) for roadbuilding. Ibid., p. 32, note 34.

43. Goodman, *Social Investment Funds,* pp. 44–45.

44. Ibid., p. 72. The following three quotations in this paragraph are from the same source (pp. 44–45, 72, and 72, respectively).

45. Social Funds and other social safety-net programs really "leave untouched the problems of the mainline services . . . [and] . . . evade the more difficult challenges of institutional reform," because they operate outside mainline ministries, use "flexible" procedures avoiding existing problematic regulations for civil servants and for procurement, and resort to nongovernment organizations at the local level. Joan Nelson, "Reforming Social Sector Governance: A Political Perspective," paper prepared for a conference on Governance, Poverty Eradication, and Social Policy, Harvard University, 12–14 November 1997 (Washington, D.C.: Overseas Development Council, 7 November 1997), p. 5. These modes of operation, of course, are also supposed to be the source of SF strength. Nelson also mentions the explicitly temporary nature of the funds (albeit now no longer the case); and the fact that some of the programs are "used as the direct instruments of particular political leaders or parties." (She cites Peru's FONCODES and Mexico's PRONASOL as examples—though Mexico, "less clearly" so.)

Similarly with respect to the Latin American SFs, Angell and Graham ("Can Social Sector Reform," pp. 202–203) reported that they "diverted resources (both human and physical) and shifted public attention away from problems in the line ministries," thus making more difficult the process of reforming these ministries.

46. The World Bank review of African and Latin American projects reported concerns about sustainability, particularly with respect to the economic infrastructure and microfinance components of such projects, noting that such concerns had "been raised in other reviews as well." World Bank, "Portfolio Improvement Programs," p. vii. Another World Bank study (Wiens and Guadagni, *Designing Rules,* pp. xvii–xviii, 46) found that none of the three Latin American projects (DRIFs) it reviewed "performed particularly well in achieving" sustainability, and that "information from local or partial surveys suggests that a high proportion of subprojects may not be sustainable." A World Bank appraisal report for a Senegal SF/AGETIP, noted that the "sustainability of many AGETIP investments is uncertain," due to a lack

of ownership and participation in the project identification and preparation phase and in the post-project operations and maintenance phase. World Bank Senegal PAR Public Works and Employment Project, 1996 draft, page 2 notes, as cited in World Bank "Portfolio Improvement Program," p. 15, note 9.

The IDB came to similar conclusions in Goodman, "Social Investment Funds," pp. 35–41, and an earlier 1994 IDB study cautioned that, "sustainability remains a potentially serious problem." Glaessner, Lee, Sant'Anna, de St. Antoine, "Poverty Alleviation and Social Investment Funds: The Latin American Experience," p. 22, as cited in World Bank "Portfolio Improvement Program," p. 15.

One exception came from a 1990 survey of the Bolivian SF, which showed 95 percent of the social infrastructure projects still operating, and 80 percent of the social assistance projects. The survey was conducted, however, only one to two years after project completion (Goodman, *Social Investment Funds*, p. 41). The survey also concluded that the projects most likely to be sustained were those where users participated most actively, where the requesting agency had had previous experience operating this type of project, and where the requesting agency had a stable source of financing for recurrent costs.

47. World Bank, "Portfolio Improvement Review," 1997, p. 31.

48. Eighty percent of the project descriptions did not mention sustainability or concern themselves with its three key components: (1) evidence of demand (range of options offered, information made available, evidence of commitment through contribution in cash or kind); (2) appropriateness of technical standards; and (3) soundness of arrangements for operations and maintenance. World Bank, "Portfolio Improvement Program," p. 30.

49. Ibid., pp. 30–31.

50. World Bank, "Portfolio Improvement Program," 1997, pp. 15–16, note 9. The World Bank evaluators reinforce their concerns about sustainability with citations from their sister SF-financing institution, the IDB, and from other reviewers within the World Bank itself. They also question whether SF designers and managers even thought about project designs and technical standards that would be more likely to elicit user maintenance and financing for recurrent costs. They point out, it should be noted, that their findings relate more to "likely," as opposed to actual, sustainability, because only a limited number of the individual country evaluations it drew on involved SF projects with long-term objectives (p. 4).

51. World Bank, "Portfolio Improvement Program."

52. See, for example, World Bank Honduras PAR Report No. 13839-HO, 1994, para. 4.15, as cited in World Bank, "Portfolio Improvement Program," 1997, pp. 15–16, note 9.

53. Goodman, *Social Investment Funds*, p. 74. In Latin America, out of sixteen countries and seventeen SFs (Guatemala has two), Chile's FOSIS has the lowest level of external financing—11 percent. The next lowest are Guatemala's FONAPAZ (12 percent), and Colombia's RED SOLIDARIDAD (20 percent). (The IDB evaluators, as noted above, ranked these three as the most successful in terms of innovative practices.) For the rest, external financing ranges from 58 percent to 94 percent, with only three countries being between 60 percent and 80 percent (Peru, Uruguay, and Venezuela) (ibid., p. 10, table 2.1). The Mexican SF, PRONASOL, is also one of the SFs

most "owned" by its government. It was initiated by the Mexican government without donor funding and is one of the largest in terms of absolute resources, share of the budget, and coverage (Cornelius et al., *Transforming State-Society*, p. 14). It does not appear in this particular table of the IDB because it is currently not receiving donor funding; it has received funding from the World Bank in the past.

54. Goodman, *Social Investment Funds*, pp. 64, 74.

55. The studies report little of this problematic nature with respect to the new role of private firms, though this may have been due to a simple lack of analytical interest in this matter. See Tendler, *Rise of Social Funds*, sections 3 and 4 for case evidence and discussion of the private firms.

56. Ibid., p. 39. In many communities, the report said, NGOs are not very active. In addition, NGOs tended to specialize more in training and community development programs than in managing the construction projects that constitute an important activity of many SFs. In the SFs where NGOs played a greater role, then, it was because the program did not focus on building infrastructure (like Chile's FOSIS). Other exceptions were cases in which the government was "institutionally extremely weak" to the point that NGOs had more capacity to generate projects than government (Haiti) and, in general, because the SF was formally required to use them. The usual tension that exists between NGOs and government also seemed to get in the way. The NGOs disliked being the "mere executors" of a "paternalistic" government program, and wanted to participate more in early phases of the project cycle. SF managers and staff, presumably, were not anxious to do this.

57. Reddy, *Social Funds*, p. 58.

58. According to a Project Completion Report cited in Subbarao et al., *Safety Net Programs*, p. 107, the projects were in health and education, and the study was conducted one to two years after completion. This same finding was cited in Goodman, *Social Investment Funds*, p. 41. Lower performers on the "sustainability" measure also included projects requested by regional government institutions as opposed to central-government institutions.

59. Subbarao et al., *Safety Net Programs*, pp. 101, 109.

60. World Bank, "Portfolio Improvement Review," 1997, pp. 38–39. The report suggested that microfinance components are "best administered by an existing agency as an apex institution . . . " because "[e]xperience shows that NGOs, generally, are not capable of providing the range of financial services required by the poor on a sustainable basis (particularly deposit services)." (p. 39)

61. World Bank, "Portfolio Improvement Program"; Goodman, *Social Investment Funds*.

62. Stewart and van der Geest, "Adjustment and Social Funds."

63. Goodman, *Social Investment Funds*, pp. 15, 43. There may also be an inherent tendency for exacerbation of this problem in that the better-off communities that are successful in getting one project will come back for subsequent ones and prepare them better, while communities that are turned down or have a difficult time will become discouraged and desist, a point made by Schady, "Seeking Votes."

64. Goodman, *Social Investment Funds*, p. 15.

65. Alec Ian Gershberg, "Distributing Resources in the Education Sector: Solidarity's Escuela Digna Program," in Cornelius et al., *Transforming State-Society* (1994), pp. 249–251.

66. World Bank, "Portfolio Improvement Program," p. 47.

67. For example, ibid., pp. vii, ix, 15.

68. Goodman, *Social Investment Funds.*

69. World Bank Honduras PAR Report No. 13839–HO, 1994, para. 4.15, as cited in World Bank, "Portfolio Improvement Review," 1997, pp. 15–16, note 9.

70. Goodman, *Social Investment Funds,* pp. 35–36.

71. Ibid., p. 34, and Raczynski, *Chile: Fondos* (pp. 38–76, particularly pp. 46, 48, 73, and 74). Also different, the Chilean government viewed FOSIS as a *permanent* program from the start (it was created during a time of high economic growth of 7 percent a year); this contrasts with the temporary status of the majority of Latin American SFs and the origins of most SFs in "temporary" periods of low growth, high unemployment, and structural-adjustment or other crises.

72. Angell and Graham, "Can Social Sector Reform," p. 203. They attribute this greater integration in Chile to the fact that a whole series of new safety net programs undertaken during the Pinochet government—particularly public employment programs—were integrated into the line ministries and hence "did not create a separate and competing bureaucratic layer." Also, these sectors had been "historically relatively efficient and had provided widespread coverage" (p. 203).

73. Goodman, *Social Investment Funds,* pp. 35–36.

74. World Bank, "Portfolio Improvement Program," pp. 28, 34–35, and executive summary; Goodman, *Social Investment Funds,* p. 43. A similar finding was reported by Angell and Graham ("Can Social Sector Reform"), namely that SF project units were strongest in the area of health and education.

75. World Bank, "Portfolio Improvement Program," p. 35.

76. Ibid., p. 28.

77. Goodman, *Social Investment Funds,* p. 43; World Bank, "Portfolio Improvement Program," p. 28.

PART 2

CASE STUDIES

6

Overcoming Poverty in Chile[1]

Dagmar Raczynski

If poverty is defined in terms of the degree to which people's basic needs are met and they have access to education, health care, housing, utilities, and basic sanitation, then the situation in Chile is very positive. The country leads the way in human development within Latin America and continues to make significant progress. Social services and sanitation infrastructure reach a wide sector of the population.[2] Primary education covers more than 95 percent and secondary education close to 70 percent of the age specific population; more than 90 percent of births occur with professional assistance; potable water reaches 86 percent of private homes; (75 percent have water available within the home); sewer systems serve 70 of every 100 homes; and 88 of every 100 have access to public lighting.[3]

Poverty levels in Chile, measured by per capita income per home and the cost of a basket of essential foodstuffs, have declined over the last ten years from 5.5 million people in 1987, to 5.2 million in 1990, to 4.3 million in 1992, to 3.9 million in 1994, and to 3.3 million in 1996. The evolution of poverty in the 1990s in both absolute and relative terms compares favorably with other countries in the region. Nevertheless, in terms of percentage of poor, according to data from the Economic Commission for Latin America and the Caribbean (ECLAC), Chile is somewhere in the middle. Costa Rica, Argentina, and Uruguay have a smaller percentage of poor homes, while Mexico, Brazil, Venezuela, Colombia, and Bolivia have a higher percentage.[4] In Chile, as in the rest of Latin America, the rate of the decline in poverty is fundamentally associated with variables in the labor market: variations in unemployment levels, new job creation, growth in the number of workers per home (labor supply), and changes in salaries.

Income distribution in Chile, on the other hand, did not improve during the 1990s, but it did not worsen either, as it did in the

119

1970s and 1980s. The difference between the average family income for the fifth quintile and the first quintile, the value of the Gini coefficient, and the percentage of income that the poorest quintile receives have all been maintained.

This chapter reviews the poverty alleviation strategy carried out during the 1990s, describing initial conditions, the policy's main orientation, characteristics of its implementation, and lessons and future challenges. But first it considers earlier efforts to overcome poverty: during the period of state-led import substitution industrialization, which extended from the 1930s until 1973, and under military rule, from 1974 until 1990, a period of neoliberal thought and authoritarianism.

The Consolidation of a
State System of Social Policies (1925–1973)

From the beginning of the century until 1973, public spending on education, health care, and retirement programs and benefits was gradually expanded. The state assumed an increasingly important role in the financing, administration, and direct provision of these services or programs. It developed employment policies, dealing with salaries, working conditions, labor unions, and collective bargaining. Price subsidies were applied to basic goods and services. Toward the end of the period, the state implemented programs that supported urban neighborhood organizations and rural labor unions, and it intensified reforms that affected private land (agrarian reform) and industrial ownership.

Until the mid-1960s, the policies and programs implemented did not incorporate a vision or special treatment for the poor. It was assumed that general policies and standardized and homogeneous programs, defined, financed, and executed directly by the state, would benefit the poor and vulnerable and enhance equity.

Growing state intervention during this period responded to the political-representation system, to its relationship with the state and with the social base. Organized sectors of society, the middle strata, the industrial bourgeois, urban workers, and miners pressured the state through their organizations and associations for greater benefits: salaries, social security, health care, better working conditions, education, and housing. Political parties sought followers who would provide them with the necessary electoral support to bring them to power, and they promised social and economic benefits in return. These benefits were later negotiated within the government and parliament. This resulted in the growing intervention of the state in all social and economic areas, and political parties were given the central, practically exclusive, role as intermediary between the people and the state. Political parties were aided by the fact that popular organizations were weak and did not quite represent their constituencies.[5]

Expansion of the system led to partial successes for the diverse groups and segments of the labor force at different moments in time: first, organized labor, then the urban middle class and urban lower-income groups and finally, and to a lesser degree, the rural population. Thus, an internally fragmented and stratified social-policy system with expanding coverage was established. Toward 1970, the population had access to nominally similar benefits that concealed differences in the amount and quality of benefits and eligibility requirements. Throughout the decades there were attempts to streamline the system, to make it more equitable and efficient. There was a tendency to integrate diverse institutions—assisting various social sectors—into larger organizations. This resulted in the formation of large, centralized public entities, slow both in making decisions and in implementing them. This led to difficulties in responding to the needs and demands of the population as the social arena became more diverse and complex.

Furthermore, the expansion of the system was accompanied by an increase in public spending that was not always adequately financed. Budget imbalances appeared that intensified inflationary pressures within the economy. This situation became very serious in 1972–1973 when public spending (not only on social policies) grew by more than six percentage points of the GDP and the fiscal deficit became unmanageable, reaching 30 percent of GDP. In the early 1970s a set of factors—economic imbalances; the growing demands of the population to solve housing, health care and education needs; mobilization of neighborhood and community organizations; agrarian-reform policies; and expropriation in the industrial and service sectors—led to a growing ideological polarization of the population and culminated in the military coup of September 1973.

In spite of the accumulation of socio-political and economic difficulties, economic development and the expansion of the social-policy system during the first six decades of this century were successful and completed the first stage in the social development of the country. Basic infrastructure for social services was created, and demand for these services was generated. Around 1970, 84 percent of the population between six and fourteen years of age had registered in primary schools and 38 percent of the young between fifteen and eighteen

years of age in secondary schools. Eighty percent of births were as-
sisted by professional help. A similar percentage of children under
the age of six took part in the preventive "Healthy Child Check Ups"
and the national food distribution program. The percentage of the
active population affiliated and regularly contributing to social security was 50–55 percent. Potable water and sanitation systems covered
66 percent and 31 percent of urban areas, respectively. The state either built or aided in the financing of 60 percent of new housing
units annually. Furthermore, the number of new housing units covered close to 85 percent of the new homes formed each year.

The Neoliberal Attempt
to Dismantle the State System (1974–1990)

The military government, which gained control through a coup in
September 1973 and remained in power for almost seventeen years,
introduced radical changes to both the economy (liberalization,
opening to the world, privatization) and to the social policy system.
The changes were shaped by neoliberal philosophy and the idea of
a subsidiary state: The size of the state should be reduced, and the
market should assume the greatest role possible in making decisions
concerning resource allocation and the provision of services.

The military government tried to dismantle the old social policy
system in order to build another. The policies that were implemented were viewed as opposite to and in conflict with those of the
previous period.

The military government, pressured by powerful international
organizations, the neoliberal credo of its economic advisers, and the
urgent need to control inflation and regain and maintain macroeconomic balance, reduced and narrowed the focus of public spending,
privatized public companies and social services, deconcentrated ministries, and transferred the administration of primary health and education to the municipalities.[6]

Characteristics of Neoliberal Social Policy in Chile

The main changes introduced by the military government to the
social-policy system were the reduction and redirection of social
spending, decentralization of the state, privatization reforms, and
promotion of demand-driven subsidies.

Reduction and redirection of social spending. The objectives of social
policy were subordinated to the needs of economic policy, in particular

the need to control inflation. The goals of economic adjustment and growth were given priority over goals of achieving equity. Statements were frequently made that economic growth was the best social policy and that social spending presented an obstacle to growth.

There was a drastic reduction in social spending, which severely affected investment and salaries. Social policy was primarily seen as a poverty alleviation tool. Expenditures on education and health care underwent intrasectoral restructuring that emphasized spending cuts on advanced services (universities and hospitals) rather than on basic services (primary education, health care programs, maternal and infant nutrition). Geographically isolated areas with fewer services were given priority to receive basic services. Portions of the population that up until that time had been poorly covered by social services were now obtaining more benefits. Simultaneously, a safety net was strengthened for those among the poor who were most severely affected by unemployment and lower family income (emergency employment programs, unified family subsidies, pensions for destitute senior citizens receiving negligible or no social security payments, preference for children at risk of malnutrition in nursery schools, and nontraditional forms of infant care, among others). A screening tool that separated the extremely poor from the rest of the population was designed and applied.

The reduction in public spending and the targeting policy fueled an intense debate on the benefits and difficulties of the strategies, highlighting the need to clarify goals in order to formulate effective social programs. Among the criticisms levied, most of them associated with the screening system, were the following: stigmatization; social-structure polarization or dualization; suppression of initiatives for solving the problems of the poorest; and administrative costs. It became evident that increased targeting did not necessarily result in more effective social spending.

Targeting was introduced at a time when the population was suffering from overall impoverishment and the government was reducing its spending. This led to a relative end to state protection for those sectors not in extreme poverty. At the same time, while the impoverishment of the poorest sector of the population was partially halted, there was no reduction in the absolute or relative magnitude of poverty.

Parallel to the targeting policies, other social reforms were initiated at significant cost. These reforms benefited the upper-middle and upper classes and negatively affected the availability of government resources for the poor. Among those reforms were creation of a privately administered, individual-capitalization pension system and a private health care system (the ISAPREs).

Decentralization of the state. The principal ministries and public services were geographically decentralized. Resources and responsibilities were transferred to the municipalities. Up until this time, the municipalities had been weak. Their functions had been limited to trash collection and beautification of neighborhoods, design of urban-development plans, and issuance of commercial and other permits. Municipalities began to manage primary and secondary schools, primary health care, and components of the safety net. Thus, the municipality became a new and mandatory element in the lives of the poor.

This process did not develop along a straight line. It suffered from imperfections and was blocked during the 1982–1983 crisis. It was not completed until 1987 in the areas of education and primary health care. The municipalities were not prepared and had neither the human nor technical resources required to undertake their new duties properly. They generated significant deficits in managing health care and education due to the devaluation of state subsidies and administrative inefficiencies. Studies on the municipalities' performance during the 1980s reveal that local administrators were overwhelmed with demands and instructions from the central government, and work teams were weak and fragmented and had neither the conceptual nor material tools to support their social work.[7]

Ties between the municipality and its constituents and territorial and functional organizations within the municipality were weak. Mayors were appointed and subject to strict political control. Neighborhood organizations ceased to operate or functioned with appointed leaders. Citizen participation was limited to financial contributions for paving alleys and sidewalks and other public works benefiting the neighborhood.

Privatization reforms. The military government introduced privatization reforms in three areas: (1) the transfer of specific services from the public to the private sector, such as janitorial services for hospitals and the preparation and distribution of school meals; (2) the private administration of publicly financed services or programs: schools, job training courses, day care for disadvantaged children, etc.; (3) the creation of an individual-capitalization pension system administered by the private sector and a private health care system (ISAPRE) serving the upper and upper-middle classes.

The results were varied. The creation of the ISAPRE system had negative and disproportionate effects on health care for the poorest sectors. ISAPRE specialize in curative medicine. Clients—25 percent of the population in 1990—belong to the upper-middle and upper-income brackets and represent families with low health risks (young people with low rates of chronic illness). Today, these groups have easier access to health care. Nevertheless, they express concern for the system's low transparency, the uncertainty associated with health care contracts, and the lack of regulation in the sector.

The poor, the lower-middle class, and a portion of the middle and upper classes, about 60 percent of the population, are served by the public system. This system experienced a deterioration in infrastructure, personnel, and material resources while, at the same time, patients were required to make higher direct payments upon receiving care. The deterioration of the public system was due in part to the creation of ISAPREs because those with higher incomes shifted to the private health care system, transferring their mandatory contributions away from the public system. On the other hand, the ISAPRE system only took off when the state injected a number of subsidies: It underwrote the cost of maternity leave for working mothers and created a tax-deductible additional employer contribution of 2 percent. The creation of the ISAPREs was consistent with the principle of privatization and in conflict with that of targeting. Priority was given to privatization.

The pension system reform was positive in a number of ways: (1) its effects on savings and the development of the capital market; (2) the reduction in nonsalary labor costs to approximately 20 percent, a figure that is much lower than prior to the reform and below the international level; and (3) its resolution of the demographic impasse that pay-as-you-go systems inevitably face as the population ages.

However, the reform did not lead to a significant increase in the percentage of the workforce affiliated with the system (new or old) who made regular contributions. The percentage is not significantly higher than immediately before the reform. In addition, uncertainty surrounds the future value of pensions. The value of paid pensions in the new system has been greater than that of the old system. Yet, the new system so far pays only a small number of pensions, and recipients have higher paying jobs than average. The value of future pensions depends primarily on the performance of capital markets and the administrative costs of the new system, which are high.

Under the new system the state guarantees a minimum pension to those who have twenty years of contributions and a welfare pension for destitute people that have not contributed. The resources involved most likely will be significantly higher than estimates in the 1980s (2 percent of GDP), given the characteristics of the labor market (a greater number of seasonal and short-term contracts), difficulties in increasing social security coverage of the economically active population, and noncompliance with mandatory-contribution obligations.

The policies of hiring out and the private administration of services had positive results—provision of higher-quality goods and services at lower costs where standards are both easy to define and measure (for example, the caloric-protein content and hygiene of school rations). When these standards do not exist, control is limited to monitoring the use of resources and fulfilling obligations. The quality of services or benefits is relegated to a lower priority.

It should also be noted that privatization reforms faced obstacles that blocked their fruition. Among these obstacles two stand out. First, the long-standing tradition that the state play a crucial role in the financing and direct provision of social services hindered the government from extricating itself from its historical responsibility in this area. Second, the response of the private sector to the privatization process was much slower than the government had anticipated, so much so that it had to inject additional resources into the private sector in order to make their participation in social services more attractive.

As a result, at the beginning of the 1990s social services continued to be primarily financed and provided by the state. Approximately 60 percent of the population continued to receive health care in the public system, a percentage only slightly lower than during the 1970s. Ninety percent of registered students in elementary schools received state subsidies (a percentage similar to that of 1970). Sixty percent of students attended municipal schools and 30 percent private, subsidized schools. The remaining 10 percent attended high-income privately-paid-tuition schools, a percentage similar to that which existed at the beginning of the 1970s. In other words, the state continues to be the main provider and financier of health care and education. Provision of these services is, to a greater degree, under the control of substate entities.

Subsidizing demand. In line with its market philosophy, the government incorporated market mechanisms into the management of the public sector through the promotion of demand-driven subsidies—housing subsidies, school subsidies (USE), billing for provided health care (FAP). The logic behind these measures was that subsidizing demand would encourage competition for clients and, as a consequence, improve the quality of services and benefits.

Subsidized demand for housing benefited the poorest sectors only when the state adopted measures that guaranteed the availability of affordable housing and access to credit from the financial system. The problems facing the USE and FAP were different: (1) difficulty in determining a fair price that reflected the actual cost of providing the service or benefit; (2) the failure to incorporate a pricing scale based on location—rural or urban, isolated or accessible—and level of poverty among the population; (3) unstable monthly revenues (based on the number of customers serviced) while facing stable fixed costs (labor costs and equipment upkeep); (4) high administrative costs of allocating resources (the need for records and their oversight); and (5) emergence of adverse incentives associated with the system, primarily "inflation" in the number of patients seen or students registered, which demanded greater supervision, in turn increasing administrative costs.

Some Results

Available information confirms that the new system did not reduce poverty or existing inequalities. The number and percentage of indigents and poor in terms of income in 1990 was significantly higher than in 1970 and throughout the entire period (Table 6.1). Therefore, if this period is evaluated in terms of the magnitude of poverty based on income, the outcome is indeed bad. In spite of greater targeting in social spending, the number of poor increased. Moreover, the gap between the highest- and lowest-income brackets widened, and income distribution became more highly concentrated (Table 6.2). Safety net subsidies played an important role in the survival of the poorest sectors, alleviating the deterioration in living standards, but were insufficient to offset the effects of high unemployment and fall in real wages.

The housing deficit increased dramatically. Estimates indicate that the housing deficit doubled between 1973 and 1987.[8] At the same time, however, progress was made in expanding potable-water and sewer systems. Moreover, an "extreme-poverty" index, compiled by the military government, showed an improvement. This index is based on factors such as housing, number of people per housing unit, sanitation, and possession of one of a number of domestic electrical appliances or a vehicle. The index dropped from 21 percent of the national population living in extreme poverty in 1970 to 14 percent in 1982 and 12 percent in 1992. The improvement between 1970 and 1982 can be explained by the fact that 80 percent of homes owned at least one of the indicated goods, most often a television.[9]

Table 6.1   Chile: Percentage of the Population That Is Indigent or Poor (1969–1996)

Year	Indigent	Poor[a]
1969	6	17
1983	30	
1985	25	45
1987	17	45
1990	13	39
1992	9	33
1994	8	28
1996	6	23

Sources: O. Altimir, "La Dimensión de la Pobreza en América Latina," *Cuadernos de la CEPAL,* no. 27, (Santiago: United Nations, 1979); Rodríguez (1985); A. Torche, "Distribuir el Ingreso para Satisfacer las Necesidades Básicas," in F. Larraín, ed., *Desarrollo Económico para Chile en Democracia* (Santiago: Ediciones Universidad Católica de Chile, 1987); Ministry of Planning and Coordination, Republic of Chile (MIDEPLAN), *Balance de Seis Años de las Políticas Sociales 1990–1996* (Santiago: August 1996); MIDEPLAN, "Pobreza y Distribución del Ingreso en Chile, 1996, Resultados de la Encuesta de Caracterización Socioeconómica Nacional," Report for the Press (Santiago: July 1997).
Notes: a. Includes indigents.

Another side to the situation in poverty-stricken areas are the unexpected results of the social cost of the policies applied. Two new interrelated phenomena developed as a consequence of the cut in public spending, the rise in the unemployment, the fall in wages, higher-income-based poverty, increased housing needs, and the lack of respect for human and socioeconomic rights. The first was the spread of individual and collective actions by the poor to meet their most urgent needs, ranging from private and family coping activities to collective-community-based initiatives for survival.[10] The second was a proliferation of agents, activists, promoters, church organizations, nongovernmental organizations, and political associations that aided those sectors most severely affected by the social costs of the economic policies and the reduction in social spending.

The combination of these two phenomena resulted in a greater variety of popular organizations in poor areas at the neighborhood and community level. In spite of the fact that social organizations were controlled politically by the government, the community social network was diverse and dynamic. Meanwhile, external agents tested new working methods, gained experience and knowledge, searched for new types of relations with the poor and tried new ways of implementing social programs: participatory, flexible, more comprehensive, and better suited for addressing concrete social problems. The experience accumulated in this area nourished the social policy later formulated in the country from 1990 onward.

Table 6.2 Household Income Distribution

A. *Chile: Distribution According to Per Capita Quintiles, 1987–1994*[a]

Quintile	1987	1990	1992	1994
1 (lowest)	4.5	4.6	4.9	4.7
2	8.2	8.6	8.7	8.5
3	12.1	12.5	12.5	12.3
4	19.0	18.5	18.5	18.4
5 (highest)	56.2	55.9	55.4	56.1
Total	100.0	100.0	100.0	100.0
Q5/Q1 Quotient	12.5	12.2	11.1	11.9

B. *Greater Santiago, 1959–1992*[b]

Quintile	Alessandri Government 1959–1964	Frei Government 1965–1970	Allende Government 1971–1973	Pinochet Government 1974–1989	Aylwin Government 1990–1993
1 (lowest)	3.2	3.2	3.1	2.7	3.4
2	7.5	7.1	7.5	6.4	6.7
3	11.3	11.4	12.5	10.6	10.5
4	20.1	19.7	21.5	18.3	17.9
5 (highest)	57.9	58.6	55.4	62.0	61.5
Total	100.0	100.0	100.0	100.0	100.0
Q5/Q1 Quotient	18.1	19.5	17.9	23.0	18.1

Source: MIDEPLAN, *Balance de Seis Años.*
Notes: a. Distribution of declared monetary income per household adjusted to include the amount of rent for those who do not pay rent and also to adjust underdeclared income to national accounts figures. This information is provided by the CASEN surveys for 1987, 1990, 1992, and 1994.
   b. Distribution of declared monetary income per household, which has not been adjusted. This information is provided by the University of Chile's Employment and Unemployment Survey.

The 1990s: A New Social Strategy

Conditions at the Beginning

In March 1990, following almost 17 years of military dictatorship, the first government of the Concertación de Partidos para la Democracia, headed by President Patricio Aylwin Azócar, took office. In 1994 a new government of the same coalition of parties, led by President Eduardo Frei Ruiz-Tagle, assumed control.

   The socioeconomic legacy of the military government had two sides. On the positive side, it left an economy with balanced basic macroeconomic variables, no major distortions in the price system, a private sector that was planning investment for the medium term and, since 1986, had experienced growth alongside low inflation and new job creation. In other words, the economy had completed the adjustment period, had recuperated, and had started on a growth track.

However, poverty levels were higher than they had been twenty years earlier; income distribution was more highly concentrated; public services lacked sufficient funding; the housing deficit had increased; the education system reached much of the population yet was of a low and uneven quality; the public health care system was in crisis; and teachers and health care workers were in distress over the reforms of the 1980s and their impact on labor. Moreover, economic growth, globalization, and the internationalization of society were accompanied by the pressing problems of urban congestion, environmental deterioration, delinquency and violence in the cities, mental health problems, drug use, etc.

The government that took power in March 1990 intended to reduce poverty, improve the distribution of wealth, and strengthen democracy within a capitalist free-market economy while maintaining macroeconomic equilibrium and long-term economic growth based on private ownership and exports. The government program proposed a continuation of the economic policy, gradual changes in the social policy, and a new style of making policy decisions.[11] The goals were to gain/preserve the confidence of private investors, both domestic and international, and maintain macroeconomic equilibria, while simultaneously responding to middle- and lower-class demands. To achieve these goals, the government promoted a political and social understanding among business leaders, workers, and political parties never before seen in the country. The objective was to reach a common vision on economic, social, and political development that would bring social demands in line with macroeconomic and external restrictions. The new government's first projects were the "Framework Agreement," tax reform, and labor reform. Under the Framework Agreement, workers, business leaders, and the government met every year, over a period of four years, to try to agree upon changes in the minimum salary, minimum pension, and public-sector salaries. Labor reform was aimed at equalizing power between workers and employers on issues such as labor contracts, unionization, collective bargaining and the right to strike.[12] The tax reform introduced a tax increase in order to raise spending on social projects and to respond to some of the demands of the population. The greater availability of resources permitted the readjustment of the benefits of the safety net, an increase in fiscal contributions to health, education, and housing, the creation of new institutions and instruments for implementing social policy, and program innovation.

The Approach to Social Policy and to Overcoming Poverty

The priorities, focus, and content of social policy under the democratic government were modified from those of the military government. Innovations were also made in selected tools and in program administration. The most important differences have been in the following.

The relationship between economic policy and social policy. Both the military and the Concertación governments have regarded good economic performance as an essential element in reducing poverty. The Concertación government has viewed growth as being insufficient to overcome poverty and achieve equity. Investments in basic services, such as education, health care, and sanitation systems, and in specific policies targeted at the poor and vulnerable sectors are also deemed to be essential. These investments should help the economy to grow because they strengthen human and social capital.

For the military government, a decline in social spending was a goal in and of itself. The Concertación government believed that the country urgently needed more spending in this area, but it had to be financed in a way that would not negatively affect macroeconomic balances. Political decisionmakers must take both revenues and expenditures into consideration in determining the amount of public spending and its allocation among social programs. Decisions regarding these topics must be national in nature, have the support of the population, and be sustained by consensus among the main actors. The government must take the appropriate actions, initiating and negotiating concessions to build this consensus. The 1990 tax reform (and its renegotiation in 1993) illustrates this point.[13]

Goals, priorities, and content of social policies. The Aylwin government called its social strategy objectives "Incorporation into the Process of Development." The Frei Ruiz-Tagle government called its program a "Policy of Enhanced Opportunities and Quality of Life." The goal of both has been to strengthen opportunities for social integration and to mitigate the exclusion of the poor and vulnerable. Reducing poverty is a central component, but not the only one.[14]

The social policy has two central components:

1. Strengthening sectoral policies that ensure a basic level of citizenship of the entire population with regard to education,

health care, housing, social security, and justice. New priorities were set in each sector. Quality and equity of education were given high priority and seen as the main mechanism to generate equality of opportunity.

2. The design and implementation of specific programs for vulnerable groups to overcome poverty. The focus of these programs has shifted away from that of the military regime in important aspects.

One important shift in focus is to social investment over social welfare. Contrary to the emphasis on "providing help" (subsidies to the poorest sectors), programs attempt to provide the poor and vulnerable sectors with the tools to overcome poverty on their own. The goal is to enable these sectors to have a voice and to participate in solving their own problems. Support provided to groups and organizations is preferred over individual assistance.

Another shift of focus is in the recognition that the poor and vulnerable face a variety of distinct situations and that it is important to respond with more flexible, decentralized, and participatory programs. The main tool designed to deal with such diversity is competitive bids for which potential implementing agents (social organizations, municipalities, nongovernmental organizations, for-profit private firms, and others) present social-projects proposals following terms defined by the government (ministries and services).

A more complex and diverse notion of targeting. A social policy and its programs must be selective and clearly define the target population. As a result, a larger number of target groups is defined. In addition to those living in extreme poverty, there are "vulnerable groups," such as women, youth, indigenous groups, senior citizens, and the disabled.

Another new recipient group is that of microenterprises and small rural producers. Studies are conducted on the characteristics of each group and the discrimination/exclusion to which they are subject. Then specific programs are designed and implemented.

Targeting is indispensable for programs directed expressly at the most vulnerable sectors. The specific criteria used to select the beneficiaries (income, housing, malnutrition, education, etc.), the unit (individual, family, region, school, etc.), and the targeting tool employed (socioeconomic screening, poverty map, self-targeting design, etc.) will vary according to the program's intentions and priorities, the problem that needs to be overcome, and related factors. Furthermore, the criteria employed will also be based on institutional capacity to support targeting, of which data-gathering and information systems are an integral part.

With respect to the poverty alleviation programs that are the focus of this chapter, there has been growing attention in recent years on geographical targeting criteria (poor municipalities and poor communities within them).

It is understood that it is not appropriate to target all social spending since there are important issues that cannot be resolved by targeted programs, such as quality of education, strengthening of technical-professional education, and inequalities that stem from the coexistence of public and private health care systems. Also, expenses in basic social services that are designed to improve the welfare of the population at large and that have important externalities, such as education and health, should not be targeted. Adequate basic operation and coverage of these are considered requisites to guarantee a minimal level of access for the entire population.

Furthering decentralization. The objectives of the Concertación government are to strengthen and expand the deconcentration process initiated by the military government—incorporating a political dimension, improving economic-financial instruments, strengthening technical capabilities at the regional and municipal levels, and promoting social and community participation. At the local-government level, municipalities were democratized. Mayors and council members are now elected according to the Supreme Decree associated with the Basic Municipality Law of 1992. Two years later, in 1994, the Law of Municipal Revenue was modified and property taxes were adjusted, which increased the municipalities' tax base. In 1993, the regional governments, a territorial political unit, acquired a legal status (*personalidad jurídica*) that gave them relative autonomy and their own assets. The political body of the region, the regional council, is elected, though in an indirect manner, by municipal-council members. Decentralization is strengthened by the transfer of authority for allocating resources from the national to the regional level and from the regional to the local, the ISAR and IRAL instruments.[15] Simultaneously, measures are being taken to strengthen the municipalities' administrative and technical capabilities.

Decentralization of poverty alleviation programs is seen as essential for responding to the needs and demands of the poor in specific areas and for incorporating the participation of the poor in needs assessment and prioritization and the formulation, design, and execution of projects.

Stimulating public-private-NGO collaboration. The military government promoted private management of schools and day care centers as well as the transfer of a number of traditionally state-run services to the private sector. The Concertación governments proposed a partnership between the state and private organizations, including NGOs, foundations, universities, consultants, trade unions, community organizations, and private firms, to address social issues and combat poverty. The most frequent form of collaboration—the transfer of responsibility for implementing social programs to the private sector—has been intensified. The state sets priorities and defines programs that are then implemented by decentralized state bodies, municipalities, or private entities. This is done either through direct agreements or through public bidding in which potential private intermediaries and social organizations compete for project funding.

Policies to overcome poverty. New institutions were created to design programs aimed at specific social sectors and/or situations of poverty. Among others are the Solidarity and Social-Investment Fund (FOSIS), the National Office on Women (SERNAM), the National Youth Institute (INJ), the National Corporation for Indigenous Development (CONADI), and the Commission on the Disabled and Senior Citizens. Each of these institutions has designed programs specifically for its target group. Ministries and traditional public services have also created new programs for these groups.

FOSIS deserves special mention because it is a specific tool in the poverty alleviation policy. FOSIS supports programs that complement sectoral social policies. It was established to respond in a flexible manner to the problems and needs of specific social sectors, to stimulate their active and direct participation, and to strengthen their ability to solve problems. It is active in poor areas and sectors of the population unaffected or insufficiently influenced by sectoral policies. The targets are poor homes, low-income youth, ignored geographical areas, and productive activities that generate little income. FOSIS promotes the formulation and implementation of small-scale projects that build upon local initiatives.

Initially, the various lines of action within FOSIS operated independently. Beginning in 1995, the institution has made efforts to strengthen cohesion among its programs as well as collaboration among various agents at the local level (municipalities, public services, the private sector, social organizations). FOSIS, like other institutions that were created to address specific target groups, does not implement its programs directly. Rather, it holds competitions and calls for bids by third parties (social organizations, NGOs, municipalities, the for-profit private sector) who present project proposals and compete amongst themselves. Proposals are technically evaluated and funding is granted according to previously determined selection criteria.

In 1994, the Frei Ruiz-Tagle government announced the "National Plan to Overcome Poverty." This plan attempted to change social-program administration by better coordinating government assistance to the most poverty-stricken municipalities. For the first time, an official inventory of sectoral social programs, infrastructure programs, and productive programs targeted at the poor was taken. In addition, a Special Program for Municipalities (*comunas*) was designed. This program, with the support of regional governments, selected seventy-eight poor municipalities and pushed the ministries and services to give preferential treatment to these areas when allocating resources.

Assessment of Poverty Programs:
From Initial Discussions to Implementation

Post-1990 innovations in poverty alleviation policy led to a significant increase in public resources available for financing sectoral social policies, antipoverty programs, and projects directed at vulnerable groups. Per capita public social spending grew 51 percent between 1990 and 1996, a number that rose to more than 75 percent for education, health care, and poverty alleviation programs (Table 6.3). Similarly, there was a significant expansion in the number of programs. In 1996, 125 programs were registered. Of these, 73 percent had been created after 1990. The goal of almost all of these programs is to enhance the productive and social capabilities of the poor and vulnerable. Two-fifths of these programs incorporate community participation, particularly in the areas of administration and implementation of projects and of financial support. One-third employs geographical targeting criteria.[16]

The task of evaluating the results of social and poverty alleviation programs has only recently begun in Chile.[17] Very few evaluations have been made. They are scattered and have not been published. Rarely do programs have an evaluation scheme incorporated into their design.[18]

In 1994, an analysis of social programs implemented by the first Concertación government concluded that "Chile enjoys a coherent and elaborate social strategy, which has resulted in supportive political and economic decisions and also innovative and congruent social programs. However, this strategy is weakened in the implementation

Table 6.3   Per Capita Public Social Spending, 1987–1996 (in 1995 Chilean pesos)

Year	Education	Health	Social Security	Housing	Other	Total	% of Total Public Spending[a]	% of GDP
1987	37,779	24,928	83,278	11,828	17,266	175,079	65.1	14.6
1988	36,886	28,529	83,993	15,232	15,870	180,511	64.4	14.1
1989	35,943	28,198	84,971	14,252	14,224	177,588	63.2	12.7
1990	33,797	26,473	85,074	13,998	13,843	173,186	67.4	12.2
1991	37,194	30,662	86,975	16,357	15,043	186,230	67.1	12.4
1992	42,016	35,246	90,705	17,679	16,937	202,583	65.9	12.4
1993	44,981	38,866	96,743	18,881	18,918	218,389	67.0	12.8
1994	48,250	42,155	98,460	19,618	16,582	228,065	67.1	13.0
1995	53,087	43,256	102,785	20,310	22,308	241,746	67.8	12.9
1996	59,081	46,310	109,089	22,338	24,666	261,484	67.9	13.2

Sources: Public Finance Statistics 1987–1995, Finance Ministry, Department of the Budget. Estimates and projections for the population by gender and age, entire country: 1950–2050, Instituto Nacional de Estadística (INE), *Censo de Población y Vivienda Chile 1992, Resultados Generales* (Santiago: 1992).

Notes: a. Total expenditures exclude interest payments on the debt.

process. Programs achieve their immediate goals (the three analyzed), but they have not converged in the area of poverty alleviation."[19] This study, together with others, concludes that there are
two problems with the implementation of these programs: (1) coordination between programs and services; and (2) the pertinence
of the programs in the specific sociocultural and economic arenas
in which they are executed and where it is hoped they will produce
a change in the quality of life. The two issues are tightly interwoven, hence it is difficult to provide a comprehensive response to
the problems of poverty.

These two issues have been of major concern to the government since 1990. Various ways of solving the first problem have
been tested: the creation of the Ministry of Planning and Coordination in 1990, specifically in charge of the coordination of poverty
programs; the signing of collaborative agreements between public-
service agencies; the creation of the Social Interministerial Committee (CIS), presided over by the president; and the design of the
National Plan to Overcome Poverty. These actions have not
achieved the desired results, having come into conflict with the established decisionmaking areas of each of the ministries and
services, departments, or programs within them. The experience
surrounding the implementation of the Special Program for Municipalities suggests that coordination succeeds when those directly
responsible for a program in one territory work together with others in their area toward common local-development goals. This requires that a local agent, with the power and legitimacy to act, promote and facilitate the collaboration among the various actors.
Coordination must be achieved directly at the local level, which
once again implies that the municipality plays a central role. Weaknesses within the municipalities—weak professional teams, segmented organization of activities, bureaucratic administrations, inadequacies in technical and administrative tools, scant resources,
etc.[20]—hinder their ability to guide the complex and difficult challenge of combating poverty.

The ability to respond effectively to various types of poverty depends upon program flexibility, greater involvement of municipalities in local development, and the participation of the poor in prior-
itizing local needs and designing and implementing programs to
meet those needs. The principal tool used to achieve all of this is "project competition." The central government designs the programs and
lays the ground rules for project competition. The regional government selects high priority geographic areas or communities, and, depending on the bid, intermediate bodies such as social organizations,

NGOs, municipalities, and for-profit firms formulate projects that respond to the needs of the population. This mechanism, which results in short-term (rarely lasting more than one year), small-scale projects (in terms of resources and number of beneficiaries), has both advantages and disadvantages.

These can be seen in the results of an impact study of a sample of 180 projects backed by FOSIS.[21] The study concludes that seven of every ten projects had a positive impact because they achieved all or a large percentage of their goals and because the beneficiaries and qualified local observers recognized and valued the project. Moreover, half of the projects showed signs that the results are sustainable and/or have triggered new group or individual initiatives to solve existing problems and to look for new opportunities. The study indicates that projects have a positive and sustainable impact when the following conditions are present:

- Projects recognize and respond to the priorities and concerns of poor sectors, providing support (in terms of ideas and materials) and involving beneficiaries in the formulation and execution of the project.
- Projects are a part of local dynamics and are linked with previous, concurrent, and future initiatives. This depends to a large extent on the ability of the implementing body to insert itself into the local scene, the knowledge it has of the development needs and potential for the area, its ability to interact with other agents active in the area, particularly but not limited to the municipality, and the specific characteristics of the poor.
- Projects are technically appropriate and take into consideration and respect regulations and the law (permits, standards, formalities, etc.).
- Projects are implemented with efficiency, quality (including opportunity), and transparency from the point of view of beneficiaries and local agents.

The study reveals some problems: duplication of projects in the same locale; irrational project sequence; widely dispersed projects; areas that are overwhelmed with projects and not given suitable opportunities to collaborate and participate; projects initiated at an inappropriate time; projects unfulfilled because essential complementing support was not provided in time or was not believed to be needed; projects lacking participants; and projects that weaken existing local social organizations and intensify conflicts within the area. These situations emerge because the favorable conditions mentioned earlier are lacking.

Problems associated with the project competition mechanism as well as with the body of social programs itself are also evident. The project competition mechanism contributes to the following situations:

- Initial enthusiasm surrounding the definition of a proposal and ensuing expectations are transformed into indifference and skepticism when the project is not financed.
- Small, dispersed projects that seldom relate to each other are allowed to multiply.
- There is a high risk that the investments do not mature because the necessary complementing support did not attract financing.

The supply of social programs is profuse and diversified, created independently by different public entities. In 1995 there were 125 national programs related to poverty. Various programs overlap and duplicate efforts. At the same time they apply different rules and criteria and put different demands on the population. This varied and overlapping supply is confusing to the public, social organizations, implementing bodies, municipalities, and even to the regional government. Furthermore, each program tends to have a rigid design that defines its requirements in detail. With only a few exceptions, the social programs predefine specific products, for example, a training course for microbusinesses for n hours and covering x information. This makes it difficult to suit programs to the local situation or to combine two or more programs. Adjusting programs to local needs and coordinating programs depends upon the initiative or boldness of the authorities and/or municipal teams or public and private professionals who are working on-site. It is not demanded by the programs themselves. In sum, programs are designed by the central government, are top-down, and arrive at the local level in search of predefined beneficiaries. The local level is a mere recipient for programs.

In conclusion, there is an imbalance between traditional administration—centralized, vertical, divided according to sector or programs—and a decentralized form of administration that incorporates social participation and the support of social organizations, favors public-private collaboration, ensures flexibility in design and procedures, and is concerned with achieving results more than with complying with rules and procedures.

Lessons and Challenges

We have presented an analysis of the path that Chile has followed in the area of social policies and poverty alleviation during this century, focusing on poverty programs in the 1990s. Since the mid-1980s, statistics on the indigent and the poor have shown improvements, while the distribution of income remains highly concentrated. The evolution of poverty-related statistics is associated fundamentally with the labor market (unemployment rate, salaries) and economic growth. Larrañaga estimated that between 1987 and 1992, 80 percent of the decrease in poverty could be explained by these two factors. This has given rise to doubts about the distributive implications of economic and social policies, particularly when public opinion polls reveal that the public does not feel involved or protected by the state and its policies and programs. There is a sense of malaise, discomfort, and insecurity.[22]

It is essential to conduct an analysis of the societal and social policy model that is being built in Chile. Is the country effectively constructing a social-welfare system directed at equity and social integration? Or rather, are the prevailing market mechanisms in the economic arena neutralizing the distributive effects of social policy?

Chile has an innovative standpoint and strategy on social policies that, when implemented, come into conflict with prevailing practices in state institutions and society. Results could be better; however, this does not mean that social policy is ineffectual. There are several reasons for this. First, income distribution data refer to household incomes. In Chile (and in a majority of countries), the main impact of social policy is felt through the provision of education, health care, and housing, which do not have a direct correlation with household income levels. The allocation of resources for education and health care in Chile is progressive, and income distribution adjusted for these expenditures is less unequal than figures that are based solely on monetary income (Table 6.4).

Second, income distribution in Chile worsened under the military government but stabilized during the 1990s (Table 6.2). This must be viewed as an achievement.

Third, indicators of human development have shown gradual improvements, with minor fluctuations, over the past thirty years (Table 6.5). Thus, poverty in the 1990s is associated with higher education levels, lower infant mortality rates, and greater life expectancy than thirty years ago. Moreover, poverty is also linked with greater access to modern consumer goods (television, electrical appliances, private vehicles, shopping centers).

Table 6.4   The Distributive Impact of Social Spending, 1994

| Type of Income | Income Quintile | | | | | Quotient Q5/Q1 |
	1 (lower)	2	3	4	5 (higher)	
1. Autonomous income[a]	4.3	8.2	12.0	18.3	57.3	13.3
2. Monetary subsidies	33.4	27.8	19.6	13.1	6.1	.2
3. Total monetary income (weighted average of 1 and 2)	4.5	8.3	12.1	18.2	56.9	12.6
4. Social programs[b]	39.1	28.3	20.0	10.4	2.2	0.1
Health care	49.3	33.4	23.5	4.1	-10.3	-0.2
Education	34.8	26.2	18.5	13.1	7.5	0.2
5. Total Income (weighted average of 3 and 4)	6.3	9.4	12.5	17.8	54.0	8.6

Source: K. Cowan and J. De Gregorio, "Distribución y Pobreza en Chile: ¿Estamos Mal? ¿Ha habido Progreso? Hemos Retrocedido?" *Estudios Públicos* No. 64 (spring 1996):127–56, based on data from the Ministry of Planning and Coordination, Republic of Chile and the Office/Dept. of the Budget.

Notes: a. Generated by the household or family without state support.

b. Distribution is estimated based on the assumption that programs in 1994 were targeted similarly in 1992.

Fourth, the direction of social policy experienced a change in the 1990s: more public resources for social ends; a greater diversity of programs with an accent on social and productive investment; the incorporation of new topics and issues; more consideration given to quality in education and youth training; greater support to small productive units; strengthening and expanding capabilities of social organizations; and greater emphasis on justice, mental health, and senior citizens. These are long-term programs. Their goals are complex and ambitious and can only be achieved through deliberate and incremental actions. Results and impact can only be measured in the medium and long term.

Fifth, an assessment of poverty programs in Chile comes into conflict with the method of measuring poverty. The definition of poverty is based on household income levels and does not take into account changes in the quality of life, in opportunities, and in people's ability to solve their own problems, all of which are goals of the social policy. Agreement upon valid, reliable, and accepted indicators for these factors is needed urgently as is the development of monitoring systems and impact evaluation mechanisms, in order to acknowledge accomplishments and make any necessary corrections.

From a large list of complex problems that must be resolved, two stand out. First, how to speed up the changes from vertical, centralized, and sectorally segmented social policies to a decentralized,

Table 6.5 Chile: Social Indicators (Selected Years Between 1920–1995)

Year	General Mortality Rate (per 1,000 inhabitants)	Infant Mortality Rate (per 1,000 live births)	Life Expectancy from birth Men	Women	Illiteracy (%)	Gross Rate of School Registration Basic	Secondary	Higher Education	Education level of the Economically Active Population (PEA)	Working Population that contributes to social security	Urban Population with access to: Drinking Water	Sewer Systems	Estimated Housing Deficit (thousands of homes)
1920	30.5	250.0	31	32	36.7								
1930	24.1	200.0	40	42	25.3								
1940	21.3	170.0	41	43	27.1								
1950	13.0	129.0	53	57	19.8								
1960	12.5	120.0	54	60	16.4						44.8[f]	21.3[f]	
1970	8.7	82.0	58	64	11.0	94.4	37.9	7.8	4.3		66.5	31.1	508
1974	7.7	65.2			10.2	102.3	51.2	12.8			69.2	38.2	572
1978	6.7	40.1			8.9	97.7	51.8	10.2	7.5[e]	76.9	86.0	56.3	766
1980	6.1	23.6	67	74	8.7	93.6	55.5	8.7	7.6	53.6	92.1	70.0	912
1986	5.9	19.1			6.2	92.9	68.2	10.4	8.2	57.6	97.0	77.2	1,095
1990	6.0	16.0	71	77	5.4	89.2	75.5	11.3	8.6	58.7	98.0[g]	80.9[g]	
1991	5.6	14.6			5.1	88.3	71.3	12.4	8.6	61.3			
1992	5.5	14.3			5.2	88.1	71.5	14.3	9.2	62.2			
1993	5.5	13.1			5.0	88.0	69.2	15.6	9.4	60.7			
1994	5.4	12.0			4.8	87.4	67.1	17.0	9.5	61.7			
1995	5.5	11.1			4.6	87.1	68.5	18.0	9.6	62.6			

Sources: INE. Estimates and Projections of the Population by Sex and Age: 1950–2050. Yearly Demographics, Central Bank. Economic and Social Indicators 1960–1988 and Monthly Bulletins, Ministry of Education. Statistical Information Summary for 1995, and J. Scherman, *Techo Abrigo: Las Organizaciones Populares de Vivienda: Chile, 1974–1988,* Colección de Experiencias Populares 7 (Santiago: Programa de Economía del Trabajo, 1990). Information could not be obtained for those spaces left empty.

Notes: a. Ages 6 to 14. The rate falls because of early promotion to secondary education (a significant percentage of 14-year-olds are already attending); b. Ages 15–18; c. Ages 19–24, registration levels in universities and professional institutions. Technical schools are excluded); d. The number of contributors to both the old and new systems divided by the working population; e. 1976; f. 1963; g. 1988.

more horizontal and participatory scheme, and, second, how to make social programs flexible enough to respond effectively to diverse situations of poverty and vulnerability.

Clearly it is not sufficient, as was attempted with the Special Program for Municipalities under the National Plan to Overcome Poverty, to concentrate the resources of different programs in one geographical area. Rather, solutions must be sought with the participation of the poor, so that their specific living and working conditions are taken into account, expanding and strengthening social, productive, and organizational skills in poor areas and promoting individual, family, and community responsibilities in the resolution of problems.

To succeed, an economic and social strategy must address and ensure stable economic growth while simultaneously creating jobs and increasing productivity and salaries. Additionally, a successful strategy will emphasize sectoral public policies (in education, health care, housing, justice, infrastructure) that ensure a minimum level of quality of life and opportunities for the entire population and the existence of a safety net that can be activated in times of extreme need, such as economic recessions, natural disasters, and other emergency situations.

A successful strategy will require new ways of operating at the local level. The starting point should be the local situation—its inhabitants and organizations, their needs and resources, their development potential. The principal stakeholders in the area, including the poor, must be identified and share their vision for the area, forging a common understanding of the factors and processes that make development and policies to overcome poverty difficult. If local actors develop a shared vision of the situation and an idea of what is desired and possible in the future, they will join efforts. The resulting social intervention will most likely be relevant and positively linked with prior, concurrent, and future initiatives, facilitating local development. Somebody must guide the process. Depending upon the initial situation, this actor, in certain cases, can be the municipality or an NGO, a local teacher, or a professional whose interests are tied with that of the community. It is a slow process in which the various actors get to know each other, recognizing similarities and differences, defining common objectives, organizing themselves, and making commitments to achieve shared goals.

Another essential aspect is revising, ordering, and simplifying the supply of public programs, making them more transparent and simpler to promote. It requires a redefinition of programs, merging some, eliminating or changing the lines of authority in others. This is a political-technical task that directly touches the decisionmaking spaces of ministries and services and is not easy. The goal is to define a basic menu of flexible programs. The specificity of each local situation—its needs and potential for development—will indicate the combination or sequence of programs most pertinent to that area. Experience suggests that the menu should include programs that (1) strengthen organizational skills and the ability to create and manage solutions; (2) invest in community infrastructure programs (social centers, public spaces, sports areas, and recreation areas); (3) support basic services (water, electricity, sanitation, telephone, police, and streets and sidewalks); (4) develop small-scale production activities (productive infrastructure, technical assistance, skills training, credit); (5) offer training and retraining opportunities; and (6) provide a safety net in cases of extreme need.

The overhaul of the supply of social programs includes making their design more flexible and opening up areas for regional or local decisionmaking. Program formulation at the national level should limit itself to the definition of objectives, main orientation, and results expected.

This leads to a fourth requirement: the urgent need to develop systems for monitoring results and measuring program impact on local development and poverty in the short, medium, and long term.

Finally, this proposal implies a break with the way in which the national budget is designed and controlled in Chile (by sector and program and not by region or municipality). The allocation of resources by geographical area and to regional and local funds is greatly needed.

Appendix: Chile—Three Stages of Social Policy and Poverty Alleviation (1940–1996)

	Pre-1973	1973–1990, Military Government	1990– , Democratic Government
Role of the State	"Benefactor"	"Subsidiary"	"Integrator"
Social Policy/ Economic Policy	Social policy takes precedence over economic policy	Social policy subordinate to economic policy	Social policy integrated with and complementary to economic policy
Level of Social Spending	Growing	Decreasing	Growing, subject to macroeconomic balances. Efforts to secure more resources for social policy purposes properly financed.
Decentralization	Absent. Central and vertical administration.	Deconcentration of services. Municipal administration of primary health and education.	Political decentralization. New financial instruments. Strengthening of administrative decentralization.
State/Private Sector	State regulates, finances, and implements social policy.	State regulates and financially supports programs for the poorest sectors. Municipal and private-sector implementation. Privatization of social services for the middle- and upper-classes.	Similar to previous phase. Greater emphasis on the regulatory role of the state.
Allocation of Resources	Subsidies for services. Pressure by interest groups. Historical allocation.	Preference for demand-driven subsidies. Payments for services provided.	Both demand- and supply-driven subsidies and per capita allocation, depending on the program.
Targeting	Low priority. Emphasis on programs with universal (*even in nominal terms*) coverage	High priority. Implementation of a socioeconomic screening tool.	High priority. More diverse and complex approach. Implementation of new targeting mechanisms.
Social Policy Priority	Social infrastructure. Coverage of social services.	To reach pockets of poverty. Development of safety nets.	Quality of services, equitable results. Investment in human and social capital. Support given to small productive activities. "Give a voice" to the beneficiaries. Enhance social participation.
Main Target Groups	Ambiguous definition. Mothers and children.	Extremely poor. Mothers and children.	Poor sectors. Children, youth, women, senior citizens. Poor municipalities and localities.

Notes

1. This chapter was written in 1998. The facts and statistics presented in the chapter should be viewed accordingly.
2. UNDP (United Nations Development Programme), *Informe de Desarrollo Humano* (Santiago: 1994, 1995, 1996).
3. Dagmar Raczynski, "Social Policies in Chile: Origin, Transformations and Perspectives," *Democracy and Social Policy Series,* Working Paper no. 4 (Kellogg Institute, University of Notre Dame, Indiana, 1994, updated in 1998); and INE (Instituto Nacional de Estadística), *Censo de Población y Vivienda Chile, 1992: Resultados Generales* (Santiago: 1992).
4. ECLAC (Economic Commission for Latin America and the Caribbean), *Panorama Social de América Latina 1996,* LC/G, 1946–P (Santiago: February 1997).
5. P. Oxhorn, *Organizing Civil Society: Popular Organizations and the Struggle for Democracy in Chile,* (University Park, Pa.: Pennsylvania State University Press, 1995). These characteristics are not exclusive to Chile. For further discussion on the expansion and growth of social security in various countries of the region, see Carmelo Mesa-Lago, *Social Security in Latin America: Pressure Groups, Stratification, and Inequality* (Pittsburgh, Pa.: University of Pittsburgh Press, 1978); M. A. Garreton, "New State-Society Relations in Latin America," in C.I. Bradford, ed., *Redefining the State in Latin America* (Paris: OECD, 1994); and B. Kliksberg, ed., *El Rediseño del Estado: Una Perspectiva Internacional* (Mexico: Fondo de Cultura Económica, 1994) present a more general discussion on the role of the state, political parties, and private entities in the development of Latin America.
6. T. Castañeda, *Combating Poverty: Innovative Social Reforms in Chile During the 1980s,* International Center for Economic Growth, (San Francisco: ICS Press, 1992), discusses in detail the ideological proposition that formed the basis of the new social-policy focus and describes the principal measures adopted. P. Vergara, *Políticas Hacia la Extrema Pobreza en Chile, 1973–1988* (Santiago: FLASCO, 1990), and D. Raczynski, "Social Policies in Chile" provide a critical analysis of these same topics.
7. D. Raczynski and C. Serrano, "Administración y Gestión Local: La Experiencia de Algunos Municipios en Santiago," *Colección Estudios CIEPLAN* (Santiago: CIEPLAN, 22 December 1987) and "¿Planificación para el Desarrollo Local? La Experiencia de Algunos Municipios de Santiago" *Colección Estudios CIEPLAN* (Santiago: 24 CIEPLAN, June 1988); V. Espínola, *Descentralización del Sistema Escolar en Chile,* Centro de Investigaciones y Desarrollo de la Educación, CIDE (Santiago: CIDE, 1991).
8. J. Scherman, "Techo y Abrigo: Las Organizaciones Populares de Vivienda: Chile, 1974–1988," *Colección de Experiencias Populares 7* (Santiago: PET, 1990).
9. D. Raczynski, "¿Disminuyó la Extrema Pobreza Entre 1970 y 1982?" *Notas Técnicas* no. 90 (Santiago: CIEPLAN, December 1986).
10. L. Razetto, *Economía Popular de Solidaridad* (Santiago: Programa de Economía del Trabajo, 1986); Dagmar Raczynski, "Social Policy, Poverty, and Vulnerable Groups: Children in Chile," in G. A. Cornia, R. Jolly, and F. Stewart, eds., *Adjustment with a Human Face, Ten Country Case Studies* (Oxford: Clarendon Press, 1987); G. Campero, *Entre la Sobrevivencia y la Acción Política* (Santiago: Instituto Latinoamericano de Estudios Transnacionales, (ILET),

1987); C. Hardy, *Organizarse para Vivir: Pobreza Urbana y Organización Popular* (Santiago: PET, 1988).

11. The book edited by Pizarro et al., eds., *Políticas Económicas en el Chile Democrático* (Santiago: CIEPLAN–UNICEF, 1995), describes the principles that guided the first Concertación government, the main policies implemented, and some results, as seen from the point of view of the authors of the adopted strategy. R. Cortázar, *Política Laboral en el Chile Democrático: Avances y Desafíos en los Noventa* (Santiago: Ediciones Dolmen, 1993) analyzes the achievements and remaining challenges in the area of labor. More recently, books by R. Cortázar and J. Vial, eds., *Construyendo Opciones: Propuestas Económicas y Sociales para el Cambio de Siglo* (Santiago: Ediciones Dolmen–CIEPLAN, 1997), and C. Toloza and E. Lahera, eds. *Chile en los Años Noventa* (Santiago: Presidency of the Republic and Dolman Ediciones, 1998) provide a retrospective and prospective balance of the two Concertación governments.

12. Cortázar, *Política Laboral.*

13. The first Concertación government was faced with a budget predetermined by the military government in which the amount of total resources and those for the social sector were 7 percent lower than in 1989.

14. Ministry of Planning and Coordination, Republic of Chile (MIDE-PLAN), *Balance de Seis Años de las Políticas Sociales 1990–1996* (Santiago: MIDEPLAN, August, 1996).

15. See Jorge Rodríguez and Claudia Serrano, "Cómo Va el Proceso de Descentralización del Estado en Chile," in R. Cortázar and J. Vial, eds., 1997.

16. CIS (Comité Interministerial Social), "Programa Nacional de Superación de la Pobreza: Seguimiento y Evaluación" (Santiago: CIS Executive Secretariat, October 1996).

17. During 1997, at the request of the Chilean Congress, the Budget Department, in association with the Ministry of Planning and Coordination and the General Ministry Secretariat of the Presidency, contracted out for an evaluation of twenty social programs. For each program, a panel of experts from both the private and public sectors was chosen. Each panel, employing a common methodology over a period of two months, had to complete a report on the administration and results of the program based on the information available and on interviews with those in charge of the program. In 1998, forty more programs were added for review.

18. One of these is the "Youth Training Program," which was implemented by the Ministry of Labor with the aid of the IDB between 1991 and 1995.

19. D. Raczynski, "Focalización de Programas Sociales: Lecciones de la Experiencia Chilena," in C. Pizarro and others, eds., *Políticas Económicas y Sociales en el Chile Democrático* (Santiago: CIEPLAN–UNICEF, 1995). The programs analyzed were the "Program to Improve the Quality and Equity of Basic Education" (MECE-Basica), the "Youth Training Program," and the FOSIS "All Together Program."

20. Other obstacles have also been pointed out: the ambiguity or lack of precision in rules and standards controlling local government and local administrations, in particular the central-regional, central-local, and regional-local relationships; and contradictions in some of the decisions made at the central level, where there is a strong push for deepening decentralization within the social field (more decisionmaking powers and more

resources for the municipalities) alongside the recentralization of human resource administration in education and health (Statute for Teachers and Primary Health Care Statute). C. Serrano, "Gobierno Regional e Inversión Pública Descentralizada," *Colección Estudios CIEPLAN 42* (Santiago: CIEPLAN, June 1996); V. Espínola and others, "Evaluación de la Gestión Educacional en Educación en el Contexto de la Descentralización," *Estudios Sociales* no. 91, first quarter (Santiago: Corporación de Promoción Universitaria, 1997); Serrano and Rodríguez, 1997.

21. Dagmar Raczynski and others, "Proyecto de Fortalecimiento Institucional del Fondo de Solidaridad e Inversión Social (FOSIS) de Chile: Evaluación y Rediseño de Programas, Informe Final" (Santiago: CIEPLAN and FOSIS, January 1996).

22. United Nations Development Programme (UNDP), *Human Development Report* (New York: Oxford University Press, 1997).

7

Chile: The Dark Side
of a Successful Housing Policy

María Elena Ducci

Chilean housing policy is exemplary. It is meeting many of the goals set by all developing countries, such as bringing an end to the illegal occupation of land, providing housing solutions for all families that need them (including the poorest), and making basic services available to almost the entire population. Why, then, is it important to disclose what is not working in the sole developing country whose government has been able to give solutions to the urgency of the poorest to obtain a home? It is because these amazing results have led to Chile's housing policy being imported by other Latin American countries. It is desirable to identify those aspects that are not working so as to prevent avoidable mistakes from being repeated.

Fully recognizing the merits of the Chilean housing policy, particularly those associated with the housing allocation system, it is necessary to acknowledge the emergence of new kinds of problems that, in the short or long run, will become difficult to resolve. Intangible yet valuable assets of developing societies, already lost in northern countries, are disappearing as a result of Chile's housing policy. Today, many "advanced" or industrialized societies are trying to artificially recover some of these assets, now considered essential for quality of life in cities. Values such as extended family life, solidarity, and community work, which have seemed to be an integral part of life in poor societies, have been lost in the wealthier countries and are vanishing swiftly in Chile.[1]

The analysis of the effects of these housing programs on the Chilean population reveals a dark side of this successful policy. This critique should not lead to the erroneous conclusion that what is not working is the concept of public housing itself. It is essential that governments continue to aid poorer families to find adequate dwellings. However, certain adjustments are needed so that housing

149

programs can effectively improve the quality of life for the most vulnerable sectors of society.

Achievements: An Example for the Developing World

An End to Illegal Land Occupation

One of the most striking results of the Chilean policy was the cessation of illegal land occupation, a cornerstone of urban development in all developing countries. This is no small achievement, given that this result has not yet been achieved by any other developing country.[2] Many of the problems afflicting developing cities, such as high costs of urbanization, inadequate location and inaccessibility of low-income housing, and lack of urban services are attributed to illegal land occupation. However, not all of these problems disappear when occupation is legal, as the Chilean experience demonstrates.

Beginning in the 1960s, Chile—as well as the rest of Latin America—experienced a great number of illegal land occupations, which increased to the point that it became common practice during the Allende administration (1970–1973). It is estimated that up to 400,000 people obtained a plot of land in this manner during this period, when "invasions" (*tomas*) were occurring not only on the periphery of the city, but also on centrally located and more valuable pieces of land.[3]

The situation changed drastically in 1973 when the military government seized power. Social activism disappeared, political parties were forbidden, and all takeover attempts were promptly curbed.[4] Therefore, it is understandable why the Chilean poor were not "building their own cities" during this period, as were their counterparts in other Latin American countries. During the seventeen years of authoritarian rule, only one important invasion took place. It was later gradually dismantled under a government program to eradicate illegal settlements (*campamentos*).[5] Then, in 1975, the military government introduced a system of housing subsidies for the poor and gradually began to develop housing and basic-services programs. Near the end of the dictatorship, these programs were used as electoral tools, as they have been in many democracies.[6]

When the democratic government took office in early 1990, the housing authorities deeply feared the resurgence of takeovers. This never happened, and after more than eight years of democratic government, there have been only isolated cases involving small groups. Illegality has become outdated. There are objective reasons behind the peculiar behavior of the Chilean poor, so atypical in the Latin American context. The spirit that prevailed during the first years following the return to democracy quelled any spontaneous impulse for the poor to disregard the law and create their own cities. They wanted to believe in democracy and its many promises, so they waited patiently. At the same time, the democratic government, instead of dismantling the housing subsidy program, recognized its merits and opted to improve the system. The number of available housing units increased year after year, and an information and application system was created that was so efficient that, over a period of six years, more than 260,000 low-income Chilean families obtained some form of public housing.[7]

The Ministry of Housing and Urban Development estimates that currently only 90,000 houses in the country lack basic services, and even those houses should have services within a few years.[8] A campaign entitled "Operation Neighborhood" was launched in 1997 to bring about the complete eradication of the remaining *campamentos*.

Provision of Basic Services to Almost the Entire Population

A major difference between the housing situation of the Chilean poor today and the illegal land occupations of the past is that all new housing developments sponsored by the government include the provision of basic services. The implementation of an intensive sanitation program over the last two decades has placed Chile first among all developing countries with respect to the provision of drinking water and urban sewage systems (see Table 7.1).

An important part of the improvement observed in the health levels is due to the effectiveness of the public-housing programs in providing drinking water and sanitation. The health benefits of having access to basic services are so great that, in spite of extreme overcrowding and multiple families living in one house (the result of the suppression of illegal urban growth during the military regime), health indexes, particularly those associated with enteric diseases, have dropped consistently. These statistics place Chile at the head of the developing world, with figures comparable to those in Cuba and Costa Rica.

Table 7.1 shows how the low-income housing programs implemented by the government have resulted in the widespread availability of drinking water and sanitation throughout the country. This has not been achieved in Latin America even by countries with per capita incomes as high as or higher than Chile's.

A direct consequence of the availability of basic services—in addition to programs such as free nutrition for children, pregnant women, and breast-feeding mothers; widescale vaccinations; preventive care for healthy children; and so forth—has been a remarkable improvement over the last three decades in the health indexes for the Chilean population, making them comparable to those in many developed countries. The mortality rate among younger groups dropped dramatically; for those under six years of age, it fell by over 80 percent (see Table 7.2).

The infant mortality rate for Chile was among the highest in Latin America until 1960. The rate dropped from 109/1,000 that year to 17/1,000 in 1990, a figure comparable to that in many developed countries. The infant mortality rate in Chile is well below the average for Latin America (55/1,000), surpassed only by Cuba and

Table 7.1 Percentage of the Population with Access to Drinking Water, Sanitation, and Health Services in Selected Latin American Countries

Country	Per Capita GNP 1994	Drinking Water 1985–1995 (percent)	Sanitation 1990–1995 (percent)	Health Services 1990–1995 (percent)
Haiti	230	28	24	50
Nicaragua	340	58	60	83
Bolivia	770	55	55	67
Colombia	1,670	87	63	60
Costa Rica	2,400	92	97	80
Chile	3,520	85	83	85
Mexico	4,180	83	50	78
Argentina	8,110	71	68	71

Source: UNDP, *Report on Human Development;* World Bank, *Information About World Development;* and WHO, "Most Recent Values of WHO Global Health for All Indicators."

Table 7.2 Percentage of Deaths per Age Group, 1960–1990

Age	1960	1970	1980	1990	Percentage Change 1969–1990
Less than 1 year	35.9	25.0	11.0	6.2	-82.1
1–4 years	9.1	4.4	2.7	1.2	−86.6
5–14 years	2.8	2.4	1.8	1.0	−64.3
15–44 years	13.1	13.2	13.0	11.7	−10.7
45–64 years	16.6	20.4	22.7	22.7	+26.9
Over 64	22.5	34.6	49.8	57.2	+60.1

Source: PAHO/WHO, *Informe Mundial de la Salud,* 1990; INE, *Anuario de Demografía,* 1992; World Bank, *Chile: The Adult Policy Challenge,* 1995.

Costa Rica (see Figure 7.1). The most important reason for this decline is the significant reduction in the occurrence of infectious and parasitic diseases, which is directly linked to the provision of drinking water and sanitation. Figure 7.1 shows infant mortality rates in a number of industrialized and Latin American countries.

Mortality among children below the age of five years dropped to a rate of less than 1/1,000 in 1990, and malnutrition (measured as weight-age ratio) for children below the age of six years dropped from 15.9 percent in 1976 to 6.9 percent in 1990. The occurrence of moderate and severe malnutrition in Chile is among the lowest for developing countries, afflicting less than 1 percent of children below the age of six years. Maternal mortality dropped drastically from 30/10,000 live births in 1960 to about 4/10,000 in 1990—a figure comparable to 3.9 in Cuba, 1.5 in western Europe, and 0.7 in the United States, and surpassed in Latin America only by 1.8 in Costa Rica.

Figure 7.1   Infant Mortality Rates in Selected Latin American and Developed Countries, 1991 (Per 1,000 Inhabitants)

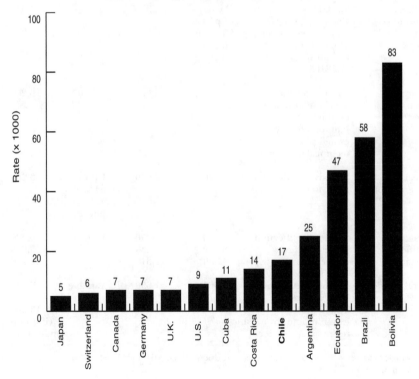

Goals Surpassed

One of the positive elements of the Chilean housing policy is the variety of housing solutions being developed and offered to applicants. The main programs currently administered by the Ministry of Housing and Urban Development are summarized in Table 7.3.

Table 7.3   Chile: Public Housing Programs, MINVU/Chile, 1996

Program	Features	Savings[a] (minimum required)	Subsidy[a] (maximum)	Credit[a] (maximum)	Cost[a] (maximum)
Progressive Housing— First stage/ SERVIU	Plot and services (electricity, sewer, pavement) area: 15 m^2 (bath, k, 1 room)	264	4,356	—	4,620
Basic Housing	Plot and services area: 40 m^2 (semi-detached, 1 to 2 stories or blocks, 3 stories)	330	4,620	2,640	7,590
Progressive Housing— First stage/ "Private"	Subsidy certification (bath, k, 1 room) services remainder of mortgage technical assistance (US$165)	Ownership of plot or 99 to 364 and mortgage	4,356	—	4,620
Basic Housing, Free Choice	Subsidy certification purchase of new or used house built on already owned plot technical assistance	660	4,620	3,300	13,200
Special Program for Workers (PET)	Subsidy certification area: 40 m^2	1,320	2,970	Up to 65% of value of house	13,200
General Unified Subsidy	Subsidy certification purchase of new or used house	1,650 3,300 4,950	4,290 3,630 2,310	Variable	16,500 33,000 49,500
Rural Subsidy	Subsidy certification built on already owned plot legalization of ownership technical assistance	1,665	1,650	Variable	8,580 or 13,200 (if group application)

Source: Synthesis based on interviews and documents; MINVU, 1994–1996.
Notes: a. In 1997 US$.

As can be seen in Table 7.4, the housing deficit in Chile has been somewhat constant between the 1960s and the 1980s. The sudden increase in 1990, when a democratic government resumed power, was due mainly to changes in the criteria for assessing the deficit.[9]

The total number of housing units produced within the country has increased more than 120 percent in ten years. The number of square meters per unit also increased by more than 25 percent during the same period (see Table 7.5). Even though the table includes all houses built in the country (by public and private sectors), the Ministry of Housing and Urban Development estimates that between 1990 and 1995, more than 80 percent were constructed with either the direct or indirect support of the state (see Table 7.6).

Considering that each year between 90,000 and 95,000 new families are formed and that the total production of houses is higher than this number (more than 130,000 units have been built per year in recent years), for the first time in Chile's history it is possible to predict an end to the accumulated deficit and provision of legally owned housing for the entire population. This is unheard of among developing countries and would indicate Chile's passage to a more developed stage.[10]

Actually Reaching the Poorest

Another aspect of Chile's housing policy that deserves special attention is that it is actually responding to the needs of the poorest,

Table 7.4   Evolution of the Housing Deficit in Chile, 1952–1996 (Official Figures)

Year and President	Total Deficit (housing units)
1996 (Frei R.)	600,000
1952 (Ibáñez)	156,205 (including shantytowns, collective dwellings, and houses "in bad shape")
1960 (Alessandri)	538,700 (11% as a result of reconstruction needs following 1960 earthquake)
1964 (Frei M.)	420,000
1970 (Allende)	592,324
1975 (Pinochet)	419,000
1988 (Pinochet)	422,000
1991 (Aylwin)	800,000

Sources: MINVU, *"Vivienda, una Tarea de Dignidad";* MacDonald, *"La Vivienda en Chile, Hoy";* MacDonald, Declarations to "El Mercurio"; and Official Address by the Minister of Housing and Urban Development, June 1996.

Table 7.5   Housing Built by the Public Sector, Chile 1990–1995

Year	Total Public Sector	Public and Private Housing	Percentage[a]
1990	79,342	73,559	92.7
1991	88,541	93,673	—
1992	108,482	94,235	86.8
1993	122,062	98,297	80.5
1994	124,785	98,719	79.1
1995	135,600	97,597	71.9
Annual Average	109,802	92,677	84.4

Source: Ministry of Housing and Urban Development/Division of Housing Policy, "Vivienda, una Tarea de Dignidad"; and V. Fernández, "Edificación Aprobada e Iniciada, Sector Público y Privado, Total Pais," MINVU/INVI Seminar, April 1997.

Notes: Public housing: contracted projects or subsidies granted by MINVU each year.

Table 7.6   Number of Housing Units and Average Surface Area, 1985–1995

Year	Number of housing units	Sq. meters/housing unit
1985	61,223	49.9
1986	58,082	55.6
1987	60,316	58.9
1988	77,501	51.8
1989	83,819	57.5
1990	79,342	56.5
1991	88,541	59.5
1992	108,482	64.7
1993	122,062	59.6
1994	124,785	59.3
1995	135,600	62.7

Source: INE, Anuarios Estadísticos; V. Fernandez, "Edificación Aprobada e Iniciada"; and MINVU/INVI, Statistical Bulletin, no. 223 (March 1997):11.

focusing an important part of housing production on them. The two public-housing programs specifically oriented to the lowest-income groups, the Basic Housing Program and the Progressive Housing Program, have been consistently supported by the government. Table 7.7 shows that, over the last seven years, the government has produced nearly 148,000 houses for the very poor through these two programs. An unintended consequence of this, discussed below, is the very high number of delinquent mortgages.

A number of studies found that a significant percentage of those families that benefit from housing programs are the extremely poor or indigent, yet they were able to procure the minimum savings required by the Ministry of Housing and Urban Development to qualify for a house. Also, a comparison of national levels of poverty and indigence with the levels found in a typical neighborhood produced through the Basic Housing Program, such as Villa Los Navíos, found a high concentration of poverty within the community (Table 7.8). Forty percent of the national population was under the poverty line in 1990 compared with 82 percent in Villa los Navíos in 1992.[11] Moreover, nearly 44 percent of the households in the villa were considered

Table 7.7   Housing Allocations for Low-Income Families, 1990–1996

Year	Basic Housing	Progressive Housing
1990	11,902	—
1991	17,276	920
1992	23,583	6,736
1993	19,997	3,736
1994	20,072	4,525
1995	17,008	2,778
1996	17,548	2,004
Total	127,386	20,699

Source: Ministry of Housing and Urban Development, *Statistical Bulletin no. 223,* March 1997, p. 11.

Table 7.8   Levels of Poverty According to Family Income (National Levels Compared to a Typical Basic-Housing-Program Project)

Type of household	National (1990)	"Villa Los Navios" (1993)
Nonpoor	60.0	17.9
Poor	26.2	38.3
Indigent	13.8	43.8
Total	100.0	100.0

Source: M. E. Ducci, *Salud Mental en Mujeres de la Periferia Pobre de Santiago de Chile,* Working Paper, Urban Studies Institute, 1995.

indigent according to traditional methods of poverty measurement.[12] This shows that, even though they have no capacity for payment, almost half of the families of the neighborhood have been able to save enough to receive a subsidized house from the government.

Feasibility of Obtaining a Publicly Subsidized House

Several studies indicate that the poorest groups are obtaining a legal housing solution with basic services in a quite short period of time compared with any other developing country. Although there are no official data about the average time between request and procurement of housing, most of the population thinks that they can obtain a house in a reasonable period, and once the applicants comply with all the requisites, the process moves expeditiously. For example, an evaluation of the Progressive Housing Program showed that the average waiting period from the time an application was made until a house was obtained was two years. [13] Even considering that the program was new and relatively few people were taking advantage of it because it does not grant a complete house, it has been extremely effective. It offers a legal solution to the housing problem, providing basic services and a small room. Furthermore, the Villa Los Navíos study found that 83 percent of the families wait less than six years to procure their house and 44 percent obtain it in less than three years.[14] Moreover, a study done for SERNAM (Secretaría Nacional de la Mujer) in 1994, found that "on average the Basic Housing beneficiaries waited 1.5 years to obtain their house; beneficiaries of the PET program, 2.6 years; and those served by the Unified Subsidy, 4.2 years."[15]

Here lies what may be the most important explanation for why the poor are not illegally occupying land in Chile: their confidence that they will be able to legally acquire a house within a few years just by showing the ability to save a small amount of money and fulfilling the requirements set forth by MINVU. In conjunction with the accelerated economic development of the country and almost no unemployment, this explains why low-income Chileans find illegal land occupation an unappealing alternative.

Problems: The Other Side of the Coin

The preceding panorama is well-know. It is no surprise that other Latin American and developing countries want to learn from the Chilean experience. Therefore, it is important to gain a deeper understanding of the problems generated by the Chilean housing policy in order to avoid their duplication in other places as well as to improve the quality of life for the poor in Chile. The different situations and issues presented here cannot be understood in isolation; they are organized to facilitate better understanding of the living conditions of the Chilean poor who have benefited from the public housing policy.

The Emerging City: The New Ghettos

Even in Chile, where the city growth has been legal, within the boundaries of any city there is another city, the city of the poor. It is different from the central city, where business is conducted and where the middle and high-income sectors live. Here, the city of the poor has been created by the state, by the successful housing policy of the Chilean government, and has its own physical expression: the "projects" (*poblaciones*), which house a specific social reality.

There is a clear rationale behind the origin of the Chilean city of the poor. To increase the number of solutions, costs needed to be reduced. One way of achieving this has been by locating low-income housing projects on the cheapest urban land available. In developing countries, where the housing for the poor sprouts illegally all over, it is assumed that squatting causes inadequate land occupation. In Chile, where the land market has defined the location of public housing, the results have been quite similar: located on the outskirts of the city, away from commercial areas, with no nearby facilities; over land of poor quality, prone to floods and sinking, or near undesirable land uses such as dumps, sand pits, water treatment plants, and cemeteries. In this respect, the most pressing problems for the residents are the isolation (especially for women who stay in the barrio) and the long distances to work for the heads of the households.

The term "ghetto" was coined in 1517 in Venecia, when the Jews were forced to move to an old abandoned foundry.[16] The modern concept of ghetto denotes neighborhoods or inner cities where minorities or marginalized groups live, as a consequence of socioeconomic segregation and, in some countries, racial segregation. In Robert Moses's New York the term *ghetto* "took on the barely submerged meaning of 'those who have been left behind'. . . . To belong to a ghetto came to be seen as a matter of sharing a common failure."[17] They are generally areas in a state of disrepair that are (or appear to be) unsafe for outsiders. Considering that in every country, urban planning is struggling to transform these areas into more livable spaces, it is of concern that a modern housing policy such as Chile's is actually creating these results.

The new low-income housing projects can be regarded as ghettos because of their isolation, rapid deterioration, lack or inadequacy of facilities (education, health care, security), insufficiency or abandonment of green areas, lack of personal safety in their streets, and vacant lots.[18] The housing projects (whether apartment buildings or individual houses) present high concentrations of poverty, reflected in the premature deterioration of the housing units and neglected common areas. This is not solely the result of the scarcity of resources of the people who are beneficiaries of these projects ("lack of culture" of the poor), but is due to the absence of an ongoing process of improvement characteristic of irregular popular settlements in other developing countries (*barriadas, villas miseria, favelas*). Conversely, in this type of project, there is a feeling of abandonment and despair, resulting in an unpleasant urban environment. The Chilean government recognizes that these poverty enclaves are an undesirable byproduct of a well-targeted housing policy, and some solutions are being considered.[19]

Public-housing projects in Chile consist of hundreds of units. As the scarce resources are concentrated in producing the housing itself, a common feature is a lack of adequate facilities, leading to a low quality of life for the residents. Most of the zones labeled "green areas" have never achieved that color and have no equipment: There are no sports grounds or facilities to host community group activities. This absence of adequate spaces to facilitate social interaction at the local level makes it difficult to establish relationships with neighbors, a key element in developing a sense of belonging and interest in improving the quality of life in the neighborhood. Children play on the street, and adults meet in inadequate and often makeshift facilities. When the young have no place to gather and no programs available to guide them, they "seize the streets," making them unsafe for other residents. Security is a serious problem in poor neighborhoods, closely related to the increase of drug addiction among the youth. In many ways, new housing projects are transformed into ghettos.

A comparable situation has been found in developed countries, where the "ghettoization" of poor neighborhoods has been discussed for several years. Countries like France, Germany, and Sweden

> paint a fairly common picture of these areas: neighborhoods of a thousand or more flats, constructed on virgin soil, monotonously designed, and built with prefabricated materials. These estates are characterized by inadequate public and commercial services and, despite the relative newness of the dwellings, severe maintenance problems. These deficiencies are caused by poor or non-existent maintenance or faulty construction methods. The transportation

systems serving these estates are often inefficient, which isolates these neighborhoods from regional and city centers and work places. In combination, such conditions often gave these areas a poor reputation right from the start.[20]

The Sort of Housing Solution Supplied

Another mechanism used to abate costs has been a reduction in the size of the plots and the units, lowering the cost of design and construction. This has had effects both on the quality of the product and on the beneficiaries' quality of life. Although there are no studies to scientifically demonstrate that a minimum area is needed to sustain an adequate quality of life for a family, it has been found, for example, that there is a strong correlation between a crowded indoor environment (measured in square meters per person and persons per bed) and increased health problems. "We are talking about internal crowding, which has implications on stress in social relations, on mental and physical health, and epidemiological risk."[21]

In Latin America, a plot of land of fewer than 100 square meters does not appear to be large enough to induce a spontaneous improvement in the quality of housing. The population values a good-sized plot of land; in all invasions or illegal purchases of land, plots have at least 100 square meters in size.

The dimensions of the housing units have been reduced in different ways. The Basic Housing Program provides low-income families with finished houses that have an average area of between 30 and 40 square meters on two floors (see Table 7.6).[22] These houses are so small that it is not uncommon for families to discover upon moving in that their furniture does not fit. The Progressive Housing Program in its two forms (SERVIU and private) provides a bathroom and a "dry unit," which can be either a small adjacent room or two or three walls that the families must complete before moving in. The average area ranges from 9 to 14 square meters per family. The Land with Services Program provides a bathroom of about 6 square meters and is generally used to upgrade existing houses originally built without facilities in the *campamentos*. These would be satisfactory solutions if the unfinished houses were actually expanded and improved upon, but this does not usually happen.

One of the most serious negative effects of the small housing size is its insufficiency to shelter families' daily life; children constantly spend time on the street, in contact with drugs, alcohol, and gangs.[23] This situation is seen as one of the most pressing problems by the residents of popular neighborhoods and tends to grow without any apparent solution. The tiny size of the houses also diminishes privacy, creating problems for couples. Furthermore, there is a negative impact on mental health, particularly among women, who spend most of their time at home and remain within the neighborhood.[24] Another problem associated with the modest size of the homes is the impossibility of sheltering members of the extended family (grandparents and married children) or celebrating family events (parties, weddings, funerals, and christenings). This is radically altering the way of life for low-income families, fomenting individualism, gangs, and disruption of family bonds.

When analyzing the type of product that is being turned out by the housing programs for the poorest, it is essential to consider the serious problem of the quality of design and construction. Although low-income housing is built by various construction companies and the design is, theoretically, open, there is a striking uniformity to the thousands of houses being produced across the country. This is because, in order to minimize costs, designs follow the minimum standards set by the construction codes and are repeated ad infinitum. This is especially apparent in houses produced by the Basic Housing Program, as the other programs offer incomplete solutions that are finished by each family, with chaotic and precarious results.[25]

Poor construction has become one of the main reasons for dissatisfaction on the part of the families that live in these houses. One of the means to reduce construction costs has been to use the cheapest materials available, so simple panels are used as dividing walls, and bathrooms are located near the entrance of the house to shorten the run of pipes from the street. Consequently, one of the priorities of the beneficiaries is to move the bathroom to a more private place. Foundations are built with insufficient amounts of cement, so they erode easily; bricks in walls become loose; the roofs cannot tolerate more than a certain number of hours of rain; and so on. Poor insulation reduces privacy between apartments, so it is impossible to ignore the activities of neighbors. This, in addition to the small size of the houses, is a source of stress and tension in family and social relations and has lowered the quality of life for the residents.

There is an almost complete lack of quality control in state-sponsored housing, which is reflected in its accelerated deterioration. Thus, many of the classic problems associated with the old illegal settlements have appeared in housing developments in a very short period of time. These problems have attained such a high level of political notoriety that, in 1993, the government created the National Commission on Housing Quality. Moreover, in September 1996 a new law was passed regarding construction quality, which protects the owners and holds the original construction company responsible for any problems eventually affecting the house. The law raises the levels of technical information regarding the product and establishes a system of guarantees.[26]

In June 1997, as a consequence of heavy and excessive rains, the poor quality of public housing generated a political crisis at the national level. Public-housing buildings protected by plastic rolls and enraged residents protesting became daily news of that winter and a symbol of the failure of a social policy considered until then to be a complete success. The conflict resulted in the resignation of the officials in charge of the housing production (minister and undersecretary) and in the reformulation (until now, only in theory) of the housing policy. As winter 1998 was marked by drought, the social conflict did not recur, but without any doubt it remains latent.

The Loss of Social Capital

The destruction of the family ties that has been caused by the housing allotment system is an issue that only recently is beginning to be considered. The efficiency of the housing allocation system is based partly on the use of modern technology. A computerized database has been created and contains complete information on all of the applicants to the various housing programs; it classifies the families according to their declared socioeconomic characteristics (which must be updated every two years at their municipality) and includes information such as savings levels and date of application. Based on this information, the allocation system operates impartially, assigning houses to those families who best meet the requirements. However, the location of the house assigned to a family is determined by availability within the projects built by MINVU or the private companies. So, a happy family that has finally achieved the dream of having its own home may find itself relocated to the outskirts of the city, away from friends, relatives, and the old neighborhood.[27] In an income sector in which transportation expenses are heavily constrained (limited to cover trips to school or work), opportunities to visit relatives or friends are almost nonexistent; this causes a breakdown in the ties between relatives and friends and disrupts the systems of solidarity and trust established among old neighbors. The most dramatic effect of this change is experienced by women, who strongly resent the isolation and loss of family support.

In any other Third World country, the extended family is the basis of the self-help system that allows the poor to improve the quality of their lives. But the success of the Chilean allocation system has had the negative effect of contributing to the destruction of the extended family. The tiny size of the plots and houses, as well as the excessive regulation that makes it almost impossible to legally enlarge houses, prevents residents from giving shelter to family members (grandparents, children of unwed mothers, relatives going through a difficult time).

More worrisome is that, even among the poorest, the extended family has become a symbol of the inability of young couples to succeed. Thus, there is now a negative connotation to the concept of "sheltering" (*allegamiento,* from *allegar,* to put in close proximity; in this sense, to bring relatives or friends into one's home).[28] This new attitude has been imported from the countries of the north, where "modernity" is associated with the nuclear family and with the displacement of the elderly, who have lost their traditional role within the family. It is important to note that two of the main problems facing developed societies are abandonment of the aged and the surge of homelessness, which has become a distinctive feature of downtown areas in big cities. Both phenomena are directly related to the collapse of the extended family and its role in society.

Moreover, the limited dimensions of houses makes it impossible to host family gatherings, which tend to disappear from the daily lives of the poorest. There is not enough space to receive family visits, which become less and less frequent as traditional social rituals vanish. All of this results in a loss of social capital, understood as the network of reciprocal relations based on trust and norms that form part of the social organization within a community. Social capital, traditionally accepted as a requirement for maintaining cohesion while undergoing social change, is now considered a key element of development; as a facilitator of economic activities it becomes a primary tool to reduce the vulnerability associated with poverty.[29]

Hindering Improvements

One of the virtues of Chilean society is that laws and regulations are observed more strictly than in most other Latin American countries. The population has a highly developed respect for the law, a positive attribute with a negative side: Excessive legalism and rigidity create insurmountable obstacles to any acts that are not clearly sanctioned by law. Construction codes are very strict in Chile; securing permits to enlarge a house requires going through a great deal of bureaucracy and expense. Thus, the remodeling or expansion of houses inhabited by the poor is often done precariously, to avoid paying fines for not building in accordance with the construction codes. The current regulations are not negative per se, but inflexible rules and complex procedures retard solutions to the urgent need to upgrade and improve the current housing supply.[30]

Social Anomie

In illegal settlements in other Latin American countries (and even in the few cases where illegal land occupation has succeeded in Chile), members of the group share a common goal: to secure control over the land and obtain basic services. As their success depends largely on the group's cohesiveness, there is a deep feeling of unity and strong interest in improving the physical environment, something entirely absent in the public housing projects. This lack of interest in participating in neighborhood improvement is mirrored in the lack of initiative on the part of the residents to improve their own homes. This is due in part to fear of being fined if they do not comply with the construction codes, and in part to the higher costs associated with compliance. As a result, most families enlarge their homes by adding only nonpermanent elements (*mediaguas*). It is interesting to observe the effect this has on the housing units that are delivered "finished or complete." As seen from the street, they look normal and neat; however, from the back, they look like huts with all manner of irregular additions. Because the families have no alternative, given that the size and type of the original unit does not meet their needs, the irregular expansion that results generates problems similar to those that plagued the illegal settlements of the past.

The lack of initiative is also fueled by the paternalistic nature of the relationship between the government and the low-income population. People expect the government to solve their housing problems (in fact, the government is doing exactly that), and there is no initiative, as can be observed in any other Latin American country, to undertake a self-improvement process. As a result, in the Progressive Housing Program, where the explicit goal is for the family to complete a very basic housing unit provided by the government (*pie de casa*), most people simply build a precarious expansion while waiting the required two years to apply for the second stage of this program. There is still no awareness on the part of the residents (or the government) that this second stage will be insufficient to meet their housing needs.

The breakdown of the network of family and social relationships is an important part of the problem. These new low-income neighborhoods, consisting of families who have only their poverty in common, are permeated by a sense of mistrust and lack of solidarity that recedes very slowly. A process of neighborhood improvement is much more difficult to achieve in an unfriendly environment and with no common cause, such as the problem of irregular settlements faced in other developing countries.

Moratorium

Delinquent debt is a growing problem—one of the most sensitive aspects of the housing programs and not properly addressed even though it affects the entire low-income housing system in Chile. To some extent, it is a consequence of the dissatisfaction of the population with the product received. A large portion of those who are beneficiaries of low-income, state-supported housing are not paying their mortgages. However, because foreclosure would have so many political costs and ramifications, an effective mechanism to deal with this problem has yet to be put into place.

A study conducted by the Ministry of the Interior in 1989 identifies the following factors as responsible for the high level of delinquent debt affecting the Land and Services Program: irregular income in the rural sector due to seasonal factors; encouragement of the "no payment" option by politicians (electoral promises of "those who do not pay will not be sanctioned"); deficiencies in the process of issuing titles; a belief by debtors that foreclosure cannot be applied; fraudulent purchase, where the buyer and seller wrongly believe that the debt has been cancelled; and inadequate set-up and management of the mortgage portfolio by municipalities (lack of coordination between municipal departments involved in recovering unpaid debt, inadequate information provided to the community on repayment of debts, and legal red tape).

The high levels of delinquent debt and the political pressure associated with this problem have led previous administrations to call for the renegotiation of housing loans. The first decree allowing such renegotiations was passed in 1989, near the end of the military government. During the Aylwin administration, two more decrees were passed, creating the opportunity for debtors to pay off their debt by actually covering only a fraction of it. This was the origin of the expression *perdonazo* (the big pardon), which creates an incentive not to pay because another perdonazo always seems to be on the way. The problem is so severe that the government is currently conducting studies aimed specifically at solving the problem of unpaid mortgages and redefining strategies to cope with it. It is a peculiar situation because, in some cases, the cost of setting up a tracking and collection system would be higher than the amount of the debt to be recovered. This situation is directly linked to the fact that a large number of houses were provided to extremely poor families who, even though they were able to save the down payment, are incapable of meeting the monthly installments. However, the high default level is also partly due to the fact that families who are able to pay refuse to do so because they feel it is unfair to have to pay when others are getting a break.

The Ministry of Housing and Urban Development decided in 1996 to address these problems by commencing a "demonstration" program to penalize those families who can afford to pay but do not, and, simultaneously, by organizing a market for previously owned houses.[31] This had not been possible before for two reasons: (1) A house could not be placed on the market until five years from the original date of purchase; and (2) the beneficiary of a housing program could not reapply for housing subsidies (efficient monitoring of the system made cheating almost impossible). In principle, creating a market for previously owned houses where subsidies would also be made available seems to be a good idea; however, it could have an unintended effect of accelerating the concentration of extreme poverty by forcing the very poor into the least desirable and most disadvantageous areas.

Conclusion

The urban environments that are being produced by Chilean housing policies show a negative balance and, even worse, demonstrate no possibility of increasing their value with time. The exceptions showing an upgrading of the housing environment (and with it, the improvement of the quality of life of the residents) are the result of the arduous work of small groups of organized residents.

Studies conducted in other Latin American countries reveal that once the inhabitants of an illegal settlement reach some degree of certainty that they will not be expelled, a process of consolidation and improvement of the dwellings begins, quickly transforming the settlement into a neighborhood. A visit to any of these areas ten years after the takeover shows colorful two- or three-story houses, shops, and rooms for rent. It has even been found that very poor families, unable to participate in the upgrading process, sell their land at market value and are expelled to the new periphery of the city, where they once again begin the cycle of securing a place to live.[32]

What can be seen in Chile's housing projects ten years after construction? With few exceptions,[33] the most obvious feature is their advanced and premature deterioration due to both the low quality of the materials used and the inability, lack of will, and/or lack of initiative on the part of the residents to make improvements.[34] This phenomenon is even more pronounced in four- or five-story apartment buildings where, in addition to the poor condition of the building itself, the surrounding yards and other common areas, neglected by residents, have become dumps.

It can be argued that the low-income housing currently being produced, especially for the poorest segments of the population, is generating a new qualitative deficit as their characteristics render them insufficient or inadequate to satisfy the needs of the population. Houses provided by these government programs are incapable of accommodating the changes that naturally take place in the life-cycle of any family: the marriage of children, parents who need to be taken in, and so forth.

This prevents the houses from becoming a social asset, a key element—as evidenced in other developing countries—in promoting economic stability and reducing the vulnerability of the poor. "Housing is an important productive asset that can cushion households against severe poverty, and land market regulation can either create opportunities to diversify its use or foreclose them."[35] Low-income families in most Third World countries use their house as an asset in two ways: to accommodate more than one generation,[36] and to rent out part of the space to secure additional income for the family. Neither of these options is feasible with current low-income housing in Chile. Moreover, as stated above, the population does not even consider such options as viable ways to resolve their needs. Only about 5 percent of the houses provided through government housing programs are being temporarily "loaned" or rented out to families other than the original beneficiaries. These units are usually owned by families who did not actually need a house as a primary dwelling, but applied to the program in order to obtain a unit to rent it out for income (this is illegal and the owners can be penalized; however, the problem is often difficult to detect).

Violence and a lack of safety have become standard features of poor neighborhoods. Violence, one of the most pressing social problems today and one that seems difficult to bring under control in the near future, is partly linked to higher levels of drug addiction, a recent phenomenon that no country has been able to successfully resolve. With no apparent alternatives for earning large sums of money, many low-income neighborhoods have become centers for dealing drugs. However, these problems are also partly linked to the nature of the neighborhoods (ghettos) where many of the poor live.

The small size of the houses forces children out onto the streets, where they learn the ways of violence and gang activity.

The social anomie that permeates low-income neighborhoods in developed countries, and in present-day Chile as well, also fuels this lack of safety. In this context, it should not be surprising that the incidence of mental-health problems among the inhabitants of low-income neighborhoods is on the rise, reflected in alcoholism and drug abuse in the case of men, and in depression and anguish in the case of women.[37] This anomie is less common in the illegal settlements of the developing world where, from the beginning, the community has fought as one to achieve a shared goal. In neighborhoods where people know each other and where spontaneous networks of support and protection are created, there is a sense of safety.

An unintended consequence of the low-income housing programs, recognized only recently, is the concentration of chronic poverty in certain areas. This is the other side of the coin to the successes of the targeted systems implemented in recent years by the Ministry of Housing and Urban Planning. By concentrating on very poor families who lack not only economic means but also a network of social support to help them overcome their poverty, the housing programs are creating neighborhoods that deteriorate rapidly, where life is unsafe,[38] and where lack of expectations is common. Families receive a partial solution to their housing needs. Economic means and the commitment of the family are required to achieve a complete solution. When the majority of the families do not possess these resources and receive no external support, the chances for reaching a satisfactory standard of living are small.

Furthermore, in spite of the overall progress, there are a number of extremely poor families who are unable to save and, as a consequence, are excluded altogether from these housing programs. It has become clear that providing them with a dwelling is not even positive, as they are unable to pay for basic services or loans. Today, the government is working to design policies aimed at providing an integral solution to "hard" poverty by habilitating these groups both socially and in terms of employment (for example, training, job opportunities).

The city generated by the Chilean housing policy is destroying fundamental components of the social fabric, some of which could be recovered with a better understanding of the underlying dynamics of the process. The lack of a sense of belonging and the inability of residents to improve their environment must be properly addressed if the streets are to be kept safe and if the neighborhoods are to be livable. It is important to reassess these low-income housing programs in order to prevent the formation of pockets of chronic poverty.

If another goal is to use ownership of a house as a tool to help low-income families leave poverty behind, the housing programs must be redesigned so that they can facilitate the creation and expansion of social capital (social assets); facilitate the use of the house as an asset (upgrading and enlarging the house to accommodate the extended family and/or to rent out certain areas to obtain additional income); and facilitate continuous improvement of the houses and surrounding areas.

There are serious obstacles to improving the situation.

1. The traditional system of production of public housing has been generating important profits for the private real estate sector and promoting the growth of the building industry (creating labor, increasing the consumption of building materials).
2. The current system is the sole means for some sectors to obtain a minimum apartment or house in ownership. Since these sectors have no possibility of participating in the formal open market, highly subsidized programs give them a solution for their housing problem. Moreover, the population considers the system an acquired right.
3. Considering that the subsidized house can be sold after five years, it is evident that the beneficiaries will exert strong pressures to maintain the traditional programs.
4. There is an inertia difficult to overcome at the international level, as multilateral organizations do not seem eager to change their approaches and continue to support traditional programs.

A different approach is needed to attain a real improvement in the standard of living of the poorest. The approach must focus on generating flexible conditions to promote community and family initiatives. After decades of experiences in developed countries and learning from the "successful" Chilean experience, it is time to recognize that neither the state nor private companies can achieve this goal by themselves without the involvement of a concerned population.

Notes

1. Approximately twenty of the world's foremost experts in the field of urban studies discussed this topic at the "Solidarity Forum," one of the main fora organized by the June 1996 United Nations Conference on Human Settlements, Habitat II, held in Istanbul.
2. Cuba has not been considered due to its radically different condition.

3. Alfredo Rodriguez, "Cómo Gobernar a Principados que se Regían por sus Propias Leyes Antes de Ser Ocupados," *SIAP* 17, no. 65 (March 1983).

4. Andrés Necochea, "Los Allegados, una Estrategia de Supervivencia Solidaria en Vivienda," *EURE* 13-11, no. 39–40 (October 1987): 87.

5. The only "successful takeover" during the military government took place on 22 September 1983 when 8,000 families (approximately 32,000 people) occupied two large empty plots of land and founded the "Cardenal José María Caro" and "Monseñor Juan Francisco Fresno" settlements. This was the largest illegal land occupation to occur in the history of the country. Due to the number of people involved and their resolve, the government failed in its efforts to remove them and opted to incorporate them into the settlement eradication program.

6. Beginning in 1975, a number of measures were taken, such as the formation of communal housing committees (CHCs), to create low-income housing, housing subsidies programs, basic housing programs, a settlement eradication program, etc.

7. This is an estimate of the number of basic and "progressive" (step-by-step) housing solutions produced and/or subsidized by the public sector between 1990 and 1995 aimed at low-income families. Viviana Fernández, *International Seminar: Sustainable Urban Housing Development,* working paper, University of Chile, 1997.

8. This is the goal set by the Ministry of the Interior for its "Land with Services" program (*Lotes con Servicio*), funded by the Inter-American Development Bank and aimed at upgrading settlements that do not have basic services. Another study, conducted in 1996 by the Housing Institute of the University of Chile for the Ministry of Housing and Urban Development, found that about 100,000 families live in houses without sanitary services. Drago Domancic, Ministerio del Interior, Subdirección de Desarrollo Regional, Interview, 1996.

9. In 1985, the Ministry of Housing and Urban Development (MINVU) estimated a deficit of 380,000 housing units, while other sources estimated 800,000 units. Newspaper *La Segunda,* cited in "Hechos Urbanos," SUR Profesionales, Chile: October 1985. Three years later, Joan MacDonald, who would become Undersecretary for Housing and Urban Development in 1990, estimated the deficit to be 1,330,000 units. The remarkable difference between these estimates is due to methodological discrepancies, both with regard to the number of social units (families) needing a house and to the number of existing housing units.

10. Prior to 1990, the Ministry of Housing and Urban Development considered the household (any group of people who lived together and cooked meals together) as the basic nucleus needing housing. The ministry ignored the large number of housing units being used to shelter more than one family. Moreover, the ministry underestimated the pace of the increase in the size of families, assuming that the size of the homes was increasing, when the actual tendency was clearly to the contrary. Finally, MINVU used in its calculations a replacement rate (i.e., housing that needed to be built to replace what had deteriorated) of 0.5 percent per year, even though the traditional replacement rate is 1 percent per year. Joan MacDonald, "La Vivienda en Chile, Hoy," CPU Working Paper no. 12, 1989.

11. María Elena Ducci, "Salud Mental en Mujeres de la Periferia Pobre de Santiago de Chile," working paper, Urban Studies Institute, 1994.

12. The levels of poverty in the neighborhood (nonpoor, poor, indigent households) were measured by the basic purchasing power, calculated according to their per capita income. Nonpoor households have a per capita income higher than the cost of two "basic nutritional baskets." (A basic nutritional basket reflects the minimum food intake necessary to fulfill the basic needs for calories and protein.) In the poor households, per capita income allows them to purchase between one and two basic nutritional baskets, and for indigent households per capita income is lower than the cost of one "basket." This method was developed by ECLAC; the cost of a "basket" (Ch$ 12,699) in February 1993, when the survey was conducted, was applied.

13. María Elena Ducci and M. Greene, "Evaluación de Consolidación Habitacional del Programa de Vivienda Progresiva, Modalida Privada, Primera Etapa" (Chile: Ministry of Housing and Urban Development, 1994).

14. María Elena Ducci, "Salud y Habitat: Capítulo Chile, Informe Final," working paper, Urban Studies Institute, 1994.

15. María Elena Ducci, "Políticas de Vivienda y Mujer," *EURE* 20, no. 59 (March 1994): 73–91.

16. "Ghetto" means "foundry" in Italian and comes from "gettare," to pour. Richard Sennet, *Flesh and Stone* (New York: WW Norton & Company, 1994), p. 231.

17. Sennet, *Flesh and Stone,* pp. 367–368.

18. Although the number of children receiving an education is high at the national level, there is a large gap between the quality of the education provided in the poorer areas compared to the middle- and upper-income areas. Something similar occurs with the quality of health care and police services.

19. José Manuel Cortinez, Undersecretary of Housing and Urban Development, *International Seminar: Sustainable Urban Housing Development,* University of Chile, April 1997.

20. Goran Cars, "Introduction: Comparisons and Counterparts," in Rachel Alterman and Goran Cars, eds., *Neighborhood Regeneration, an International Evaluation* (London: Mansell, 1991), pp. 3, 4.

21. Claudio Accioly and Forbes Davidson, "Density in Urban Development," *Building Issues* 8, no. 3 (Lund University, Lund Centre for Habitat Studies, 1996), p. 7.

22. This is the only housing program aimed at the poorest sectors that provides "completed houses," i.e. all walls are built, there is a bathroom, a kitchen space as part of the living room/dining room area, doors, windows, drinking water, and a sewage system, all of which are finished and working. This is the ultimate goal of low-income families, who only apply to the "Progressive Housing Programs" when they have no other alternatives or when they think that it is the quickest way of obtaining a house.

23. In interviews and polls conducted in May and June of 1996 in 35 settlements nationwide, youth and drugs were cited in all cases as the main problems affecting the neighborhood. M. Greene and María Elena Ducci, "Seguimiento y Evaluación del Programa de Mejoramiento de Barrios y Lotes con Servicios" (Chile: Ministry of the Interior, 1997).

24. Ducci, "Salud Mental en Mujeres."

25. "They look like huts with a bathroom" was the comment of a housing expert while visiting a project of "progressive" houses.

26. Cortinez, *International Seminar.*

27. MINVU has tried to address this problem. For close to a year, families that have been allocated houses can request specific municipalities. Furthermore, they will not necessarily lose benefits (such as their place on the waiting list) if they choose not to accept a house in an area where they do not want to live.

28. In other Latin American and Third World countries and even in Chile before the authoritarian government, *allegamiento* has been and is a functional social mechanism that allows low-income families to support recently wed children or relatives who have just moved to the city. Sheltering as a transitory stage that provides the new families with an acceptable living environment becomes an efficient mechanism to allow the insertion of the new families into the socioeconomic system.

29. Robert D. Putnam, *Making Democracy Work: Civic Traditions in Modern Italy* (Princeton, N.J.: Princeton University Press, 1993). Caroline O. Moser, "Confronting Crisis: A Comparative Study of Household Responses to Poverty and Vulnerability in Four Poor Urban Communities," ESD Studies and Monographs Series no. 8 (Washington, D.C.: World Bank, 1996).

30. The goal should be to encourage a "self-managed" upgrading process as a viable option to overcome the problems afflicting low-income housing in Chile. One of the recommendations put forth by Habitat II in Istanbul 1996 was the need to review and adapt existing legislation to facilitate the process of enlarging and upgrading low-income housing.

31. Cortinez, *International Seminar.*

32. Jorge Montaño, *Los Pobres de la Ciudad en los Asentamientos Espontáneos* (Mexico: Siglo XXI Editores, 1976). María Elena Ducci, *La Colonia Popular, una Manifestación del Problema de la Vivienda* (master's thesis Universidad Nacional de México, 1978).

33. Some of the best examples of this kind of situation have been collected in Montserrat Palmer and Francisco Vergara, "El Lote 9x18 en la Encrucijada Habitacional de Hoy" (1990).

34. In the last two or three years, and as a result of the country's rapid economic development, it is possible to observe an accelerated upgrading and enlarging process. This is true especially in houses that are suitable to accommodate small shops.

35. Moser, "Confronting Crisis," p. 44.

36. This, according to the World Bank, can be used as an indicator of lower vulnerability. Caroline O. Moser, "Situaciones Críticas: Reacciones de las Familias de Cuatro Comunidades Urbanas Pobres ante la Vulnerabilidad y la Pobreza," ESD Studies and Monographs Series no. 8 (Washington, D.C.: World Bank, 1996), p. 3.

37. Ducci, "Salud Mental en Mujeres."

38. The payment of a "toll" is common in certain neighborhoods on the outskirts of the city where it is dangerous to pass even in the light of day.

8

What Significance Hath Reform?
The View from the Mexican Barrio

Susan Eckstein

In the early post–World War II period, Mexico was a model Third World country. It had the highest growth rate in the world for a time, a low inflation rate, diverse exports that minimized dependence on world market prices of a single commodity, and a manageable foreign debt. The government had also staked out space for local capital by preventing foreign capital from majority ownership in key sectors and by directly assuming ownership of certain industries. The industrial sector was especially dynamic. Tariffs protected firms from foreign competition, while a large internal market and political stability created an attractive investment climate.

The discovery of large oil reserves in the early 1970s proved both a blessing and a curse. It enabled the country to borrow heavily in international markets and thereby finance economic expansion and an array of public programs. The relatively unprofitable agricultural sector, however, was neglected. As a consequence, in the midst of the bonanza rural poverty increased, inducing urban migration and illegal immigration to the United States. When later in the decade interest rates soared and oil prices plunged, Mexico was left with one of the largest foreign debts in the world. In 1982 the government temporarily ceased payments on its external debt. It then devalued the peso, prioritized exports, and implemented structural adjustment reforms that Washington and the international banking community advocated.

By the 1990s, Mexico had experienced a new revolution of sorts, one that, from the vantage point of the poor, was partially counterrevolutionary in effect. President Carlos Salinas (1988–1994) buried the nationalist, populist, import-substitution economic model that had guided governments since World War II. His reforms altered the economy, the society, and the polity. Mexico followed key features of the Chilean model introduced under General Augusto Pinochet Ugarte's rule.

Neoliberal restructuring had begun already under Salinas's predecessor, Miguel de la Madrid (1982–1988), but Salinas "perfected" it. He slashed tariffs that had protected inefficient industries, promoted exports, privatized state-owned enterprises, removed price controls, and reduced state subsidies. He also opened the economy more to foreign investment by removing earlier nationalist restrictions. Most noteworthy, he formalized free trade and investment with the United States and Canada through the signing of the North American Free Trade Agreement (NAFTA). The accord, which went into effect on January 1, 1994, allowed for the free mobility of capital, though not labor, between the three countries.

Government efforts to liberalize the economy so as to compete in the globalized economy of the 1990s appeared to pay off. Foreign investors flocked to Mexico. Direct investment jumped from $750 million in 1982 to $8 billion twelve years later. Exports skyrocketed, with the value of manufactured exports increasing seventeen-fold between 1986 and 1996.[1]

Some Mexicans benefited handsomely from the reforms. The country generated new entrepreneurs, including twenty-four new billionaires. And in cities, the richest 10 percent's share of the national wealth rose from 26 to 35 percent between 1984 and 1992.[2]

But the "popular sector," already hit hard by the austerity policies of the 1980s, suffered more in the 1990s. Indeed, 90 percent of the population experienced a precipitous drop in living standards. The reforms barely generated a net growth in employment. Almost two million jobs were lost in 1995 alone.[3] Liberalized trade policies hurt inefficient but labor-absorbing businesses that could not compete with imports in a more open economy. The contraction in government spending, along with the sale and closure of state enterprises, cost tens of thousands of employees their jobs.

Meanwhile, poverty rates rose; the portion of the labor force earning at least the minimum wage and who held jobs guaranteeing health care, unemployment compensation, and pensions decreased (as "formal-sector" employment contracted); and the populace suffered from cutbacks in state social expenditures.[4] Food subsidies that had guaranteed the populace an affordable minimal diet, for example, were slashed. And *campesinos* lost their revolution-fought right to land and the little security their small holdings had provided. The Salinas government terminated the *ejido* program because the community-held but individually farmed lands were considered inefficient and because inalienable holdings interfered with the administration's commitment to the free mobility of land, labor, and capital in agriculture.

His neoliberal commitments notwithstanding, Salinas concomitantly very publicly promoted PRONASOL (Programa Nacional de Solidaridad), a program of his own creation. PRONASOL was a partisan political operation designed to gain support for the PRI (the Party of the Institutionalized Revolution). It did so in a manner that benefited thousands of communities, especially in the countryside, with schools, roads, housing, nutrition, and sanitation.[5] The program did not, however, keep the poorest 40 percent's share of the national income from deteriorating,[6] and the program precipitously ended with Salinas's fall from grace shortly after his term of office expired.

Ernesto Zedillo, Salinas's successor, remained committed to the neoliberal reforms. However, he was forced to devalue the overvalued peso on which the Salinas "miracle" had been based and to deal with the economic and political crisis that ensued.

Although economic opportunities in Mexico City, as elsewhere in the country, deteriorated following the peso devaluations of the 1980s and 1990s, the megalopolis continued to expand. The population of the greater metropolitan area rose to an estimated eighteen million, one-fifth of the national population. However, the rate of migration to the capital began to taper off. As economic conditions deteriorated, city-dwellers looked to the United States and even the provinces for work.[7] An incipient reverse migration process began. When unable to get into the United States under official immigration quotas, Mexicans went illegally.

Within Mexico City demographic settlement patterns shifted. The center city lost population to surrounding rings. The innermost of the "rings" surrounding the center came to house approximately half of the city's population. Outer rings, in the state of Mexico, also grew.[8] The newer settlements lack the range of urban and social services of the older neighborhoods.[9] Fiscal constraints, together with a decline in the influence of the popular sector within the ruling coalition, contributed to government cutbacks in urban and social outlays.

The new economic model modified how and where Mexico City residents earned their livelihood. Not surprisingly, factory and artisan employment options associated with production for the domestic economy declined in Mexico City in general, but above all in the center city.[10] Industrial employment in the city became increasingly concentrated in the inner ring, whereas in the past it had been in the center city. The newer, *maquila* export industries tended to locate in the north of the country, though some located on the periphery of the capital.

As industrial opportunities tapered off, employment in the city shifted to the service and, secondarily, the commercial sectors.[11] And as formal-sector options contracted, increasing numbers of city dwellers turned to self-employment, drawing upon the labor of unpaid family members. Much of the labor force, especially the younger generation, found themselves underemployed.

The deteriorating economic conditions created social problems. Armed robberies, muggings, burglaries, kidnappings for ransom, and car theft became universal experiences. Youth gangs took over streets. The social order disintegrated to the point that public security became a major concern of rich and poor alike. Police defected to the side of the criminals. Reflecting the breakdown of law and order, reported crimes increased 30 percent in 1995 and a similar percentage in 1996. Yet, most crimes were believed to go unreported, for the populace saw the police as part of the problem, not its solution.[12]

The economic and social dislocations fueled political change. In response to pressures from civil society, the government had been gradually democratizing the formal political system since the 1970s. Because of both greater government tolerance of dissent and mounting opposition, the PRI—the so-called official party—gradually lost its monopoly control over the electoral system and the legislative process. Authorities honored electoral defeats. Although it is widely believed that the PRI stole the 1988 presidential election, authorities allowed parties besides the PRI to win municipal and state government offices. And Mexico City acquired its own elected legislature (the *Asamblea*) in 1988, which in 1997 assumed legislative functions. In 1997 the city also attained the right to elect its own mayor (renamed governor) for the first time.

At the municipal level the democratic opening included administrative reforms as well. There was some devolution of power within the system of governance. New administrative layers were added between the population at the grassroots and district-level offices. Reforms allowed people in the neighborhoods to elect the cadre who both oversaw the administration of local urban and social services and represented the community to higher authorities. And while the city budget was halved in the 1980s, the portion allocated to district administrators (*delegados*) increased somewhat.[13]

The neoliberal initiatives, combined with the political reforms that formally deepened democracy, were intended to revitalize the economy in a manner that would preserve the PRI's hold on power. Indeed, from the PRI's vantage point, both the economic and the political reforms initially paid off. In 1991 the PRI won all of Mexico City's *Asamblea* seats based on direct representation and 290 of the 300 seats based on direct representation in Congress.[14] In the 1994 election the majority of Mexicans supported Zedillo, the PRI candidate. The party appeared to rebound from its weaker showing in

1988, from a much-publicized rebellion in Chiapas on the first of January 1994, when NAFTA went into effect, and from the assassination of the initial 1994 PRI presidential candidate, Luis Donaldo Colosio (and shortly thereafter the assassination of the PRI party secretary, Francisco Ruis Massieu).

The political situation changed soon after the election. Guerrilla activity picked up. In at least seven states besides Chiapas, small guerrilla groups had significant local support; demonstrations became common throughout the country but especially in Mexico City; and drug lords became more powerful and violent. The peso devaluation of the 1990s that caused living standards to plunge stirred anger, and in the changed political climate, the populace became intolerant of newly disclosed corruption that included Salinas and his close collaborators (including his brother).

Both the PAN (the National Action Party) and the PRD (the Democratic Revolutionary Party) that Cuauhtemoc Cárdenas founded, after breaking in the 1980s with the PRI, capitalized on the growing intolerance of PRI misbehavior and official policies that hurt most voters economically. By 1997 the PRI lost its historical majority in Congress, it lost the governorships of two key states (Querétero and Nuevo León), it lost all seats in the Mexico City Legislature by direct representation, and it lost the first city mayoral election, to the PRD. The 1997 elections were a watershed. They shattered the PRI hegemony. The economic reforms had weakened the federal government and eroded the PRI's base of power. Just as the neoliberal economic restructuring had not averted—and partly contributed to—the country's worst economic crisis since the depression of the 1930s, the political objectives of the Salinas reforms, from the vantage point of the PRI, had backfired.

The electoral democratization, moreover, masked mounting internal PRI and government problems. Politicians vested in the old oligarchic political system did not willingly concede power, and economic interests tied to the growing drug economy fueled political violence. Human-rights abuses rose. Former PRI loyalists in record numbers followed Cuauhtemoc Cárdenas's lead and defected. Among those remaining within the party, divisions deepened between so-called *técnicos* and *políticos* (derogatorily called "dinosaurs"). The *políticos* pushed through a reform in party policy under Zedillo that required presidential candidates to have previously held elected office. Heads of state since 1982, reflecting the rise in influence of the *técnicos*, had not run for political office before the presidency.

How did Mexico City's poor experience these changes? To get a sense of how they did, I revisited three urban neighborhoods in April of 1997 that I had come to know over a thirty-year period: an old inner-city slum, an area settled by an organized squatter invasion in the 1950s, and a government-built housing development officially intended for the popular sector. I selected the three areas initially to assess how diverse housing environments might offer different opportunities for, and impose different constraints on, city poor. While I did my most extensive research in 1967–1968, I returned to the communities in 1971–1972 and 1987, as well as in 1997.

The analysis below relies mainly on about 160 in-depth, open-ended interviews with local organization and institution officeholders and "influentials" (and their district-level superiors) over the years. Some interviews took four to eight hours and several appointments. The people interviewed were asked about the activities of their groups, the history of the communities, and their personal experiences and backgrounds. My earlier research also included a survey of one hundred residents in each area regarding political, economic, and social matters; detailed interviews with a smaller sample of male residents about their work experiences; and a survey of local businesses. In addition, I attended group meetings, talked informally with many community residents, and consulted printed sources, including documents, newspaper articles, and other surveys.[15] The longitudinal research provides a unique opportunity to see how changes at the macro level are experienced at the grassroots level—and why.

Neighborhood Impact of Neoliberal Economic Restructuring

The number of shantytowns and squatter settlements mushroomed during the import-substitution era and the urbanization that accompanied it—in Mexico as in other Latin American countries. Such settlement growth reflected poor people's own solution to a need for affordable housing as well as populist government tolerance of a politically popular and fiscally practical solution to the mounting demand for inexpensive shelter. Urbanists praised the new type of housing. They argued that such areas offered relatively inexpensive dwellings that could be adapted to family needs, access to property usable for income-generating rental and business purposes, experience in participatory politics owing to mobilizations for much-needed urban services, and a safe environment.[16]

The same commentators argued that older center-city slums were stagnant and decadent and characterized by blight, apathy, and despair. They attributed the inner-city social conditions both to the effect of the decaying physical environment and to the types of people who settled there. The areas purportedly housed the poorest of the urban poor: recent migrants; the unemployed; the unskilled and illiterate; and alcoholics, vagabonds, and delinquents. Once residents had the economic means they allegedly moved to outlying shantytowns.[17] The upwardly mobile purportedly did not stay long enough to shape the local culture. Those who did stay—the vagabonds, alcoholics, and petty delinquents—shaped community norms and values.[18] But the commentators theorized about the inner city typically without studying it empirically. They inferred life from its outward manifestations, not street-level reality.[19]

Urbanists at the same time looked askance at government-financed housing projects. They argued that such housing was cost-inefficient, priced beyond poor people's means, and not designed with recipients' social and economic needs at heart.

By the latter 1980s, conditions in the state-subsidized housing developments confirmed critics' claims, but conditions in the other two areas defied earlier theorizing. The shantytown depiction was too upbeat, the slum depiction too downbeat. Life in the two areas changed with macro political-economic dynamics. The changed macro conditions worked to the advantage of inhabitants of the inner city in comparison with residents of outlying areas. The former were better situated to adapt to the national economic crises and to the neoliberal economic restructuring. As formal-sector opportunities contracted in the capital and as the purchasing power of formal-sector jobs deteriorated with austerity policies, center-city residents were better placed to adapt to informal-sector alternatives.

The Center-City Area

Most residents in the inner-city area lived there by choice, not default, the congestion and poor quality of the housing notwithstanding. By the mid-1980s, heads of households had lived in the district, on average, thirty years, and when an earthquake left tenement dwellers homeless, they fought for the right to stay.[20] Although the area did contain vagabonds, alcoholics, drug addicts, and delinquents, it also contained a dynamic informal economy, and residents enjoyed lives embedded in dense local social networks. The ne'er-do-wells were not the dominant social, cultural, or economic force.

Center-city residents were hurt by 1980s and 1990s austerity policies and peso devaluations that reduced formal-sector employment options, lowered earnings, and increased consumer prices. But the area had a comparative advantage in the informal commercial sector. By the latter 1990s, it was bustling with some 10,000 *tianguis* street merchants (merchants without fixed stalls), in addition to vendors in four large, permanent market structures (each with about 700 stalls).

Local commerce intensified both because of and despite the country's economic problems. As formal-sector opportunities contracted, ever more city dwellers turned to street vending in this well-situated market area that had a long tradition of commerce. When I first visited the area in the latter 1960s, residents there already had been heavily involved in commerce, along with other forms of self-employment. Residents there were more likely to do small-scale independent work and to earn more at such work than people of comparable educational backgrounds in the other two areas I studied.

Center-city merchants are not dependent solely on local clientele. Customers come from the provinces and from other urban neighborhoods because the produce, secondhand goods, and new consumer durables all sell here for less than almost anywhere else.

This commercial dynamism was rooted in a combination of legal and illegal activity. Secondhand goods included recycled stolen items, while factory-new consumer goods included contraband, until the government slashed tariff taxes in conjunction with the neoliberal reforms. Once trade liberalization lowered tariffs, local *comerciantes* continued to have an edge over vendors and shop owners in outlying districts. They could still sell their goods for less and profit more, because of the volume of their business and the better terms on which they obtained credit.

Some commerce was so lucrative and so well organized that vendors could obtain easy credit. One of the most influential local *comerciante* leaders, for example, operated an informal savings and loan association that entitled members to borrow up to three-fourths of the money they paid into the *caja de ahorros* (credit association), with only nominal interest charges (1 to 2 percent). Members were expected to deposit about twelve dollars per week into the *caja*. Merchants with access to inexpensive credit were at a competitive advantage within the informal commercial economy. They could acquire more and better stock and pay lower interest on the money they borrowed. In the peripheral areas of the city, and in the weaker economic associations in the center city, vendors needed to rely on loan sharks and more costly supplier credit. Thus, a stratified informal banking economy evolved in the interstices of the informal commercial economy. The center-city area offered more than locational vending advantages within the informal sector.

Because of these advantages the informal value of stalls rose over the years. The transfer price for the best locations went for the equivalent of $12,500 by the latter 1990s, up from $5,000 just ten years earlier.

The spillover of commerce from the indoor, officially regulated markets into the streets occurred in an organized manner, somewhat akin to the formation of squatter settlements on the city's periphery. People were not free to sell wherever and whenever they chose. To sell, vendors needed to belong to a *comerciante* or *tianguis* association. Otherwise, they risked costly encounters with the police. By the latter 1990s there were sixty to seventy *tianguis* groups in the center-city area, organized by street. The largest had a thousand members. Would-be vendors typically paid weekly dues to a "street organizer" for several months while the organizer negotiated with the government for rights to work on a specific site. In the period before attaining official rights, the prospective merchants patiently sat in the spot they claimed. While investing time, the monetary cost of entry into local commerce through such street invasions was minimal, especially in comparison with the cost of subsequently buying transfer rights.

Because inner-city commerce can be lucrative, many local families took advantage of market opportunities even when the head of household held a formal-sector job. The household head helped out on weekends, the busiest business days, while other family members maintained the stalls the rest of the week. Families also sought multiple stalls, when possible.[21] Business expansion typically occurred through the acquisition of multiple stalls rather than growth at a single site, partly because of space limitations but also because of a tendency to diversify in a manner that minimized risks.

Residents were not the only people to work in this bustling locus of informal commerce. The very success of local commerce indeed came to squeeze out opportunities for residents. "Each day," noted a long-term merchant, "fewer vendors are from here." By 1997, 70 percent of the *tianguis* merchants were estimated to live elsewhere. While some of the nonlocal merchants used to live in the area or had resident relatives, moneyed people with no local claims increasingly paid the original *tianguis* squatters to rescind their claims to street space. Some *asiaticos,* as locals called them, from South Korea even made their way into the local retail sector. Their entrance had been through the lucrative contraband commerce, before tariff reductions eased legal access to their source of goods. Locals were not forced to sell their informal claims to vending locations, but many found the opportunity to make a quick profit enticing.

By the latter 1990s, nonlocals also were renting or purchasing center-city condominium units that had been built for people of the community after the 1985 earthquake. Local residents had fought hard for the housing, but as of 1997 about 25 percent of the units built for *damnificados,* as earthquake victims were called, were used instead by new occupants who typically used the apartments not as residences, but for commercial purposes such as stocking merchandise, since street vendors had to disassemble their stalls and pack their wares daily.

Community reconstruction after the earthquake proved to provide residents with an asset of considerable worth. The value of the new apartments rose fifteen-fold (in current dollar value) in one decade. Politics here had intertwined with invisible market forces to residents' advantage. The government built new housing for former tenement tenants in response to public pressure, although authorities insisted on political quiescence before new construction began.[22] The value of the well-situated new condominiums quickly rose. The center-city experience thus suggests both that poor people need not move to outlying shantytowns to enjoy the economic benefits of home ownership and that inner-city areas are not inherently places of blight.

Yet, the transformation of dwellings into commercial units contributed to the area's depopulation. Such depopulation was characteristic of the central city in general, as previously noted.

The vibrancy of commerce also squeezed out local craft production. The area used to be a center of the leather and shoe trades. Sweatshops had proliferated as the city population mushroomed after World War II and demand for shoes increased.[23] Shoe artisans were displaced neither by more-efficient shoe manufacturers nor, in the main, by cheaper imports resulting from trade liberalization. Rather, craft production relocated outside the capital, where labor was cheaper and fewer alternative employment options existed. The shoe activity that remained in the inner city centered on its more lucrative commercialization. That commercialization came to include two weekly evening shoe *tianguis* markets, along with street stalls and a dedicated permanent market. Here too, local changes mirrored citywide deindustrialization, but the local deindustrialization was not entirely by default. Commercially savvy businesspeople came to concentrate on the more lucrative, if less productive, aspect of the shoe trade.

These new commercial opportunities replaced earlier rags-to-riches channels of mobility. The area had been known a generation earlier for such prize-winning boxers as "Raton" Macias. Residents came to view commerce as an easier and more viable, if less prestigious, means of enrichment.

As vibrant as local commerce had become, vendors were hard hit by the Zedillo 1994 peso devaluation. Their income was immediately halved, as demand for their wares dropped with the precipitous decline in customer purchasing power and as their import capacity suffered. The devalued peso drove up the cost of foreign inventory. Shopowners also were left with commercial debts contracted when the peso had been stronger. The local merchants who came to be most weighed down by debt were those most invested in import trade. Nonetheless, to the extent that they relied on local low-interest, informal, financing, they were shielded from the full adverse effects that merchants elsewhere experienced with the devaluation.

Economic hard times spurred new illegal activity. Mexico's drug economy, traditionally tied to U.S. demand, expanded to include a secondary domestic market. A niche developed in the center city for the cheaper drugs such as marijuana. Residents became caught up in this economy, both as consumers and distributors—especially the younger generation who had difficulty finding work. By the latter 1990s, about a third of local youth were estimated to be involved in narcotrafficking. They could earn more in the drug trade than elsewhere.

Not only was drug dealing illegal, it also was violent. There came to be, on average, three drug-related homicides per week in the center-city area. The narcotrafficking had such a corrosive effect on the local social order that even families long committed to the area, who had overseen its renaissance after the mid-1980s earthquake, moved to more-peripheral areas to provide a safer haven for their children.

In sum, the local informal economy offered opportunities that more peripheral areas did not, but residents found it increasingly difficult to compete economically within their own neighborhood. Market forces, both legal and illegal, were eroding a community that just a decade earlier, after the earthquake, had fought for its own preservation. The government, meanwhile, inadvertently undermined community vitality when its rebuilding of the area after the earthquake allowed individual families to gain by giving up local vending and housing rights. Mounting problems notwithstanding, at the century's end, when neoliberalism prevailed, the area still offered advantages that more peripheral settlements did not.

The Shantytown

Much of urbanists' optimism about shantytowns was premised on home ownership. But the shantytown that I came to know over a thirty-year period increasingly housed tenants who were poorer than the homeowners. While the proliferation of tenancy in such areas has been noted in other studies of Latin American cities, its implications have heretofore not been analyzed.[24]

Two countervailing socioeconomic trends occurred in the shantytown since its formation. The homeowner stratum "upgraded," partly as original squatter settlers and their children became more economically successful, but also as middle-class families moved in after the government provided the area with urban and social services and legalized property rights. Some individuals capitalized on the opportunity to build income-generating *vecindades* (rental units). Although *vecindades* typically housed only six families, a small rentier class evolved that included absentee owners. There were landlords with as many as ten *vecindades*.

Many homeowners used their property not for income-generating purposes but as a family asset. Children of the first generation of homeowners often stayed on their parents' plots when marrying and having children of their own, to minimize living costs and avoid the inconvenience of moving to affordable but more distant areas in the city's outer ring, in the state of Mexico. They benefited from the stakes their parents claimed when the area first was settled, before market forces drove up the value of the inner-suburb land beyond their means. In essence, as housing prices rose, nuclear-family living became a luxury few second-generation local families could afford.

At the same time, though, the growing tenant stratum contributed to a community socioeconomic downgrading. Tenants were poorer than homeowners, and for them housing was no economic asset.

Urbanists had argued that shantytowns offered not merely inexpensive housing but economic opportunities as well. Properties could be used for income-generating businesses, and residents could sell goods and services in local markets. However, local informal-sector opportunities did not begin to compare to those in the inner city.[25] First, the 1980s and 1990s peso devaluations drove up merchant operating costs and debts here more than in the inner city. Shantytown vendors lacked access to low-interest-charging informal credit associations.

Second, consumer demand contracted more here than in the center city in response to the peso devaluations. The growing tenant population was poorer than the typical center-city resident, and shantytown merchants were almost entirely dependent on local clientele. Unable to offer the price advantages that inner-city merchants could, they attracted only customers for whom propinquity was important.

Third, shantytown income-earning opportunities were undermined by mounting competition. *Colonos,* as shantytown residents are called, were not faced, in the main, with wealthy intruders who bought into the community, as in the center city. Most competition came from a growing number of humble *tianguis* vendors who lived elsewhere but sold locally on designated streets on designated days. The *tianguis* vendors belonged to associations that negotiated itinerant citywide street vending rights.[26] By the latter 1990s there were five *tianguis* groups with 100 to 500 members. The ambulant vendors typically underpriced resident *comerciantes* who sold in the indoor markets and in home shops, and they located close to where many residents lived.

Even more than in the inner city, shantytown youth were hard-pressed for work. With fewer options, they increasingly looked to the United States for economic opportunities, often going as *mojadas,* "wetbacks." But immigration did not necessarily resolve their economic quandary. Some experienced unemployment, imprisonment, and deportation. Others went back and forth, trying to eke out a livelihood on both sides of the border.

With prospects increasingly perceived as limited both in the United States and Mexico City, residents began to look to the provinces for economic respite—a growing urban trend, as noted above. Incipient urban-to-rural migration replaced the initial rural-to-urban social base of the community.

Meanwhile, as local economic opportunities deteriorated, social problems proliferated. Drug addiction, violence, theft, and assault all increased with the austerity policies and peso devaluation of the 1990s. Unemployed youth with nothing to do and no means of livelihood, from the shantytown as well as from poor areas in the neighboring state of Mexico, committed much of the local crime and violence. As one resident noted, "Delinquency has become so prevalent that we no longer know who is good and who is not." Streets were dangerous at night, when gangs took over. The social decay was further reflected in new centers of prostitution and vending of unlicensed liquor.

Here, too, narcotrafficking made inroads. The younger generation became involved in it, as both consumers and distributors. "They sell drugs as if they were tortillas," one resident complained. Addicts, needing money for their addiction, contributed to the rise in theft.

Thus, the shantytown had come to be described more aptly as a "slum of despair" than a "slum of hope," the opposite of what urbanists had theorized.[27] With the economic crises in the 1980s and 1990s, many residents experienced economic hardship. In the neoliberal and deindustrialized urban economy, shantytown residence gave no locational advantage. Any gains and optimism experienced during Salinas's short-lived economic "miracle" vanished with the dramatic peso devaluation shortly after his term of office ended. And the community esprit among squatters when they first staked claims to the area in the latter 1950s had long since disappeared. Political dynamics, elaborated below, eroded collective grassroots activity that might have countered the moral, economic, and social decay.

The Housing Development

The housing development, comprised of freestanding homes, was from its inception more prosperous than the other two areas, and differences in the socioeconomic profiles of the communities became more accentuated over the years. For one, authorities allocated homes in all but one section of the development to functionaries and to formal-sector unions for their members. Politics influenced dwelling allocations soon after the development opened for settlement. Although allegedly intended for poor people and families displaced by public-works projects, authorities quickly came to give preference to groups more influential than the poor. Allotments reflected the regime's class bias. Sold at cost to the original housing recipients, the area became a middle-class subsidy—as urbanists could have predicted.

The "invisible market" came to further accentuate differences in the socioeconomic profiles of the communities. Private home sales over the years further contributed to the development's upgrading. The market value of the homes quickly exceeded the subsidized price that original home recipients paid. Initially, the homes were to be inheritable but otherwise not transferable; however, as more well-to-do families illegally bought into the well-serviced community, they pressured the government to legalize their property claims and make home ownership alienable. Accordingly, market and political dynamics came to marginalize poor people from the settlement.

Indeed, the planned community quickly came to house lower- and working-class families in only one section, the only section I therefore continued to study in the 1980s and 1990s. This one area contained the smallest and least expensive units.

As in the shantytown, residents in the poorer area transformed their homes designed for nuclear-family use into multigenerational households—also for economic reasons. Few local families, however, converted their homes into rental units, because of space limitations and less-severe economic need.

Though it was a planned community, the chief architect had not addressed the most fundamental socioeconomic issue—employment creation—and market forces did not on their own generate many local work opportunities. Within the informal local economy, residents, again like shantytown dwellers, lacked prospects comparable to those in the center city. The younger generation, though more educated than their parents, here too experienced unemployment and underemployment.

Not surprisingly, in the absence of economic opportunities social problems set in. By the latter 1990s, the community was haunted by the drug addiction, alcoholism, and theft that architectural blueprints had been designed to prevent. The formation of a Drug Addiction Anonymous program reflected how severe the drug problem had become. Almost all addicts were young. Meanwhile, public security disintegrated as aggressive youth gangs formed locally for the first time. Residents attributed the "social decomposition" to poverty.

Good intentions of the architect to create a socially viable and meaningful community notwithstanding, the planned project proved no more successful than a self-built, squatter shantytown in addressing poor people's economic needs and in creating and maintaining a moral community. Broader market, political, and social forces eroded the positive effects the state-subsidized, planned community was to have.

Democratization for Whom?

If the neoliberal reforms left the city poor worse off economically than in years past, especially after the 1994 peso devaluation, did the political reforms provide a means to correct market injustices? Residents of the three areas contributed to the erosion of PRI hegemony that became so transparent by 1997. However, informal political dynamics limited the distributive and redistributive effects of formal democratization.

Administrative Changes

There were two citywide administrative reforms that affected governance in the three communities. In the 1980s, a *Juntas de Vecinos* (Resident's Council) initiative officially deepened administrative democratization, from the district to the community and block levels. The reform proved to democratize governance, however, more in form than fact.

An official devolution of power from the mayor's office to the city districts (*delegaciones*) accomplished little. The district-based *delegados* received insufficient funds to exercise much discretionary power.

Community-level governance was, however, democratized. Each block elected, as it had for years, a *jefe de manzana,* a block representative. In the 1980s, the *jefes de manzanas* in turn elected for the first time presidents of newly formed community-wide residents' associations. And the democratization of governance officially extended "upward," from the community to the *delegación* level. The presidents of residents' associations within each *delegación* elected district-wide *Juntas de Vecinos* officers from their ranks. The electoral procedure assured that the leadership lived within the district. Mayor-appointed *delegados* who oversaw district affairs, by contrast, rarely resided in the areas they administered.[28]

The administrative reform appeared to make local-level governance more democratic also because the nationwide principle of "no reelection," enforced since the consolidation of the revolution, was applied to the *Juntas de Vecinos* and their community-based residents' associations. The administrative reform accordingly allowed the populace to have greater input into who governed, while the reelection restrictions constrained incumbents from monopolizing leadership and perpetuating their own rule.

Nonetheless, the extension of formal democratic rights served, in practice, more to regulate the communities than to provide residents with real power, access to resources, or the means to decide how resources were utilized. The presidents of the residents' associations had no budget or decision-making power. They mainly channeled grassroots solicitations for urban services to central authorities, as had *delegado*-appointed community-based *subdelegados* before them. And they were expected to deal with higher authorities in the same manner as their predecessors before the reform. They were to solicit, not demand, goods and services, and they were not to go in large groups when soliciting favors from authorities. These norms limited pressure on higher authorities to respond. As a consequence of continued compliance with these norms, residents' association presidents accomplished no more for their neighborhoods than had appointed *subdelegados* in the past.

Second, the democratically elected officers relayed information downward and sought local support for concerns of their superiors. In the late 1980s, for example, the citywide head of the *Juntas de Vecinos* spoke at a meeting with residents' association presidents against the formation of an elected city congress with lawmaking power. The Mexican president at the time opposed such a congress. The citywide leader also discussed possible presidential candidates. Cuauhtemoc Cárdenas's newly formed Democratic Current had no voice at the meeting. Thus, the democratically elected *Juntas de Vecinos* served as

a channel through which national political elite sought to undermine democratizing trends that threatened PRI's hegemonic base of
rule. Elected, the *Juntas de Vecinos* leadership legitimated a chain of
command that in practice remained hierarchically dominated.

Third, the principle of "no reelection" kept leaders from building up an effective local political base that could strengthen their
bargaining position with city and national officials. In the political
competition of the 1960s and early 1970s, the hierarchical nature of
organizational relations, the multiplicity of groups, and the personal
style of politics all constricted poor people's ability to form an effective political bloc.[29] The principle of no reelection served the same
end, at the same time that it prevented an antidemocratic oligarchy
from establishing itself at the grassroots level.

The power-dampening effect of the no-reelection principle could
be seen in the center-city area. There, the main leaders of street vendors could serve for life and even pass on their leadership position
to their children. They owed their position to the people they informally served and represented, not to authorities or to formal political status. Powerful within the informal economy, and commanding
as many as 1,000 members, the leaders were in a strong bargaining
position vis-à-vis the government. Their informal clout enabled them
to successfully negotiate rights to street vending and community reconstruction after the earthquake.

At the same time, in the two most heavily populated areas, the
housing development and the center city, multiple residents' associations impaired community-wide organization for common concerns. In
these areas formal as well as informal channels of communication and
coordination were vertically structured. The democratically selected association presidents in the different sections of the two areas did not all
report to, and deal with, the same administrative superiors. The associations were organized by *delegaciones,* and both areas were incorporated
into more than one *delegación.* Even the democratically elected presidents incorporated into the same *delegación,* though, did not interact
and collectively organize for common concerns. They never met on
their own. The only contact they had with each other was through the
district *Juntas de Vecinos* office (and through PRI offices at the district
level). Compounding problems, the bureaucracies that provided urban
and social services were also hierarchically organized, but along lines
not coinciding with residents' association boundaries. This further constricted community mobilization for collectively shared concerns.

Insufficiently effective at preventing an erosion of PRI hegemony, authorities introduced yet another administrative reform in
the 1990s: *consejeros ciudadanos* (citizen advisers).

In principle, *consejeros ciudadanos* deepened administrative democratization and decentralization in that not only were the new local officers elected, as had been their *Juntas de Vecinos* predecessors, but they also received public funding. They were officially paid for their services so that they could dedicate themselves full time to community service.

But the *consejero ciudadano* initiative, like the preceding administrative reform, proved more democratic in form than practice. Elections were manipulated by higher-ranking nonlocal authorities. PRI district activists influenced who ran and who had the most campaign support. Also, elected officers had no independent base of power. They continued the tradition of channeling local grievances to, and soliciting favors from, higher-ranking government and PRI authorities.

Meanwhile, at the community level the reform proved divisive. Presidents of still-functioning residents' associations resented that *consejeros ciudadanos* received pay for the same work they did pro bono.[30] Also, the two local authorities competed informally both for local followings and for the favor of higher-ranking officials.

Creating new problems while not resolving old ones, the central government brought the *consejero ciudadano* reform to a precipitous halt in 1997, three years after formation. No one in the center-city area, shantytown, or development understood why the reform ended, not even the *consejeros ciudadanos*. From the government's vantage point the reform had failed to curb informal pressure for further citywide democratization: for a mayoral election and for the transformation of the *Asamblea* into a legislative body. And the reform was inconsistent with neoliberal fiscal belt-tightening insofar as the *consejeros ciudadanos* became a new paid administrative stratum. The residents' association presidents had performed, as noted, most of the same functions as the *consejeros ciudadanos* free of charge. Since the reform did not empower residents more than in years past, they did not oppose or resent the termination of the initiative.

Political Changes

Locally, the PRI sought to fend off the electoral appeal of political parties that were gaining national preeminence. For decades both the PRI's routine involvements and its campaign activity were able to contain opposition parties. Its ability to do so caved, not with the political reforms per se, but with the plunge in living standards following the peso devaluations and implementation of neoliberal reforms and with growing revelations of large-scale corruption. In the changed political, economic, and social milieu, everyday political and administrative dealings no longer had the same effect as in years past. They no longer served to deliver votes come election time.

The party, for example, continued locally to operate in its long-standing machine-like manner. It sought to buy votes in exchange for material favors. District offices offered occasional legal, medical, dental, and haircutting services, plus meals and gifts on major holidays and during political campaigns. PRI officers gave out juice, napkins, T-shirts, pots, and pitchers, and they organized raffles for servibars, bicycles, and gas stoves. Desperate for votes, as other political parties became serious and no longer merely nominal political contenders, PRI district functionaries went so far as to pay cadres to go door-to-door to convince residents to vote for the PRI. Politics, as one politico noted, became profitable. And in the center-city area, functionaries reminded vendors that they owed their street location claims to PRI's interception on their behalf.[31]

Meanwhile, the routine activities of local administrative cadres continued the decades-old local fusion (and confusion) of politics and governance. None of the elected *consejeros ciudadanos* or residents' association presidents went soley to their administrative superior when soliciting urban and social services. They typically first secured PRI backing because they were told to and felt it in their interest to so do. In the words of an assistant to the *consejero ciudadano* in the shantytown, "the PRI and the government are a closed circle. Both the party and *consejeros ciudadanos* solicit favors from higher authorities. The *consejero ciudadano* is like a *pequeño diputado,* a mini-congressman." Similarly, the president of the residents' association in the development noted that when he had a simple request he went alone to the district offices. Otherwise, he worked through PRI channels. He met regularly with the other residents' association presidents in his district who were PRIistas. "We presented ourselves as a block to authorities when we wanted sewage, school, and other problems resolved. As a block we pressured the *delegado* to allocate resources to us. Our work with the PRI was symbiotic." In essence, long-standing informal PRI-government relations continued and were created anew within the interstices of political-administrative reform measures. Local PRI and civic officeholders were opportunistic in mixing politics with administration, up to the eve of PRI's 1997 electoral defeat.

Similarly, prior to the 1997 elections, the *Asamblea,* the citywide body of elected deputies formed in 1988, proved at the local level not to involve a devolution of power. As long as most elected *Asamblea* representatives were of the PRI (as they were until summer 1997), deputies functioned and were seen as but one more set of

cadres through whom complaints and solicitudes could be channeled. Deputies also served to contain opposition to the PRI. They
were instruments of PRI communication and control.

Accordingly, through the spring of 1997 the political and administrative reforms gave a deepening-of-democracy veneer to a system
of governance that continued to subordinate local to nonlocal concerns and that higher-ranking authorities tried to manipulate to
PRI's advantage at a time of PRI decomposition at the national level.
Under the circumstances, residents in the three areas anticipated
just three months prior to the PRI's devastating citywide electoral defeat that little would change if the PRI lost. They did not view the
PRD, Cárdenas's reconstituted Democratic Current and a center-left
alternative to the PRI party, as a source of empowerment or a solution
to their plight. Some of them were pragmatic and understood that organizational strength, not partisan politics, was the key to political influence. Reflecting this viewpoint, an activist in a center-city *tianguis* association noted that she liked the PRD's goals but felt the party was
"run by intellectuals who did not know how to administrate." She did
not worry about a PRI electoral defeat, though, for she felt that her
tianguis group would be able to negotiate with whatever party won because "we're a large force and have tradition in our favor."

Other residents viewed all the parties as a "clan" that did not represent them. In general, the popular sector, as represented in the
three areas I studied, did not feel the electoral democratization to be
as significant as did either the middle and upper classes behind the
reforms or the political parties. Residents had learned the hard way
to be cynical about political change.

Meanwhile, as democratization rooted in party competition picked
up at the city and national levels, locally opposition parties adapted
some of the nondemocratic practices long associated with the PRI.
Intra- and interparty democratization did not evolve hand in hand.
Opposition parties followed the PRI's example and instituted ma-
chine-style vote-getting practices. They too gave out presents. If they
were less generous the reason was not their higher moral principles
but the fewer resources they commanded. In a political field where
the dominant party relied on material and not merely moral persuasion, other political parties felt pressured to do the same. Opposition
parties also continued the PRI's practice of selecting local candidates
extra-locally. People in the neighborhoods were not involved in the
selection of candidates for political office for any of the parties in
their districts. In early April of 1997, residents were just on the verge
of being introduced to the candidates who were to represent them.

Despite the continuation of old-style politics and administration, and opposition parties not offering a break with traditional rules of the game, the PRI ceased to be able to bring in the votes as in former years. Already in the 1980s, the economic crisis had contributed to a decline in local support for the PRI. The PRI experienced a partial rebound in the Salinas years, when the economy improved, but that rebound was short-lived. In the shantytown, for example, PRI electoral support dropped from about three-fourths in the 1960s and two-thirds in the 1970s to one-third in the 1980s. The PRI still polled a plurality but no longer a majority of the votes; by 1997 the PRI lost the plurality as well. The PRI did only slightly better in the development. But PRI opposition in all three areas came to be channeled through the PRD, not as in years past through the PAN. PAN voters in the past had been more anti-PRI than pro-PAN.[32] Residents welcomed a more populist option to the PAN. Cárdenas (the son of the populist reformer President General Lázaro Cárdenas [1934–1940]) symbolized a people's candidate. But residents were not convinced that having the PRD would be better than the PRI.

Most significantly, people's attitudes toward voting by 1997 had changed. In the 1960s and 1970s, the government and the PRI successfully convinced most urban poor that support for the PRI was synonymous with patriotism and that voting was an obligation and not merely a right. By the 1990s, though, the electorate came to view voting as a right, including the right to abstain or to vote for parties other than the PRI. They also came to feel that they could be public about their non-PRI sympathies without fear of reprisal.

In the changed milieu, the PRI's best hope was to portray itself as a champion of democracy. It allowed for its own electoral defeat, and made a point of blaming the PRD, which won most city offices up for election, for the plethora of unsolved social and economic problems.

People in the neighborhoods were quick to criticize the PRD they helped sweep into office. Within two months of the election they complained that local PRD functionaries were inefficient, administratively incompetent, and unresponsive to local needs and wants (especially for public security, which had become a number-one preoccupation).

Cárdenas tried to convey symbolically his commitment to the common man. For the first time the mayor (formerly appointed, now elected governor) came to the center city to celebrate the start of the new year. Late New Year's Eve in 1997 he delivered a speech from there to the people of the area, the city, and people as far away as Chiapas. His focus on Chiapas spoke to a local fear: worries that he would pay more attention to national than local concerns, with his eye on the upcoming presidential election. Political democratization had yet to work to the advantage of urban poor.

Conclusion

The neoliberal reforms and post-peso-devaluation economic downturn of the mid-1990s caused poor people's living standards to go from bad to worse—in Mexico in general and in the three communities that I studied over a thirty-year period in particular.[33] Employment and income-generating opportunities deteriorated, especially for the younger generation, and the communities experienced moral and social decay.

The three communities, nonetheless, experienced the macroeconomic and political changes somewhat differently. In the context of the shift from an industrial to a commercial and service-based urban economy, and from import-substitution to neoliberalism, the center-city area offered the best opportunities. Those opportunities, however, were confined to the informal economy.

There are historical reasons why the center city fared better than more peripheral areas, whether built by the government in accordance with seemingly well-intended planning conceptions or spontaneously by squatters in search of affordable housing. The center city had a long history of commerce and commercial networks on which to build. But area-based advantages were not all historically determined. Politics was also important. Residents sought new informal-sector vending opportunities through collective street invasions, and they organized informal credit associations. They also fought collectively for the preservation of their community after the 1985 earthquake. The center city differed politically from the two peripheral communities at the informal, not formal, political level.

Informal and formal politics intersect, however. Once formal politics prevail, urban poor are less effective politically. Government/ PRI dynamics operated to ensure this to be so. As a consequence, shantytown dwellers had been more effective in their government dealings when first invading the area. They organized spontaneously then "from below," to fight for land rights and urban and social services. While inner-city street vendors still exercise considerable clout, informal community-wide organizing for collective concerns has tapered off. Authorities demanded acquiescence and, until recently, political support as a quid pro quo for community provisioning. Less pressure is thereby placed on the regime for more goods and services,

and invisible market forces can thereby increasingly shape what tran-
spires locally.[34]

Nonetheless, formal democratization has been of some consequence. Both comparative and historical evidence suggests that democratization may create opportunities for inner-city poor that authoritarian rule does not. Earlier, when under less populist pressure,
the Mexican government had bulldozed a nearby center-city slum for
"development," replacing it with high-rise apartments priced beyond
poor people's means (in Tlatelolco). It had hoped to similarly transform the inner-city area I studied but did not when faced with popular resistance. Under authoritarian regimes in both Uruguay and
Brazil, steps were taken for slum clearance.[35] Fiscal crises put a halt to
these initiatives that were to benefit commercial and real-estate interests at poor people's expense, but not before tenements were razed.[36]

Democratization contributed to a reshaping of the political culture, not always in ways the government had intended. At the same
time that formal democratization expanded electoral and other
channels of political articulation, it also made political protest more
likely. City folk took to the streets to seek change because they felt
formal channels were ineffective and because they feared repression
less than in years past. In this respect the post-earthquake housing
movement proved a watershed. While deft government handling of
the movement made the restoration of order a prerequisite for housing, in 1996 the capital alone was the scene of more than 3,000
protest marches.[37] People do not see formal democratization as the
solution to their plight.[38]

The experiences of the areas I studied challenge urban theory
and policy in turn. Social scientists, planners, and policymakers have
all been too optimistic about shantytowns, which they portrayed as
"slums of hope," and too pessimistic about inner-city areas, which
they claimed were "slums of despair." They erred for several reasons.
One, they did not study firsthand or in depth the inner city about
which they wrote, except for Oscar Lewis. Second, their paradigm
blinded them from fully depicting and understanding "life on the
ground." Lewis's "culture of poverty" thesis led him to claim slum-
dwellers to be hopeless, apathetic, and passive, at the same time that
his extensive descriptive data showed his informants to be creative
and involved in a rich informal social network. Indeed, the very slum
dwellers who Lewis claimed were trapped in a culture of despair organized for the reconstruction of their neighborhood after the earthquake and for the rights to street commerce. Meanwhile, defenders
of squatters documented empirically the difficulties shantytown
dwellers experienced, but then did not analyze those difficulties.[39]

Third, urbanists failed to contextualize their findings. They assumed that the differences they portrayed in different urban neighborhoods were intrinsically rooted in community type, independent of macro political and economic conditions. Yet, my analysis has shown how varying macro conditions differ in their community effects.

If the longitudinal study of three communities in Mexico City calls into question prevailing urban conceptions, how generalizable are my findings? However wanting are the conditions in the shanty-town and development that I studied, they are better than in more outlying areas in the state of Mexico. In Mexico, as elsewhere in Latin America, debt-ridden and neoliberal belt-tightening governments, in the 1980s and 1990s, invested less in social and physical infrastructure than earlier interventionist, populist, and less fiscally strapped states. And the more peripheral an area, the further it typically is from viable sources of employment. Accordingly, the development and the shantytown I studied underestimate the despair of mushrooming communities on the ever-expanding boundaries of key Latin American cities. As cities expand, the inner-city area I studied represents an increasingly less common form of settlement. It was more typical in decades past. The area I studied also represents an extreme of slum vibrancy and resilience. It should be viewed as an ideal type, against which other inner-city areas are compared.

Notes

1. Luis Rubio, "Mexico's New Politics," *LASA (Latin American Studies Association) Forum* 28, no. 3 (Fall 1997): 11.
2. John Sheahan, "Effects of Liberalization Programs on Poverty and Inequality: Chile, Mexico, and Peru," *Latin American Research Review* 32, no. 3 (1997): 7–38.
3. Rubio, "Mexico's New Politics," p. 11.
4. Guillermo Trejo et al., "Mexico: Social Spending and Food Subsidies During Adjustment in the 1980s," in Friedmann, Lustig, and Legovini, *Contra la Pobreza* (Mexico City: Cal y Arena, 1993).
5. Denise Dresser, "Neopopulist Solutions to Neoliberal Problems: Mexico's National Solidarity Program, Transforming State-Society Relations in Mexico," in Wayne Cornelius, Ann L. Craig, and Jonathan Fox, eds., *Transforming State-Society Relations in Mexico* (La Jolla: Center for U.S.-Mexican Studies, University of California, San Diego, 1991).
6. Sheahan, "Effects of Liberalization Programs," p. 24.
7. Peter Ward, *Mexico City: The Production and Reproduction of an Urban Environment* (New York: John Wiley & Sons, 1990), chap. 1.
8. Ibid., preface to 2nd edition and chap. 1. Purportedly in the 1990s more people left from than migrated to Mexico City. The provinces, however, have their own problems. For an analysis of the difficult economic and

social conditions in Mexico's increasingly important "western growth pole," Guadalajara, see Guillermo de la Pena, et al., *Crisis, Conflicto, y Sobrevivencia: Estudios Sobre la Sociedad Urbana en Mexico* (Guadalajara: Universidad de Guadalajara, CIESAS, 1990).

9. Ward, *Mexico City,* chap. 1.

10. Ibid.

11. Ibid.

12. *New York Times,* 7 November 1997, pp. 1, 6.

13. Ward, *Mexico City,* p. 114.

14. Rubio, "Mexico's New Politics."

15. For a more detailed discussion of the methodology deployed in my earlier research, see Susan Eckstein, *The Poverty of Revolution: The State and Urban Poor in Mexico* (Princeton, N.J.: Princeton University Press, 1988), pp. xiv, 279–304.

16. See, for example, C. Stokes, "A Theory of Slums," *Land Economics* 38 (August); William Mangin, "Latin American Squatter Settlements: A Problem and a Solution," *Latin American Research Review* 2 (1967); John C. Turner, "Housing Priorities, Settlement Patterns, and Urban Development in Modernizing Countries," *Journal of the American Institute of Planners* 34, no. 6 (1968); Alejandro Portes, "The Urban Slum in Chile: Types and Correlates," *Ekistics,* no. 202 (September 1972); and case studies by Janice Perlman, *The Myth of Marginality: Urban Poverty and Politics in Rio de Janeiro* (Berkeley: University of California Press, 1976); Wayne Cornelius, *Politics and the Migrant Poor in Mexico City* (Stanford: Stanford University Press, 1975); Larissa Lomnitz, "The Social and Economic Organization of a Mexican Shantytown," *Latin American Urban Research* 4 (1974); Talton Ray, *The Politics of the Barrios of Venezuela* (Berkeley: University of California Press, 1969); Susan Eckstein, *The Poverty of Revolution;* and Henry Dietz, *Poverty and Problem-Solving Under Military Rule: The Urban Poor in Lima, Peru* (Austin: University of Texas Press, 1980).

17. John C. Turner, "Approaches to Government-Sponsored Housing," *Ekistics* 42, no. 242 (January 1976); Oscar Lewis, *The Children of Sanchez: Autobiography of a Mexican Family* (New York: Random House, 1961) and *Five Families: Mexican Case Studies in the Culture of Poverty* (New York: Random House, 1959).

18. Portes, "The Urban Slum in Chile."

19. See my discussion in Eckstein, "Urbanization Revisited: Inner-City Slum of Hope and Squatter Settlement of Despair," *World Development* 18, no. 2 (February 1990).

20. Secretaría de Desarrollo Urbano y Ecologia (SEDUE), *Housing Reconstruction Program in Mexico City* (Mexico City: SEDUE, 1987).

21. Rights to stall locations were de facto inherited. Accordingly, access to street rights was passed on intergenerationally (when not sold at the "going" market rate).

22. For a lengthier discussion and analysis of the housing movement, see Susan Eckstein, "Poor People Versus the State and Capital: Anatomy of a Successful Community Mobilization for Housing in Mexico," *International Journal of Urban and Regional Research* 14, no. 2 (1990): 274.

23. See Eckstein, *Poverty of Revolution,* pp. 143–148.

24. See A. Gilbert and P. Ward, *Housing, the State and the Poor: Policy and Practice in Three Latin American Cities* (Cambridge: Cambridge University Press, 1985).

25. Paul Strassman, in "Home-Based Enterprises in Cities of Developing Countries," *Economic Development and Cultural Change*, 36, no. 1 (October 1987), has argued that informal-sector earnings depend more on location than on type of economic endeavor. My study confirms his claims.

26. For more detail on Mexico City street vendors see John Cross, *Street Politics: Street Vendors and the State in Mexico City* (Stanford: Stanford University Press, 1997).

27. See Eckstein, "Urbanization Revisited."

28. The name of the top city official changed from mayor to governor in 1997, with the shift in the post from a presidential appointee to an elected officer.

29. Eckstein, *Poverty of Revolution*, pp. 78–107.

30. While the residents' association presidents were not salaried, they made money on the job because people in the community paid them for favors rendered. However, *consejeros ciudadanos* similarly made money on the side.

31. On the politics of sanctioning inner-city vending claims, see Gary Issac Gordon, "Mexico City's 'War on the Sidewalks': The Politics and Economics of Street Vending in Historical Perspective" (paper delivered at the Latin American Studies Association, Guadalajara, Mexico, April 1997).

32. PAN continued, however, to maintain its political hold in the north of the country.

33. Nora Lustig and Miguel Szekely, "Mexico: Economic Trends, Poverty, and Inequality" (Washington, D.C.: Inter-American Development Bank, 1998).

34. On local political dynamics in Mexico's Guadalajara, see de la Pena and de la Torre, "Irregularidad Urbana, Contradicciones Sociales y Negociación Política en la Zona Metropolitana de Guadalajara," in Luis Chirinos, et al., eds., *La Urbanización Popular y el Orden Jurídico en America Latina* (Mexico: Universidad Nacional Autonoma de México, 1993).

35. Laura Benton, "Reshaping the Urban Core: The Politics of Housing in Authoritarian Uruguay," *Latin American Research Review* 21, no. 2 (1986).

36. For a more detailed analysis, see Ward, "The Latin American Inner City."

37. *New York Times*, 21 January 1997, p. 5.

38. On Latin American social movements see Sonia Alvarez, Evelina Dagnino and Arturo Escobar, eds., *Cultures of Politics: Politics of Cultures* (Boulder, Colo.: Westview Press, 1998) and Susan Eckstein, ed., *Power and Popular Protest: Latin American Social Movements* (Berkeley: University of California Press, 1989).

39. See, for example, Mangin's positive analysis of shantytowns in an introductory essay of a volume he edited containing empirical descriptions of problematic life in such areas. William Mangin, ed., *Peasants in Cities: Readings in the Anthropology of Urbanization* (Boston: Houghton Mifflin, 1970).

9

The Social Consequences of Political Reforms: Decentralization and Social Policy in Venezuela

Juan Carlos Navarro

This chapter describes how a process of political and administrative decentralization led to substantial and long-term transformations in social policy in Venezuela.[1] Social reform—reform of the education, health, social-security, or safety net institutions and policies—in Latin American countries has been the subject of increasing attention in recent times, as economic reforms have become widespread across the region.[2] Yet social reforms have usually been approached through an analysis of the conditions and dynamics of reforms originated within the social sectors themselves. The question has been how an education or health sector reform proceeds, taking for granted that the will and the capacity for undertaking such a reform exists in at least some of the actors who control or have authority over the sectors. Of course, it is common to point at all sorts of political enemies and the tremendous obstacles that make these reforms difficult, but at least it is generally assumed that the minister, some technocrats, or even a president is pushing for reform, so that the process is set in motion.

Very little of such a thing can be found in the Venezuelan experience, where no formal education or health reform has been initiated with any force in recent times. Yet, the advancement of political decentralization has profoundly transformed the way social policies are defined and implemented. By creating new actors and mobilizing new constituencies, a political process that was not primarily intended as a tool for social-policy reform has in practice become one. Social sectors have thus started to be reformed from the bottom up, with little overall planning and with even less of a centrally mandated direction.

This interesting process is the subject of this chapter. In order to provide the necessary context, the chapter describes the main characteristics of social policy in Venezuela before 1989, the year decentralization started, and explains how decentralization was only one out of three simultaneous reform trends affecting social policy in the nineties. These trends, to a large extent mutually reinforcing, are described briefly and contrasted with the traditional pattern of state intervention in the social arena. After that, the discussion focuses on decentralization; the most tangible changes introduced by it are described through a close look at the evolution of social expenditures by subnational governments, and then attention is paid to the implications and prospects of the changes identified.

Social Policy in Venezuela:
The Limits of a Traditional Pattern of Intervention

Social conditions in Venezuela deteriorated continuously throughout the 1980s, as they did in other Latin American countries. This deterioration was directly related to economic decline, the result of misguided fiscal, monetary, and exchange policies that, in the specific case of Venezuela, were combined with negative external shocks affecting the oil industry. Between 1981 and 1989, the poverty index doubled, covering almost 40 percent of the population. Márquez pointed to declining real salaries, a reflection of slow growth and high inflation rates, as the main reason for the rise in poverty during the decade, in spite of the fact that the poor were working more and not overly affected by unemployment.[3]

Other factors appear to have also played an important role. Morley found that the Venezuelan economy was relatively unable to protect the poor and other vulnerable groups during times of economic decline, in comparison with other countries of the region.[4] Thus, during the 1980s, poverty in Venezuela increased more than in Argentina, Brazil, and Peru even though these countries experienced a greater decline in real salaries.

In the specific case of Venezuela, there was no severe scarcity of resources. Common sense suggests that, if the GDP remained the same and population grew, public funds for social services would decrease, aggravating social conditions. This perspective, however, is not backed up by the research.[5] Expenditures in social sectors by the central government were maintained and, in some cases, even slightly increased as a percentage of the budget during the 1980s. If the relative percentages of spending in each of the social sectors are an indication of the priority which they were assigned, then education and, to a certain degree, nutrition and health care were at least as important to the Venezuelan government during those years as they were prior to the serious economic problems of 1983. To a certain point, the overall impoverishment of the country was definitely reflected in a decrease in per capita social spending, yet, even from this point of view, the decline was not very significant and, in any case, was proportionally less than the drop in GDP during the same period.

Long after the prosperity of the 1970s and early 1980s had disappeared, per capita expenditures on social services were higher in Venezuela than in other countries at a similar development level. However, in spite of this financial support, the country's principal social indicators remained particularly low. Not only were the spot figures worrisome, but so were the trends: Various health and education indices remained stagnant or significantly slowed, and others—for example, mortality rates from certain tropical diseases and secondary-school attendance rates—deteriorated.

A majority of the analysts who try to explain this paradox—poor results in spite of the considerable amount of resources allocated to the social sectors—agree on one point: Venezuela's relative inability to protect the welfare of its citizens during economic adversity is directly related to its very weak public institutions and their poor performance in the social sectors.

Before 1989, Venezuela's social policy was based on a limited set of very homogeneous and tightly interwoven principles. The most important of these were:

• From a policy perspective, the government was not thought of as just an important provider of social services but rather as the only one. Private providers of these services were considered only marginally important. Under the best of circumstances, private providers were tolerated but rarely openly supported or incorporated into public-policy programs for the social sectors.

• Monopolization of the provision of social services was accompanied by a highly centralized administrative structure: Education, health care, poverty alleviation programs, nutrition, low-income housing, and others were highly centralized services. The central office for each sector, located in the capital, was not only responsible for planning, regulating, and financing services at the national level, but also for implementing, managing, evaluating, and processing each of the small administrative details related to the actual provision of services throughout the entire country, even in very remote areas. In general, the bodies responsible for directly providing services, such as schools and hospitals, had little or no administrative autonomy.

• Extreme centralization had traditionally been accompanied by strong paternalism in the provision of services. Users and citizens were, in general, not involved in decisions concerning the quality or quantity of services provided, nor in their evaluation or the gathering of feedback. Accountability was almost nonexistent.

• In Venezuela, as in other Latin American countries, these characteristics, in combination with certain features of the political system, has led to an extreme level of penetration—or capture—of the agencies responsible for providing social services by political parties and, especially, labor unions. To a large degree, these agencies and their policies served those who worked in them, rather than the public and society at large.[6]

These were not occasional deviations in the application of some social-sector policies, but rather features that dominated the design and implementation of social policies in Venezuela for most of four decades prior to 1989. Considerable achievements in health, education, and welfare were made, particularly during the 1960s and early 1970s, within the framework provided by this pattern of social policy. However, by the end of the 1980s most of the effectiveness of highly centralized, paternalistic, and clientelistic policies had weakened if not entirely dissipated. At the same time, their shortcomings had become apparent. Together these features formed a coherent pattern in social policy that shaped the initial conditions for the reforms of the 1990s.

Social Policy in the 1990s: Moving Towards Structural Reforms

In answer to the problems associated with the pre-1989 social-policy approach, Venezuelan society began to generate a series of responses from diverse sources—including, but not limited to, the state.

Beginning in 1989, with the inauguration of a new, reform-oriented administration, modern targeted social programs, especially in the general area of poverty alleviation, were introduced for the first time in Venezuela. With these programs, the public sector attempted to significantly alter the type of instruments used to attend to those living in difficult socioeconomic situations. These new instruments were continuously employed during the following years, with varying degrees of success. Their introduction, as well as the details surrounding their use and eventual modification, were subject to a considerable amount of controversy, political conflict, and public attention. All this took place during the period that extended, for the most part, through two constitutional presidential terms, the first of which began with President Carlos Andrés Pérez (1989–1994) and ended with provisional president Ramón J. Velázquez, and the second under President Rafael Caldera between 1994 and 1999.[7]

The particular political circumstances of 1989 allowed for the creation of a series of innovative and well-financed programs to address the impoverishment of wide sectors of Venezuelan society.[8] At the same time, and most remarkably, the programs were carried out without touching the traditional institutional structures of social policy.[9] For the most part, these programs constituted attempts to create administrative and service delivery structures for providing social benefits that ran parallel to those public entities supposedly responsible for the same task. From the very beginning, the possibility of saving, improving, or reforming traditional bureaucratic organizations in the social sectors—the line ministries and related agencies—was discarded. Working with those organizations was considered either a hopeless proposition, given the strength of vested interests, or impractical given the strong political pressure to produce quick results to compensate for the social costs of the adjustment program being implemented in 1989. Thus, initiatives in nutrition and health care were put forward without affecting the established structures of these sectors. Unemployment insurance was created without touching the financing or organization of the Venezuelan Institute for Social Security, which normally would have been responsible for it. Schools were built by parallel ad hoc agencies with few links to the education bureaucracy that was supposed to maintain the schools or fill them with students and teachers. Other examples could be mentioned.[10]

An important implication of this strategy of institutional bypassing or parallelism was that no reform was undertaken of the core policies and organizations responsible for the vast budgets and actions of the Venezuelan state in the social arena. Innovations were piled up or designed to work around old institutions, with as little contact as possible with them.

Meanwhile, other broad political and social changes began to affect the state's social policy. First, so-called civil society, operating separately from the state, became involved in providing social services, paving the way for a couple of very important developments in social policy: a growing nongovernmental organization (NGO) involvement in public social programs and, at the same time, autonomous activities by NGOs that transformed them into important suppliers of social services.[11]

Second, social policy was also affected by the decentralization process that began with the December 1989 election of governors and mayors by direct universal vote, the first such elections in Venezuela. Although not initially devised as a plan to reform social services, the process of direct elections wound up having a strong impact on the manner in which health care, education, and other public social services were organized and managed. To a large degree, again, it was precisely those sectors least affected by the deliberate reform initiatives of the central government—health care and education being the most important cases—that would benefit the most from the the new political conditions fostered by decentralization.[12]

The combination of these three trends—the introduction of a new generation of targeted poverty alleviation programs by the central government, the impact of decentralization on social policies and on the institutions responsible for providing social services, and the activities of NGOs as highly capable social-service providers to low-income groups—complete the picture of public-policy reforms in social services in Venezuela starting in 1989.

All three trends, using different methods and diverse strategies, have not so much increased the resources allocated to combat social problems or introduced improvements in specific programs, but rather have attacked the weaknesses in social policy caused by institutional, political and technical complexities. Reformers have made diverse but serious attempts to change either the type of dominant programs and policies, the nature of public institutions in charge of such programs, or the social actors involved in their design and implementation. These reforms are attempts to attack the root of the problem of Venezuelan social policy, to implement changes that could be called structural, if by structural we mean a modification not of specific programs or policies but rather of the design and implementation of social policies and of the institutions responsible for advancing such policies. Furthermore, these simultaneous and interrelated approaches were started at a time when major economic reforms were being introduced in the country.

In what follows, this chapter will focus specifically on one of the aforementioned trends, that of decentralization. I will describe and analyze the impact political and administrative decentralization has had on Venezuelan social policy with a concise synthesis of the available information on such attempts between 1993 and 1996. The discussion begins with a look at public expenditures by states and a sample of municipalities between 1993 and 1995, and also includes information provided by those responsible for social policy at the state and municipal levels for the month of August 1996. The information used for the purposes of this chapter is only a small part of the information collected for a wide-reaching project on decentralization completed by the Institute de Estudios Superiores de Administración (IESA) in 1998.[13]

Political and Administrative
Decentralization in Venezuela

The rise of the modern state in Venezuela during the twentieth century was marked by a strong central government and weak subnational governments. Health care, education, nutrition, and all types of social assistance were organized in such a way that the financial weight of the central government allowed decisionmaking power to be concentrated in the main headquarters of the ministries, even regarding the details of operating schools, hospitals, community centers, cultural activities, and every aspect of social life. Increased central government activities in the social arena produced a "crowding-out" effect on the willingness of subnational governments to take responsibility for important aspects of social policy.[14]

In areas where subnational governments were able to maintain a relative level of importance, for example in basic education, they did so in a primarily residual role: Students attended state schools when there was no nearby school run by the Ministry of Education. Along the way, social sectors administered by the central government reached such proportions that it was difficult for them to be managed prudently and efficiently, and major obstacles arose that prevented changes in their structure and behavior. In Venezuela in the 1980s, a vicious combination—the central government's quasi monopoly on social services and policies together with the declining performance of the principal public organizations responsible for these services and strong institutional inflexibilities—made it difficult to imagine any attempt at reform of health care, education, social assistance or social-security services originating from within the sectors themselves.[15]

The decentralization process begun in 1989 opened a completely new chapter on the distribution of responsibilities for social services among the various levels of government. It also presented the first and most significant opportunity in several decades for substantive reform in social-service provision. Not only did the changes in legislation provide a legal basis for decentralization, but political changes—in particular the introduction of direct elections for state governors and the recently created position of mayor in the same year—also immediately established a system of incentives for subnational governments to actively push forward in several areas, including social policy. The new and recently elected heads of state and municipal governments became, as could be expected, the targets of direct demand for social services. Many responded and tried to satisfy this demand, with varying degrees of success. Along the way, they started to reap another of the benefits of decentralizing services, that is, a certain degree of intergovernmental competition along with experimentation in new management and service provision models.

With these new political actors and processes in place, the new legislation opened up two avenues for local and regional authorities to become meaningful actors in social policy. First, practically all areas and sectors of social policy were defined as "overlapping jurisdictions," that is, different levels of government had the legitimate opportunity to take part in the same sectors along with some form of shared responsibility. As a result, the central government was, in principle, not the sole actor in extremely important sectors such as health care or education. Second, a "transfer of jurisdiction" process was established, under which, after certain steps were completed—that is, designing the transfer plan and obtaining congressional approval—social services previously under central-government control began to fall under the authority and administration of state or municipal governments.

One interesting aspect of decentralization under Venezuelan legislation is that the transfer of a specific service—for example, primary health care—is assumed to be unequal and asynchronic in different states within the country based on the will of each jurisdiction. This could result in coordination problems and can lead to regional inequalities. Yet it does have the advantage of having started from an honest acknowledgment that administrative capabilities are uneven throughout the entire country. It also recognizes that, above all else, regional and local constituencies hold different social services to be more important, or believe that certain sectors should experience a transfer of jurisdiction more quickly given the specific circumstances prevailing in a certain locality.

In reality, the path of overlapping jurisdictions has been much more important than transfer of jurisdiction during the first decade immediately following the introduction of decentralization. Although some jurisdiction transfers have taken place—most notably in health care after 1995, when more than half of the states have been given jurisdiction over health care services (generally primary-care ambulatory centers)—both the political complexity of the legal process and the lack of a transparent framework for fiscal transfers guaranteeing the economic sustainability of the services are obstacles that have held back decentralization considerably. However, governors and mayors have used their new legal powers in social services extensively and, without waiting for the transfers of jurisdiction to take place, have dedicated increasing levels of funds, energy, and human resources to establishing all types of social programs.

The Impact of Decentralization on State and Municipal Social Policies

A first impression of state- and municipal-government social policies can be obtained from the information gathered on public expenditures shown in Table 9.1. This table compares the relative importance of the three levels of government in national social spending. It compares the allocation of funds and variations within each level between 1989, the last year for which state and municipal budgets were drafted under the original power sharing and electoral system, and 1994, five years after decentralization had been initiated.

It is quite clear that social expenditures underwent a definite transformation in just five years since decentralization began. Probably the

Table 9.1   Allocation of Social Spending in Venezuela According to Level of Government

	1989	1994
Social Expenditures (Millions of US $)	3,414	5,454
Central Government	2,937	3,876
State Governments	436	1,339
Municipal Governments	42	239
Social Expenditures as a Percentage of **Total Social Expenditures**		
Central Government	86.01%	71.07%
State Governments	12.77%	24.55%
Municipal Governments	1.22%	4.38%
Social Expenditures as a Percentage of Total **Expenditures, by Corresponding Level of Government**[a]		
Central Government	32.53%	31.98%
State Governments	41.34%	69.27%
Municipal Governments	19.18%	32.61%

Source: Figures for 1994, IESA Survey. Figures for 1989, World Bank (1992) for Central Government and States. González, Rosa Amelia ("Anexos" in Janet Kelly, [ed.] *Gerencia Municipal.* Ediciones IESA, Caracas, 1993) contains figures for public expenditure in municipalities for 1986 that were used as a basis for estimating 1989 municipal social expenditures.

Note: Percentages do not total 100%.

most notable change is in the relative weight of expenditures among the three levels of government: In 1989 the central government was responsible for 86 percent of social expenditures, while in 1994, the percentage dropped to slightly more than 70 percent in favor of the municipalities, which rose from 1.22 to 4.38 percent of nationwide social expenditures, and the states, which almost doubled their relative participation, climbing from 12.77 to 24.55 percent.

This change in the relative weight of the different government levels in total social expenditures was not due to a decrease in central-government social spending during these years, which actually grew during that period. In fact, social expenditures in real bolívares for 1994 were greater than in 1989 even though the central-government portion of total social spending was reduced. Nor was it due to a decrease in the relative importance placed on social spending as a portion of total public expenditures by the central government. As can be seen in Table 9.1, it remained practically the same at about 32 percent. This is especially significant given that decentralization has often been criticized in Latin America as a disguised strategy for allowing the central government to push problems down to the lower levels of government and free itself of the corresponding budgetary responsibilities associated with those problems.

The reason for the transformation must be sought in the undeniable change in spending priorities among the subnational governments. Although public expenditures among these levels grew, in general, as a result of the increase in *situado constitutional* (the transfer of funds from the central government to the subnational level, as dictated by the constitution) during this period, the decisive factor was an increase in the relative significance of social spending as a portion of total state and municipal expenditures. Thus, in the municipalities, social spending climbed from 19.18 to 32.61 percent between 1989 and 1994. For the states, it rose from 41.34 to 62.27 percent.[16]

The same conclusion can be reached by looking at per capita spending figures. More than half of the growth registered for national per capita social expenditures for those years under consideration can be attributed to subnational governments, especially the state governments. Thus, although social expenditures increased in each and every level of government during this period, social spending by municipalities grew three times more than social spending by the central government, and social spending by state governments grew more than six times that of the central government. It is clear that these growth rates surpassed the overall increase in state and municipal public expenditures combined, which, again, clearly points to a change in public-spending priorities at the subnational level in favor of social policy.

Looking at the distribution of expenditures across sectors would show that, even though spending on education continues to be important in every state, as it was before decentralization was initiated in 1989, the health care sector gained significant ground. This sector went from being practically nonexistent to being the second most important when averaging for all the states. Given that the figures used are for 1994, when there had not yet been any transfer of jurisdiction from the central to the regional governments, this increase clearly indicates that health care became the most important priority for sub-national governments after decentralization. The product of their own initiative, this was presumably a response to the preferences of their constituents.

This is consistent with the answers of those responsible for state social policy when directly asked about priorities. The health care sector received 34.92 out of 100 points in a survey used to assess the priorities of state governments, more than any other sector. Following in importance are education (23.81) and nutritional programs (16.67). The responses also reveal considerable activity in the social sector, with a proliferation of programs that did not exist prior to 1989—just 12 percent of the programs listed by those interviewed had been established before this date. These figures coincide, in general, with anecdotal information and research on individual experiences. The state of Lara has made strong efforts over the last few years to organize a set of state government initiatives on social development and compensation. Aragua has done the same. Mérida and Bolívar, are known for their accomplishments in educational reforms, and Carabobo and Lara, for the reorganization of their health care systems.[17]

Similar trends can be seen in the municipalities, most notably the general increase in the percentage of funds allocated to the social sector. Education and health care do not dominate municipal budgets, and the per capita spending is much higher. This is due to a greater diversity among the municipalities in terms of their fiscal and demographic features. The dominant item in municipal social expenditures is the one labeled "social security." In Venezuela, the social security system, which encompasses health care provision and pension funds for retired people, is the responsibility of the central government. What then can be included under this title for sub-national government expenditures? The category is primarily comprised of the many municipal activities surrounding subsidies for senior citizens and poor families with small children and, to a lesser degree, the indigent poor and the unemployed. The municipality has traditionally played a residual—in the sense that it is not formally responsible for these types of programs—yet important role in the areas commonly referred to as "assistance" because of incomplete coverage by the national social security system. Municipal public-spending figures indicate that municipalities continue to play an active role. The fact that assistance to groups in precarious socio-economic situations has been maintained since decentralization began in 1989 can simply be an indication of the lack of reforms and improvements in coverage and efficiency in central government social security services. On the municipal side, as the survey established, such continuity does not necessarily imply a lack of innovation or change. Even though significant funds continue to be channeled to these purposes, at least some of it is spent within the framework of new programs and new administrative capabilities.

Undoubtedly, the renewed momentum given to social policy by subnational governments faces considerable obstacles. When asked about the main difficulties that they face, those responsible for state and municipal social policies tended to highlight scarce resources. This was the opinion in 20 of the 22 states and in 61 of the 64 municipalities included in the sample. This response directly reflects the notorious gap between the ability of the states to finance their expenditures and the growing expectations of their constituents regarding social conditions in their areas. In fact, a key element in the expansion of social policy among the subnational governments is that it developed together with a sharp fiscal imbalance.[18] The considerable amount of activity and program innovation and, to a lesser extent, institutional innovation in state and municipal social policies has not been accompanied by a comparable eagerness to look for new sources of financing, for instance, through the introduction of user fees for social services. There are some actual examples of innovation in this regard, but they are only exceptions. In direct connection to this problem, the slow pace of transferring jurisdiction within the larger social sectors, such as health care and education, can be attributed mainly to the lack of a framework for transparent and credible fiscal transfers that allows subnational governments to accept full responsibility for the administration of services which for decades had been the domain of the central government.[19]

In spite of the reported scarcity of resources, however, it is significant that substantial institutional innovations can be observed at both the state and municipal levels. These include association with nongovernmental providers in implementing public programs, along with efforts to introduce user feedback, targeting, evaluation schemes, program follow-up, and other technical innovations that seem to indicate a new push for modernization and reform in social-service provision by subnational governments in Venezuela.

Efficiency, Equity, and the
Political Economy of Decentralization

One clear conclusion springs forth from the information provided in the previous pages. Decentralization, which began in 1989, has had tangible and important consequences for the behavior of subnational governments regarding social policy. Probably the clearest consequence is the significant increase in subnational social expenditures. Today, both states and municipalities spend more per capita in the social sectors and allocate a greater percentage of their budgets to social spending than they did prior to decentralization.

Given the slow pace of transferring jurisdiction and, in most sectors, the lack of ad hoc policies by the central government to stimulate subnational social spending, it is plausible to conclude that the increase in expenditures is the result of autonomous decisions by state and municipal leaders, and not due to a deliberate plan that originated in central-government ministries.

Yet, if this first point is agreed upon, a number of unanswered questions remain concerning the variables that determine and the effects that arise from the increase in subnational social spending. The initial question would, naturally, have to be whether the increase in spending has been accompanied by more efficient social policy, or whether it has simply increased resource waste by putting money into poorly run or barely capable programs or government entities. In this regard, it is worth noting Campbell's distinction between production efficiency, allocation efficiency, and fiscal efficiency.[20] The first refers to how well subnational governments can produce a specific service at a low cost for a given level of quality. Allocation efficiency refers to how well fund distribution—among, for example, sectors, programs, or population groups—reflects the preferences of the electorate. Fiscal efficiency refers to whether the resources used by subnational governments have been obtained in a way that minimizes the burden on economic efficiency, that is, that the use of resources is compatible with the source and manner of collection of those resources.

It is almost impossible to evaluate production efficiency given the type of information available. Detailed and comprehensive comparisons on the cost effectiveness of services managed by the central government with those administered by subnational governments practically do not exist. Circumstances in Venezuela make it difficult to arrive at firm conclusions in this area, given important distortions in budget distribution patterns that have existed for decades without ever being modified; the absence of a system to measure the costs and effectiveness of major services; and waste of resources. These and other problems that afflict a vast majority of entities responsible for providing social services should be taken into consideration when trying to gauge efficiency in subnational government performance. On the other hand, somewhat abundant evidence from specific case studies of state-run social programs seems to point to a cost advantage, or at least an increase in quality when costs increase.[21]

With respect to fiscal efficiency, the decentralization process obviously requires a redefinition of the fiscal powers assigned to the municipalities and especially to the states. Given the overwhelming dominance of the *situado* as a source of financing for subnational governments, it is obvious that citizens are not paying optimal tax rates, which would create the appropriate size and type of demand to best satisfy their preferences.[22] As was established by Oates, a strong dependence on unconditional resource transfers can destroy incentives to make responsible decisions at the local level, so that citizens lose sight of the costs of the services they demand from the local or regional government.[23]

This does not completely exclude, however, the possibility that decentralization has improved efficiency in the allocation of resources, channeling the appropriate amount and percentage of funds in accordance with the demands of the local and state electorates and avoiding the inherent inefficiencies in the uniform, centralized provision of services. Thus, various political balances at the state and local level can lead to different combinations of taxation and spending structures in different jurisdictions.

It is important to stress that even though considerable fiscal imbalances can introduce severe distortions into local and state decisionmaking processes, such imbalances do not necessarily annul the alignment that exists between constituent preferences and the decisions made by subnational governments. In a democratic polity, such an alignment is the result of competition in electoral processes and of accountability mechanisms. The changes in subnational social policies are simply unexplainable if this premise is omitted from the discussion.

It is always possible, of course, to attribute the high priority placed on social policy to manipulations by local politicians hoping to gain reelection. Independently of constituent demands, the pure and simple distribution of various subsidies can be seen by state and municipal politicians as an important component of their popularity and a basis for their eventual reelection. The clientelistic traditions of party politics, firmly rooted in Venezuela, provide some support for a hypothesis of this kind. Certainly, the problem here is not that a governor or mayor tries to win votes by developing a specific social program appreciated by the electorate. This is not only legitimate but also desirable. The problem lies with the moment in which the search for votes through social policies distorts the institutional development of the social sector or begins to have negative consequences for the social development of the area or region where the policies are being implemented: when technical capability is sacrificed in program administration to fulfill political favors; when payroll for the social sectors is used to finance activists or to award supporters who may lack the skills necessary for the position; when a particularly visible or vocal group is favored over other groups that legitimately deserve publicly financed benefits; and so on.

The information gathered for this study does not allow definitive conclusions to be drawn in one direction or another. Using social programs for political proselytizing, nevertheless, cannot be considered an outcome of decentralization, because that type of activity existed long before 1989. However, it is clear that the introduction of direct elections for governors and mayors may have increased these practices, by increasing the number of positions subject to electoral competition. It is difficult to believe that this is not happening to some extent in many states and municipalities, but, at the same time, there is ample anecdotal evidence to suggest that there is another side to the story. In fact, some social-service reforms by certain states and municipalities are clearly opposed to clientelistic party practices while some have even expressed the explicit goal of eliminating them.[24] In several instances, for example, the governor's or mayor's party has proposed a particular reform that the labor union linked to the party has opposed because it would mean the end of clientelistic instruments under union control. In other instances, various important reforms have survived a victory by the opposition, as has been the example of education in Mérida and Bolívar, or health care in Lara. Moreover, much evidence exists of attempts by governors and mayors to stimulate participation in the design and implementation of social programs through channels other than political parties.

Still another attempt at approaching the issue of the determinants of the growing involvement of subnational governments in social policy has been undertaken through a statistical analysis of the factors affecting subnational social spending.[25] It is based on the hypothesis that the level of municipal social expenditure per capita should be a function of whether the majority of the people living in the municipality live below the poverty line—or, in terms of political-economic models of voting processes, whether the median voter (*votmediano*) is poor; the seriousness of social problems within the jurisdiction, measured by the absolute number of poor (*pobres*); the availability of resources to the municipality (*recursosPC*), measured by overall per capita expenditures and the size of the municipality (*población*); and the size of the municipality according to population. Given the possible existence of distinct social problems in rural municipalities (*rural*), another variable was added to separate out those municipalities of fewer than 10,000 inhabitants. Table 9.2 in the appendix to this chapter shows the results of a regression analysis in which the dependent variable is municipal per capita social expenditures. It is hoped that municipal per capita social spending will be higher as the availability of resources increases, size increases, and the number of citizens living below the poverty line rises and in rural municipalities and in those municipalities where the median voter is poor.

The regression analysis confirms most of the hypothesis. Its relatively high explanatory power (*r* squared adjusted by 0.48) suggests that it is a good model for trying to understand the determinants of the generosity of social expenditures by a Venezuelan municipality. All of the estimated coefficients for the variables were statistically significant at 5 percent, with the exception of constant C. The coefficient signs behaved as expected, with one remarkable exception. The number of poor within the jurisdiction has an inverse relationship instead of a direct relationship with the level of per capita spending. This could indicate that, because poor individuals presumably contribute very little or nothing to the financing of local public services due to low consumption and income levels, the higher the number of poor in a certain jurisdiction, the greater the financial burden for the rest of the nonpoor and, consequently, the smaller the tax base, which could then lead to smaller social expenditures. Apart from this exception, both the hypothesis of the median voter and the overall economic prosperity, size, and location (rural versus urban) of the municipality appear to have a clear influence on per capita social expenditures in the expected direction.

If the statistical exercise is repeated using the percentage of municipal expenditures allocated to social sectors as the dependent variable, the resulting model is a little less strong (*r* squared is reduced to 0.10 with F having a 12 percent margin of error). Both the level of prosperity for the municipality and whether or not it is rural cease to have a significant impact on the behavior of the independent variable, even though the constant C becomes statistically significant. For the other variables, the behavior of the signs of the coefficients is stable (detailed results can be found in Table 9.3 in the appendix to this chapter). The more limited results of the second exercise suggests the need to continue exploring the determinants of municipal social spending.

In sum, the hypothesis that the behavior of social expenditures depends on structural characteristics and core political processes within the municipalities more than on short-term political manipulations seems to gain credit. In line with what has been seen, factors such as the prosperity, size, and location of a municipality and whether the median voter is below the poverty line explain differences between municipalities regarding the level of per capita social expenditures and, to a lesser degree, the importance of social spending as a part of total municipal expenditures.

Conclusion: The Impact of Political Reforms on Social Policy in Venezuela

Venezuela can be viewed as a clear case of how a strictly political change within a democratic framework can have an impact on the structural aspects of social policy. The introduction of direct elections for governors and mayors in 1989 brought about changes in local and state political balances strong enough to have a visible impact on the structure of subnational government expenditures. This took place even when there was no clear decentralization policy by the national government. In other words, even though the decentralization of social services in Venezuela is unofficial, neither an expressed nor dominant national-government policy, the change in political incentives made possible by changes in electoral regulations has produced a de facto transformation in who makes social policy, who sets priorities, to which programs and groups funds are channeled, and how social services are administered.

More specifically, decentralization has clearly been accompanied by:

• A rise in resources allocated to the social sectors, as has been documented with estimates of the total and per capita amounts dedicated to social sectors by both states and municipalities. Even more interesting is that this has occurred, up to 1994, the year for which the estimates were made, without a single complete transfer of jurisdiction from the central government to the subnational governments.

• An increase in the relative importance of subnational social spending as a percentage of total social expenditures for the country. This is true in spite of the fact that between 1989 and 1994 there was a rise in social spending by the central government. This rejects the hypothesis that decentralization is actually a strategic move by the central government to resolve its fiscal problems by passing its responsibilities on to other levels of government. In Venezuela, the central government, for those years under study, increased the amount of resources allocated for the provision of social services, and, yet, these funds lost their relative importance within the realm of social spending because the municipalities and especially the states increased the amount of resources they allocated to financing social policy at an even greater rate.

• A wave of very important program innovation and sectoral reforms. Abundant experiences show that today in Venezuela reforms in health care, education, nutritional programs, and other areas are fueled largely by the states and municipalities. This wave of innovation includes not only the creation of new programs but also extends into the institutional arena, with the generation of new organizational models that reflect the search for better incentives to encourage new agents to provide social services. Social participation, the involvement of nongovernmental organizations, and the establishment of semi-independent public entities constitute a portion of these institutional innovations.

• A greater alignment of social policies with the characteristics and needs of the inhabitants of each jurisdiction, as ample anecdotal evidence illustrates and as the statistical analysis presented in the previous section suggests. Thus, in spite of the general tendency to assign greater importance to social spending and within it to specific sectors, and in spite of the consequences of certain broad tendencies in social policymaking that were identified in this chapter, both the priorities assigned to different social sectors and the substance of program and institutional innovations and reforms introduced by different state and municipal governments are very diverse. This, in turn, has resulted in experimentation, emulation of successes, and competition between jurisdictions on an unprecedented level in Venezuela. One of the most important predictions made by the advocates of decentralization, namely, that innovation would flourish, has been borne out: Mérida and Bolívar have provided educational reform models to other states, Lara and Carabobo have done the same with their health care reforms, and Aragua has received international recognition for its nutritional programs. The failures, which have also occurred, speak eloquently—and people are listening—of the considerable human, political, and cultural limitations faced by these pioneering efforts to improve social policy in Venezuela.

At this point it should be remembered that changes in social policy resulting from decentralization take place in the context of the very precarious institutional framework of the central government for practically all social sectors. The regulatory and supervisory capabilities of both the Ministry of Education and the Ministry of

Health have been extremely weakened by years of excessive central-ization, distorting partisan intervention in policy and personnel deci-sions, and by the growth of labor unions, which have gained effective control of decisionmaking in the provision of services far beyond their natural role of protecting workers. The Ministry for the Family, in spite of considerable program innovation first introduced in 1989 and its cooperation with nongovernmental organizations, has not been able to develop the basic requirements for administering a modern network of social benefits, which must be based on up-to-date infor-mation about social conditions and on precise targeting. The collapse of the social security system by itself has transformed Venezuela into a country with a low percentage of GDP allocated to social spending.

Accordingly, sectoral reforms initiated from below, due to the ac-tivism of governors and mayors, are not a part of the general na-tional policy outline for these sectors—with a rare and recent excep-tion—but rather exist in a legal vacuum. There is little indication as to what the guidelines will be for the development of health care, ed-ucation, social security, or poverty alleviation in the medium and long term, and the central ministries are for the most part unable to provide direction.

This institutional weakness in the central government simultane-ously creates great opportunities and major risks for state and mu-nicipal social policy initiatives. Opportunities arise from the freedom to create, innovate, and resolve problems in new ways, in accordance with the circumstances and the location of each case; this provides opportunities for efficiency and radical innovation. Risks arise be-cause this creativity most often occurs without the required technical support and without information systems or common denominators to facilitate evaluation of the decentralization process. An evaluation of this sort could reduce the risk of incompatible models or of un-desirable side effects such as an increase in inequalities among mu-nicipalities. Venezuela has benefited from taking risks; however, in the medium term, the decentralization agenda must include ade-quate institutional strengthening of central government bodies.

Institutional strengthening is also a pending task for states and municipalities. Although the common complaint of scarce resources clearly brings to mind the shadow of the fiscal imbalances that are the weakest component of decentralization in Venezuela, one could ask why the scarcity of qualified human resources in the social sector is not the most common and loudest complaint, given the obvious lim-itations each subnational government faces in this area. The informa-tion gathered allows us to conclude that, to a certain degree, munici-palities and states have taken initial steps toward the professional handling of social policy—creating specialized social policy agencies where they did not exist or making initial efforts to attract capable personnel to run social sectors. Yet they still do not see the problem of institutional and human weaknesses as critical. Undoubtedly, work remains to be done by both the subnational governments themselves, by technical assistance associations, and by academic institutions that provide specialized training in public and social administration. The next steps in the process of decentralizing social policy will depend greatly on the improvement of technical and institutional capabilities.

Musgrave, in his classic work on the distribution of responsibilities among different levels of government, assigned distributive policies to the central government in order to avoid different levels of generosity or efficiency between adjoining jurisdictions.[26] Such inequalities could produce unwanted migration by the poor in search of greater governmental subsidies or by the relatively wealthy in large numbers to avoid the financial burden of supporting redistributive programs. More recently, however, it has been argued that in the area of social-assistance and poverty alleviation programs, the need for decentralized entities to play an important role has to be emphasized because of their advantages in adapting to the local situation, in accountability and follow-up procedures, and in promoting constituent participation. Moreover, it has been known for a long time that there are advantages to assigning important responsibilities in sectors such as health care and education to decentralized bodies, due to diseconomies of scale and the almost insurmountable problems associated with highly centralized information systems. Everything that has been said regarding the spontaneous evolution of social policies by municipal governments in Venezuela is in line with these principles. As the process matures and becomes consolidated, a considerable contribution will be made to social-sector reform in Venezuela by drastically changing the level of government where social policy decisions are made as well as increasing citizen access and participation in policymaking. There will also be a direct contribution to efficiency in the social sectors and to their democratic legitimacy.

Once again, decentralization is not a panacea for social policy. Whatever the situation, a decentralized social policy depends upon a central government that is capable of carrying out its essential responsibilities of directing and guaranteeing equity and relevancy among the decentralized policies. In terms of which model of service provision will prevail in each of the social sectors, the emphasis must not be on decentralization per se, but rather on defining the most effective roles for each of the actors involved in social policy, and on correctly fine-tuning incentives. Developments like the creation of FIDES,[27] an institution devoted precisely to strengthening decentralization, as well as preliminary attempts by the Ministry of the Family to improve coordination among municipalities, states, and the central government in the execution of poverty alleviation programs, strongly support the need for coordination between the different levels of government. Likewise, such developments open up possibilities for improving the profile of each level in social policy. If no advances are made in this area, the natural impulse behind decentralization will still probably bring about greater efficiency in the provision of social services. However, it could be unnecessarily costly in terms of equality between jurisdictions, because the central government would not fulfill its irreplaceable role in inter-regional compensation and in defining national social policy.

These caveats notwithstanding, decentralization in Venezuela has stimulated reform in the social sector and the involvement of catalysts, new voices, and groups of people expressly interested in changing and improving social policy, whether they are mayors, governors, nongovernmental organizations, community organizations, business leaders, or simply citizens. Therefore, the contribution of decentralization to social policy reform is singularly important. The definitive or optimal organizational model of a specific social service, such as health care or education, may or may not be decentralized, but when the starting point is excessive centralization, a vigorous decentralization process such as the one Venezuela has experienced during the last ten years can be an excellent instrument for change. It creates opportunities where institutional rigidity had produced inefficiency and inequality, and it brings about innovation and new stakeholders where organized interest groups in the central government had stifled change. Finally, it sends signals to the public that things can be different and furthers the idea that reform of social services is not impossible.

Appendix

Table 9.2 **Determinants of Municipal Per Capita Social Expenditures (1994) Results of Regression Analysis**

Variable		Coefficient	Std. Error	t Prob.
C	166.3968	349.9048	0.475549	0.6376
Votmediano	921.1075	328.2827	2.805836	0.0085
RecursosPC	0.199777	0.063205	3.160753	0.0034
Rural (dummy)	−666.8181	308.0807	−2.164427	0.0380
Population	0.004509	0.001368	3.295514	0.0024
Poor	−0.021772	0.007477	−2.911932	0.0065
R-squared	0.555952		Median v.d.	1287.544
R-sq. (adjusted)	0.486569		Dev. v.d.	1109.053
Std. Error	794.6819		Akaike inf.	13.49982
Sum of squares	20208618		Schwartz crit.	13.75839
Log likelihood	−304.4163		F	8.012842
Durbin-Watson	1.957740		Prob(F)	0.000055

Table 9.3 **Determinants of the Relative Weight of Municipal Social Expenditures (1994) Results of Regression Analysis**

Variable		Coefficient	Std. Error	t Prob.
C	0.345862	0.078237	4.420693	0.0001
Votmediano	0.121909	0.073403	1.660831	0.1065
Population	7.03E-07	3.06E-07	2.296114	0.0284
Poor	−3.14E-06	1.67E-06	−1.875733	0.0698
RecursosPC	−2.03E-05	1.41E-05	−1.437932	0.1602
Rural (dummy)	−0.080255	0.068885	−1.165053	0.2526
R-squared	0.225718		Median v.d.	0.300337
R-sq. (adjusted)	0.104736		Dev. v.d.	0.187794
Std. Error	0.177687		Akaike inf.	−3.311521
Sum of squares	1.010328		Schwartz crit.	−3.052955
Log likelihood	14.99924		F	1.865720
Durbin-Watson	2.058789		Prob(F)	0.128182

Notes

At the time the author was conducting research for this chapter, he was a professor at the Institute of Advanced Management Studies (IESA) in Caracas. Currently, he is the senior specialist in Social Development and Education at the Inter-American Development Bank in Washington, D.C. The opinions put forth in this chapter should not be attributed to either of these two institutions and are the sole responsibility of the author.

1. This chapter is based primarily on the article "Decentralization, Social Spending and Social Policy in Venezuela," in *Descentralización en Perspectiva*, R. De la Cruz, ed. (Caracas: Ediciones IESA, 1998) and was presented at the November 1997 conference, "The Politics and Administration of Social Policies," sponsored by the Woodrow Wilson Center and the Institute of Advanced Management Studies (IESA) in Caracas, Venezuela. *Descentralización* provides abundant details on the characteristics of the decentralization process in Venezuela.

2. Moisés Naím, "Latin America's Journey to the Market: From Macroeconomic Shock to Institutional Therapy," International Center for Economic Growth, Occasional Paper no. 62 (San Francisco: ICS Press, 1995).

3. G. Márquez, "Venezuela: Poverty and Social Policies in the 1980s," in N. Lustig, ed., *Coping with Austerity: Poverty and Inequality in Latin America* (Washington, D.C.: Brookings Institution, 1995).

4. S. Morley, "Poverty and Adjustment in Venezuela," Working Paper Series no. 156 (Washington, D.C.: Inter-American Development Bank, 1992).

5. Márquez, "Venezuela."

6. S. Paul, *Accountability in Public Services: Exit, Voice, and Capture* (Washington, D.C.: World Bank, 1991).

7. Pérez and Caldera were known for holding opposing views on how the state should conduct itself in almost all areas, including economic and social policies. Yet, after some hesitation, the Caldera administration decided to continue with the innovations introduced by Pérez in antipoverty policies.

8. These political circumstances were a confluence of a highly reform-oriented administration that adopted swift economic-policy reforms and strong pressure to produce responses in the social-policy arena created by the serious riots and civil unrest that shook the country just a few days after the inauguration of the administration in February of 1989. Thus, the political pressure to do something in social policy and the technocratic and modernizing leadership combined to produce social policy innovation in antipoverty programs.

9. IDB/UNDP (United Nations Development Programme). *Social Reform and Poverty: Toward a Comprehensive Agenda for Development* (Washington, D.C. and New York: IDB/UNDP, 1993); Alan Angell and Carol Graham, "Can Social Sector Reform Make Adjustment Sustainable and Equitable? Lessons from Chile and Venezuela," *Journal of Latin American Studies*, 27, Part 1, 1995.

10. J. C. Navarro, "Reforming Social Policy in Venezuela: Implementing Targeted Programs in the Context of a Traditional Pattern of Public Intervention" (Washington, D.C.: Inter-American Development Bank, 1994, mimeograph).

11. J. C. Navarro, ed., *Las Organizaciones de Participación Comunitaria y la Prestación de Servicios Sociales a los Pobres en América Latina* (Washington, D.C.: Institute of Advanced Management Studies–Inter-American Development Bank, 1994).

12. R. de la Cruz, ed., *Ruta a la Eficiencia: Descentralización de los Servicios Sociales* (Caracas: Ediciones IESA, 1995).

13. De la Cruz, *Descentralización en Perspectiva*. The information covered all of the Venezuelan states and a random sample of sixty-six of a total of 282 municipalities that existed in December 1995.

14. This is illustrated by a decline in the number of primary-school students registered in municipal schools during the 1970s and 1980s. R. Casanova, M. Jaén, J. C. Navarro, and J. Corredor, *La Distribución del Poder: Decentralización de la Educación, la Salud y las Fronteras* (Caracas: COPRE/UNDP, Ed. Nueva Sociedad, 1992).

15. Casanova et al., *La Distribución del Poder; Venezuela Poverty Study: From Generalized Subsidies to Targeted Programs* (Washington, D.C.: World Bank, 1991); and *Venezuela 2000: Education for Growth and Social Equity* (Washington, D.C.: World Bank, 1993).

16. This includes, for the purposes of this chapter and unless expressly indicated otherwise, expenditures on health care, education, culture, and programs directed at vulnerable groups such as children, mothers, the unemployed, adolescents not in school, and senior citizens, for both municipalities and states. With respect to the states, expenditures on housing have also been included. Some adjustments have been made to the reported figures to reflect the fact that a certain share of the resources dedicated to social programs appears under nonsocial expenditure categories.

17. De la Cruz, 1995.

18. We define fiscal imbalance as a lack of correspondence between expenditures and the ability to collect taxes in a decentralized public finance system. E. Wiesner, "Fiscal Decentralization and Social Spending in Latin America: The Search for Efficiency and Equity," Working Paper Series 199 (Washington, D.C.: Inter-American Development Bank, 1994). In Venezuela, after almost a decade of political and administrative decentralization, the states, having almost no powers to collect taxes, continue to depend upon income transfers from the central government for up to 90 percent of their social budget. The situation is less severe for the municipalities because they collect municipal taxes that, particularly in the more highly populated areas, provide them with at least one independent source of income. At both levels, however, the vast majority of fund transfers from the central government are in the form of nonconditional en bloc transfers, stipulated only as a percentage of the central-government budget. This explains why the distribution of the budget among sectors and programs remains in the hands of state and local authorities and therefore can be used, as it is in this chapter, as an indication of priorities.

19. In addition to scarce financial resources, other significant obstacles to achieving an efficient decentralized social policy were detected: a lack of qualified personnel to manage the new social programs, very limited technical assistance from the central government or other sources, etc.

20. T. Campbell, G. Peterson, and José Brakarz, *Decentralization to Local Government in LAC: National Strategies and Local Response in Planning, Spending, and Management* (Washington D.C.: World Bank, 1991).

21. For a recent case see J. C. Navarro and R. de la Cruz, "La Organización Industrial de Servicios de Educación en Venezuela," Working Papers, Research Centers Network (Washington, D.C.: Inter-American Development Bank, 1997), which offers a comparison of national, state, and private schools in the state of Mérida. Although the results of this study are merely an initial approximation and must be evaluated with caution, they do point to a superiority among state schools that were reformed within the Integral Schools program. Furthermore, even though they are slightly more costly—in terms of recurrent costs per student—than their counterparts run by the

Ministry of Education, they are much more effective in retaining students and reducing drop-out rates and display some advantages in student performance. Private schools in the Fe y Alegría network, in turn, are the most cost-effective of the three types of schools included in the study. See also R. de la Cruz, ed., *Ruta a la Eficiencia.*

22. *"Situado"* refers to *"situado constitucional,"* the legal term used in Venezuela to refer to a constitutionally mandated, unconditioned block transfer from the central government to the states and municpalities. This constitutes a percentage of the central government budget. It is by far the main source of funds for the states, and less so in the case of municipalities.

23. W. Oates, *The Political Economy of Fiscal Federalism* (Lexington: Lexington Books, 1993).

24. De la Cruz, *Ruta a la Eficiencia;* P. Lowden, "The Escuelas Integrales Reform Program in Venezuela," in A. Silva, ed., *Implementing Policy Innovations in Latin America: Politics, Economics and Techniques* (Washington, D.C.: Social Agenda Policy Group, Inter-American Development Bank, 1996).

25. The analysis was conducted with the information available from a sample of thirty-eight municipalities during 1994, the only ones for which a complete data set existed containing the required variables. A simultaneous analysis of state social expenditures was impossible due to an insufficient number of cases in the sample study.

26. Musgrave, *The Theory of Public Finance* (New York: McGraw Hill, 1959).

27. FIDES (Intergovernmental Fund for Decentralization) is an intergovernmental agency—that is, under the combined control of the central and subnational governments—designed to finance programs for administrative development, institutional strengthening, and investment activities by state and municipal governments.

10

The Social Agenda in Argentina: A Review of Retirement and Employment Policies

Laura Golbert

Unemployment, insecure employment, and the loss of social safeguards are problems that a majority of Western nations are facing at the beginning of the twenty-first century. The forecast is not encouraging: there is a strong consensus among specialists in the field that this situation will not be reversed in one day, but rather, requires a long and complicated process over several years. While some maintain that sustained economic growth is sufficient to produce this change, others observe that economic expansion can occur without creating the jobs needed to absorb, at least in the short and medium term, the whole of the population seeking work. For them, the information revolution and globalization are paving the way for a new type of society in the industrialized world in which traditional employment will disappear completely.[1] For example, Castel states that job instability and unemployment are a given in the current dynamics of modernization. They are the unavoidable consequence of the new modes of employment organization, which produce a deficit of available places in the social structure, if we understand a "place" as a position with a social use and public recognition.[2]

The existence of job insecurity and unemployment calls into question the entire institutional framework that has been constructed over the course of the past century and has culminated in the creation of the welfare states. It was this social framework that helped overcome worker vulnerability brought about by the industrial revolution. Free workers, recognized as those that generate social wealth, lived in misery with jobs that are today considered precarious, without any guarantees for the future.

A document written at the start of the industrial revolution accurately depicted the situation: "These increasingly pressured groups of workers do not have even the security of maintaining a job. The

227

industry that has attracted them only summons them when it needs them and when it can ignore them, abandons them without the slightest concern."[3] Nevertheless, and for different reasons, concern grew among the different political sectors. Conservatives feared for social order, liberals believed that material needs turned individual liberties into bare formalities, and socialists advocated greater social equality. When the notion spread that the market was not sufficient and that state intervention was needed, a series of measures, designed to protect the worker and thereby ensure social cohesion, began to be implemented.

Today, transformations in the labor market are generating problems similar to those the politicians and intellectuals attempted to resolve during the middle and end of the nineteenth century, which became known as the "social question." The legal and institutional architecture that protected workers through unemployment security, social security, or assistance in case of illness, is being seriously questioned as employment turns into a scarce commodity and labor relations weaken.

In spite of the fact that many countries are currently facing problems in the labor market, the causes are not necessarily the same and the strategies chosen to combat these problems are different. Some try to maintain previous levels of protection while other strategies are aimed more toward "market solutions" in the belief that, in the long run, they will efficiently resolve labor market problems.

Without a doubt, the individual characteristics of the labor market as well as the institutional legacy of each country play a significant role in determining which strategies are pursued. The orientation of these policies is also influenced by the interests of the parties involved in the decisionmaking process. The choice of one or another path has repercussions not only on people's welfare, but also on class structure and varying social orders.[4] For example, government assistance that is given to someone who is temporarily unemployed yet maintains his or her identity as a worker is different from aid for someone who is considered needy. In this instance, the recipient is being assigned a different place in the social structure.

This chapter addresses the Argentine case. In the 1990s, at the moment that Argentina opened its economy, announced the convertibility of its currency, and sought fiscal balance, unemployment climbed to levels never before seen in the history of the country. However, while there has been a surprising and dramatic increase in the unemployment rate over the past few years, problems have existed in the labor market for more than two decades as indicated by the rise in self-employment and the various ways work has shifted to the informal sector.

This process, which is accompanied by an increasing polarization between the highest and lowest income brackets and a growing deterioration of the quality of benefits offered by the various social services, was a driving force behind the transformation of a society that in the 1950s distinguished itself from the rest of the countries of Latin America by its mechanisms for social, economic, and political inclusion. Today, not only is there a more pronounced concentration of incomes, but there are also pronounced differences in access to and the quality of social services offered, exacerbating social divisions.

In the area of public policies, employment issues raise a series of questions. On one hand, macroeconomic decisions must be made regarding the best strategies for generating new jobs. On the other hand, in the specific field of designing social policies to protect the population, an array of problems exist, such as lack of resources, the orientation and administration of programs, and the political viability of their implementation.

From a perspective of social protection, this chapter will analyze some of the initiatives taken by the government of Carlos Saúl Menem (1989–1999) in two areas that are key in providing incomes and that have a direct impact on the living conditions of the population: work and retirement benefits. In order to set up the institutional framework under which these reforms were conducted, the following section will provide a brief history of the development of social policies in Argentina.

Brief History of Social Policies

In analyzing the development of social policies in Argentina, two facts stand out in comparison with other Latin American countries: the early development of social security and the role played by unions.

At the beginning of the twentieth century, the first retirement funds appeared. These benefited workers who occupied a strategic location in the production chain or in public administration. It was also at this time that mutual-support associations began to appear, created by immigrants and their descendants or by unions with the purpose of caring for their members. These were joined by neighborhood first-aid associations designed to provide health coverage to their members. This is how a health system was shaped in which public hospitals—both municipal and national—were oriented toward attending to the poorest sector, while foreigners and the higher income sectors were able to receive better care, whether in the community hospitals or in an emerging private sector.[5]

During the 1940s, all occupational groups jointly achieved retirement benefits. This coverage was provided by institutions managed and maintained by workers and businesspeople. At this time, then-president Juan Domingo Perón, ignoring the proposal by the Minister of Health Ramón Carrillo to strengthen public hospitals, decided to support the expansion of union-related social-welfare programs (*obras sociales*).[6] Although these *obras sociales*, whose origins date back to the mutual-support associations, primarily were aimed at giving vital medical assistance to workers and their families, they also provided other benefits such as vacation homes, sporting facilities, association stores, and so forth.

The central role given to the unions corresponded to the labor relations structure that was formed during the Perón government. An outstanding characteristic of this government was strong state intervention in the selection of which trade unions would participate in collective negotiation processes and in the resolution of conflicts. However, its most prominent role vis-à-vis the unions was that it determined which unions—only one in each area—could participate in collective bargaining.[7]

In 1957 the Family Allowances Fund for Employees of Trade and Industry was created as a private institution. In 1963 the institutional framework for the Family Allowances Program was completed with the creation of the Fund for Stevedores.[8] Under this type of social security system, the central role of the unions was maintained during the military governments. In fact, even though in 1967 the Argentine Revolution government (1966–1973) decided to convert the pension system into a state-run system by reorganizing its administration with the objective, among others, of eliminating a union presence in the administration of the funds, this same government took other measures that strengthened the unions. In 1970, the Obras Sociales Law 18610 was passed, establishing obligatory contributions by employers and workers to their respective unions, even if they were not members of the union, hence strengthening the union's position.[9]

The ratification of this law, which institutionalized *obras sociales* by incorporating them into the health care system, caused greater stratification of demand as compared with the traditional model. In the latter, both the public and private sector had been important. The law also strengthened the negotiating ability of the unions with regard to the financing and payment of medical services.[10] In fact, the large amount of resources transferred to the unions by way of this law turned them into active protagonists, granting them a strategic role in the decisionmaking process regarding health issues irrespective of the number of their actual members.

In 1971 the National Institute for Retirees and Pensioners was created,[11] aimed at providing medical services to retirees, pensioners, and primary family members from the National Pension System. The following year the National Housing Fund was created, with the goal of financing multifamily housing, infrastructure, and community facilities for low-income sectors. It was financed essentially by contributions.

This is how the social security system appeared when it was completed in the mid-1970s. Although the military government that assumed power in March 1976 took control of union welfare programs and suspended laws allowing professional associations, collective bargaining, and *obras sociales,* it did not alter the system's inherent design. With the return to democracy, these laws were reinstated.

Nevertheless, financial difficulties quickly began to emerge as a result of persistent inflation, problems in the labor market, and the growth of the informal sector. Additional problems arose within the pension system. The aging of the population and the need to expand coverage caused a rise in expenditures at the same time that the surplus generated by the system during the 1950s dried up.[12] Under these circumstances it was impossible to comply with the level of payments stipulated by law. Payments fluctuated between 70 and 82 percent.

When democracy was reinstated, the state's inability to fulfill its legal obligations provoked protests by retirees. Many of them opted to file suit against the fund. The government responded by issuing a temporary emergency decree that recalculated payments at a lower rate and created a temporary financing facility for a period of five years to cover a pension system debt that was equivalent to 1.8 percent of the GDP. It also attempted to improve the financial situation by collecting taxes specifically for use by the retirement system.[13] When Menem assumed the presidency under these circumstances in 1989, it was obvious to everyone that the financial difficulties of the system had made reform necessary.

To summarize, in spite of the political instability—alternating between military and democratic regimes—and the financial difficulties that emerged almost immediately upon the completion of the system, the social security model designed in the 1940s and 1950s has been maintained. The quality of services severely deteriorated in the 1980s, aggravated by macroeconomic instability that made the introduction of palliative measures difficult. Financial restrictions hindered covering the start-up costs normally associated with restructuring.[14]

Reforms in the 1990s

In analyzing the reforms implemented by the Menem government, the role of the unions cannot be ignored: Many of the modifications made to the original proposal put forth by the executive branch were the result of negotiations with the trade unions. In other countries a rise in unemployment and a fall in membership weakened the unions' ability to negotiate. In Argentina, on the other hand, the leading unions, at least those with more political and/or economic pull, continued to be key actors in public-policy formation. In addition, their political affinity with the governing party had increased their influence. Therefore, when the reform process was initiated, at times the government found itself forced to negotiate with the unions, while at other times the government sought their participation.[15]

Pension System

The initial government proposal included two innovations: privatization of the system and transformation from a shared (pay-as-you-go) system to one of individual capital formation.

The government's project established that the retirement benefit would be composed of a *prestación básica universal* (PBU) or universal basic payment paid by the state and an additional payment from the capital accumulated in each beneficiary's individual retirement account. The PBU included a fixed amount for all beneficiaries who were able to prove thirty years of contributions to the pension system, to be financed by employer contributions and taxes. All workers under forty-five years of age, even those who were self-employed, would be obligated to join the individual account system financed by member contributions. Anyone over the age of forty-five who voluntarily chose to do so could also join the system. For both the public and private systems, the retirement age for both men and women was raised to sixty-five years.

This project was discussed extensively in Parliament. At the time that it was presented for consideration, it was not thought that the economic program would face difficulties, because low inflation rates and strong capital inflows were encouraging consumption. As the Argentine economy appeared to be doing well, the projects introduced by the executive branch to Parliament were not urgent nor was there a perception of being on the edge of a catastrophe as when the economic emergency laws were being discussed.[16]

When the project was presented to Parliament, the Radicals, the main opposition party, as well as deputies with links to the unions and some from the Justicialista Party, objected. The project caused a serious debate: What was being proposed was a change in the philosophical base of the system. On the one hand, it would change it from a system of payments based on intergenerational solidarity to one that emphasized individual accounts. On the other hand, it would be administered by private insurance companies, the AFJP (Administradora de los Fondos de Jubilaciones y Pensiones—Retirement and Pension Fund Administrators). Moreover, the issue of the debt, of concern to the retiree organizations, was left pending.

While this debate was being conducted, some unions became involved in the AFJP's business. Some studies suggest that this weakened the opposition camp and allowed the passage of the law.[17] Even though this analysis could be said to be correct, the following must also be taken into consideration. During the debate and as a result of the intervention of deputies from different political and union backgrounds, modifications were introduced that, from the perspective of the beneficiaries, improved the initial project.

One such modification was the elimination of the clause that stipulated that those under forty-five years of age are obligated to join the individual account system: it permitted all to equally opt for one or the other alternative. Another was the recognition of contributions made before the pension system changed (compensatory benefits). That is, when the law was finally approved, four types of benefits were defined: the universal basic (PBU), the compensatory (PC), the "permanence" benefit for those who chose the public system, and the payments from individual accounts. With the exception of the last type, the amount is determined by law. This is surprising given that one of the reasons for the reform was to do away with the contradiction of the previous pension system, which, although considered to be a shared (pay-as-you-go) system, stipulated the benefit amount as a percentage of the worker's salary.[18] Worse still, calculations show that the amount determined by the law is even higher than what the system was paying out prior to the reform.[19]

Due to these changes, the pension reform was increasingly burdensome for the public coffers. A 1994 decision to reduce employer contributions further exacerbated the problem. Thus, in 1995 the government, concerned with imbalances in the sector, pushed forward a new law called the Retirement Solidarity Law.

In accordance with this law, the state no longer guarantees payments made by the new pension system. The payments depend solely upon funds coming from the resources established by the law and those determined by the budget for each year. A debate has arisen on whether there should be a "funds availability criteria." According to some experts,

> Financial imbalances in the system will require a reform in the pension system that ensures a balance between income and costs. Because a series of payments are required by law 24241, whose value at any given moment depends upon average worker contributions (AMPO) and on the former salaries of the retirees and not on the resources available within the system, the application of this article of the retirement solidarity law will generate significant legal claims.[20]

On the other hand, as part of retirement program policy, the government also pushed forward the transfer of provincial funds to the national system. Given that these funds are, in most cases, deficits, their inclusion in the system in effect raises the deficit.

This very short analysis of the pension system highlights some serious problems. First, difficulties with its financing put into doubt its ability, in the medium term, to comply with the law. Second, the reform did not lead to substantial changes in the situation of current retirees: Although the average pension payment has slightly increased over the past few years, it is currently less than half the value of the average salary. Third, as a result of transformations in the labor market, today only 63 percent of the economically active population (PEA) is affiliated with the system. Of these members, slightly more than half, 54 percent, contribute regularly to the system.[21] The numbers are even more dramatic when looking at the self-employed: In 1996 only 20 percent contributed regularly to the system. Thus, for many the problem is not the level of payments but rather not having access to retirement benefits at all.[22]

Therefore, the reform did not translate into an improvement in circumstances for the majority of current retirees. Nor does it bode well for those who currently have unsteady employment and/or have low incomes or salaries and will be unable to sustain their contribution obligations.

Policies Directed at the Labor Market

The labor policy implemented over the past years was based on research that identified high labor costs and the obstacles posed by rigid legislation on hiring practices as the primary causes of problems in the labor market.[23] The majority of Argentine businesspeople agreed with this analysis.

The Employment Law passed in 1991 was the first of a series of measures taken by the government in an attempt to alter the situation. The law instituted unemployment security, a first for the country.[24] However, the law also introduced different ways of allowing short-term hiring, an end to or reduction in compensation at the end of a specified time period, and the elimination of or a decrease in employer contributions. In order to implement these practices, they first had to be approved in a collective-bargaining process. The law created a national employment fund to finance these measures. The funds primarily came from a portion of the contributions that previously had been allocated for family allowances (equal to 1.5 percent of nominal income) and other wage taxes.[25]

In mid-1993, the national government signed the Federal Pact for Employment, Production, and Growth with the provincial governments. The executive branch agreed to reduce the taxes and pension contributions levied on employers that raise labor costs. This agreement was part of Decree 206/93 that ordered a decrease in employer contributions in the fields of primary production, industry, construction, tourism, and scientific and technological research.[26]

In 1994, in view of the rise in unemployment, the government proposed new measures designed to heighten labor flexibility, making it easier to fire employees. Although the unions threatened legal measures to stop the decree, they agreed to negotiate the issue in talks on labor reform proposed by the minister of labor, Caro Figueroa. This resulted in the signing of the Framework Agreement on Employment, Production, and Social Equality by union representatives, businesspeople, and the executive branch in mid-1994. This agreement included a series of reforms: a statute for small and medium enterprises, a bankruptcy law that annulled collective bargaining for affected companies, and an insurance system for work-related accidents administrated by work risk insurers (ART—Aseguradoras de Riesgo de Trabajo).

It was crucial that the government achieve some type of agreement with the principal actors. Unions could block government attempts to modify legislation, as they had done on other occasions.[27] Furthermore, the party in power was not willing to face off against the unions because they always had been aligned with the ranks of the Peronists. This is why negotiation and not confrontation was the chosen strategy. The unions were primarily interested in preserving resources for *obras sociales* and blocking debate on labor reform. As a result, the unions made concessions in the labor reform, and the government—through Decree 1829/94—allowed the unions to pay their pension debts over 120 installments, double that allowed employers. Furthermore, *obras sociales* were compensated for losses suffered as a consequence of the decline in employer contributions, over a period ranging from January to May of that year.[28]

Under the PYME (Small and Medium Enterprises) statute, small and medium businesses were exempted from the collective labor agreements and from the obligation to register contracts.[29] This law also introduced such changes as the ability to make bonus (*aguinaldo*) payments in installments, modification of the established norms on vacation time, and limitations on the amount of indemnity based on seniority.[30]

In 1995 the Law on Employment Promotion[31] introduced new contracting methods. Unlike those promoted by the Employment Law, these new methods set fewer demands since neither the registration nor the intervention of the collective labor agreements were required, thus facilitating the hiring of workers under a probationary period and/or apprentice period.[32]

The application of the two final norms has had an effect on the labor market. According to a survey of labor indices by the MTySS,[33] a comparison of data from December 1995 with that from October 1996 shows a 6 percent decrease in the number of workers with stable contracts or contracts for an indeterminate period, while the number of those hired on probation grew 286 percent and those with contracts for a fixed period rose 79 percent. This growth differential in flexible employment over steady employment has been recognized by the MTySS. In November 1996, it stated that, "The progressive substitution of workers with contracts for an indeterminate period by employees with flexible contracts or in 'apprentice periods' continues."[34] In fact, in October 1996, 56 percent of those who left their jobs had had steady contracts, while 64 percent of those being hired had flexible or apprentice contracts. This tendency continued the following year: The percentage of people hired under flexible terms rose from 7.8 percent of the total to 12.7 percent.[35]

There were three problems associated with the employment programs that were implemented: discontinuity, weak coverage, and limited resources.[36]

From the passage of the Employment Law until 1996, thirty programs (not including unemployment security) were initiated under the scope of the MTySS. During these four short years, many of the programs were canceled and others implemented. During 1996, within various jurisdictions of the national government, thirty-one employment and income improvement programs were in operation, of which twenty-three were under the realm of the MTySS. However, this large number of programs significantly contrasted with their diminished coverage: In 1996, benefits distributed on a monthly basis reached 3 percent of the unemployed.

With respect to unemployment security, even though the number of payments grew from year to year—at the beginning of the program in 1992, there were 12,808 monthly payments and in 1996 the number of people who received this benefit reached 143,525[37]—coverage remains very limited, reaching only 7 percent of all of those who are unemployed. This mirrors what is occurring with the employment promotion and training programs.

Today, the resources available to the fund are inadequate—it is calculated that spending on employment programs represents about 0.2 percent of the GDP[38]—to attend to the needs of the unemployed. In spite of the fact that in the past few years the amount spent has risen, this increase was extremely small compared with the growth in unemployment and has resulted in a fall in benefits for each unemployed person.[39] The consequence, of course, is a drop in per capita spending in 1996—533 million pesos were allocated to the program, which translates to less than one peso per day for each unemployed person.[40]

Regarding the employment programs, payments do not surpass $200 per month per person and the coverage period is less than six months. To this must be added another problem: Since this benefit is not considered salary, it prohibits beneficiaries, except in those programs that specifically offer some health coverage, from receiving goods and services from social security.

In conclusion, the strategy favored by the government—to promote employment by offering incentives to firms through labor flexibility or reductions in employer contributions—actually allowed a majority of the newly created employment positions to be essentially insecure.

Current Problems

The reforms introduced over this time period were not successful in decreasing uncertainty or the level of vulnerability among wide sectors of the population. Continuing problems in the labor market explain, to a large degree, this situation. Today the unemployment level remains at 14 percent and the informalization of the labor market continues to grow. The types of intervention chosen did not improve the situation. The new jobs created by the employment programs are of low quality and do not provide access to social services. The reform of the pension system, which requires one to be part of the labor market or to have sufficient income to make the appropriate contributions, excludes a large portion of the population from the system.

Currently, the Ministry of Labor and Social Security has proposed a labor reform supported by the CGT (General Confederation of Workers) that differs from the previous policy.[41] Furthermore, financial difficulties with the pension system suggest that it must be modified once again.[42] However, this discussion is linked to the defense of private interests that has little to do with improving the welfare of those who remain on the margin. Businesses continue to defend flexibility, and unions try to preserve their power bases.

Under these circumstances, it is not easy to design a proposal that emphasizes protection of the most vulnerable. A consensus must be reached, priorities fixed, resources guaranteed, and the appropriate tools chosen to achieve the proposed objectives.

Without a doubt, most people who are involved agree that something must be done to help the most needy. Determining the amount of resources that must be invested becomes a more controversial issue. Differences mount when the type of social protection needed for improving the welfare of those on the margin is discussed. This is not a minor issue. Social policies can generate a less unequal and more cohesive society, or they can merely help the most vulnerable survive by accepting, and in fact deepening, existing societal inequalities and exclusion. Therefore, if state assistance is provided to a person because he or she is temporarily unemployed, his or her identity as a worker is maintained. If, on the other hand, that person is provided assistance as a needy individual, he or she is being assigned another place in the social structure. With growing difficulties in finding long-term employment, being helped by programs designed to help the "poor" puts the unemployed in a situation of extreme vulnerability. Their survival depends on an assistance program, but access to and continued use of such a program can slip from their hands, and the program does not guarantee their future inclusion in the labor force.

Midway through the twentieth century, with a full-employment economy, a consensus was built that allowed the social and political inclusion of workers. Without a doubt, the unions worked hard for its success. Today, with changed labor conditions, the unions do not enjoy the same power base that they did in the past. Those who remain on the margin do not have appropriate channels of expression nor the organizational capability to fight for their inclusion in the system. Political vulnerability is added to economic problems. Political parties, nongovernmental organizations, unions, and businesses must promote a consensus that favors the inclusion of those who do take part in the decisionmaking process.

Notes

This chapter is based on a paper presented at a May 7–8, 1998, Buenos Aires seminar organized by the Woodrow Wilson Center, Argentina's Ministry of Social Development, and the Centro de Estudios para el Cambio Estructural (CECE), "The Politics and Administration of Social Policies: Lessons from the Argentine Experience."

1. Andrés Gorz, "Salir de la Sociedad Salarial," *Debates* (Valencia, Spain: December 1994).

2. Robert Castel, *La Metamorfosis de la Cuestión Social: Una Crónica del Salariado* (Buenos Aires: Editorial Paidós, 1997).

3. Eugene Buret, "De la Misère des Classes Laborieuses en Angleterre et en France," (Paris: Paulin 1840). Cited in Castel, *La Metamor Fosis.*

4. See Gosta Esping Andersen, "The Three Political Economies of the Welfare State," in Jon Kolberg, ed., *The Study of the Welfare State Regimes* (Armonk, N.Y.: M.E. Sharpe, Inc., 1984).

5. See Jorge Katz and Alberto Muñoz, *Organización del Sector Salud: Puja Distributiva y Equidad* (Buenos Aires: Centro Editor de América Latina, 1988).

6. In Argentina, the social-welfare system is mostly the responsibility of the trade unions. The term *obras sociales* refers to social-welfare programs administered by unions.

7. Proper legal status was granted to a union by the state and only one union was allowed for each economic field: that which enjoyed the greatest number of dues-paying members and whose members made up no less than 20 percent of the workers that it was trying to represent. This law assured that the union would be the sole recipient of all labor rights for that field. See Adrián Goldín, *El Trabajo y los Mercados: Sobre las Relaciones Laborales en la Argentina* (Buenos Aires: EUDEBA, 1997).

8. Until the creation of these institutions, family allowances had been part of collective bargaining agreements.

9. Also included are primary family groups and those persons who live with a member and receive equal treatment as a family member.

10. According to the then minister of social welfare, Francisco Manrique, this law allowed the existence of a health care system made up of three subsectors: a private one for the wealthy, one for workers, and the public hospital for the poor.

11. On May 14, 1971, Law 19032 was passed—with implementing by-laws Decree no. 1157—which called for the creation of the National Institute of Social Works for Retirees and Pensioners. Up until this time, the majority of beneficiaries of the National Pension System, which included the entire non-union sector, did not have a right to medical services.

12. From 1950 to 1957 there was a surplus equal to 25 percent of the GDP resulting from the expansion of the system. The surplus then declined

substantially, and in 1962 there was a deficit for the first time. Deficits or extremely thin surpluses appeared during the following years. Beginning in 1978, the system started to exhibit increasingly significant imbalances. Jorge Feldman, Aldo Isuani, and Laura Golbert, *Maduración y Crisis del Sistema Previsional Argentino,* Argentine Political Library no. 236 (Buenos Aires: Centro Editor de América Latina, 1988).

13. Domestic taxes on fuel, gas, and telephone services tried to bring more resources into the system. In 1991, during the Menem government, VAT taxes of 11 percent and all taxes on personal goods not used in production were added. José Luis Machinea and Oscar Cetrángolo, "El Sistema Previsional Argentino: Crisis, Reforma y Transición," *Estudios del Trabajo,* no. 4. (Buenos Aires: ASET, second semester 1992).

14. Luis Beccaria and Ricardo Carcioffi, "Políticas Públicas en la Provisión y Financiamiento de los Servicios Sociales," Aberto Minujin, ed., *Desigualdad y Exclusión Social: Desafíos para la Política Social en la Argentina de fin de Siglo* (Buenos Aires: UNICEF/Losada, 1993).

15. Obviously the unions were not the only interlocutor: businesspeople and, in the case of the pension system, retiree organizations also played important roles. However, it is important to highlight the role of the unions because in Argentina they are quite different from their counterparts in other countries of the region.

16. Excerpted from Alejandro Rossi, "Reforma Previsional ¿Cómo y Por Qué?" (master's thesis in social sciences research, UBA, n.d.).

17. "The opposition was weakened when the AFJP negotiated with the unions and they became business partners. This presented great opportunities for some unions, given that they were part of the AFJPs or were negotiating the affiliation of their members with the administrators or offering life insurance to the retirement funds." Rossi, "Reforma Previsional." See also Victoria Murillo, "El Sindicalismo Argentino y las Reformas del Estado," *Desarrollo Económico,* no. 147 (October–December 1997).

18. This is why it was referred to as a hybrid system.

19. Oscar Cetrángolo, *El Nuevo Sistema Previsional: ¿Una Reforma Definitiva?* Serie de Notas no. 2 (Buenos Aires: CECE, August, 1994).

20. See Oscar Centrángolo, Mario Damill, Roberto Frenkel, and Juan Pablo Jiménez, *La Sostenibilidad de la Política Fiscal en América Latina: El Caso Argentino,* Serie de Documentos de Economía no. 6 (University of Palermo, CEDES, 1997).

21. In the shared system the numbers are even more dramatic: In 1997, regular contributions to this system represented only 62 percent of those made in 1994, while membership grew 30 percent. Ministry of Labor and Social Security (MTySS), *Panorama de la Seguridad Social* (first quarter, 1997).

22. In 1994, Law 24437 was passed allowing anyone over 70 years of age who had made contributions for 10 years to receive a basic pension.

23. This chapter will not analyze all of the modifications in labor relations, but rather only the new forms of hiring that emerged with the Employment Law.

24. There were two forerunners to unemployment security in Argentina: the Unemployment Fund for Industrial and Construction Workers and the unemployment subsidy implemented by the Alfonsín government. See Oscar Cetrángolo and Laura Golbert, *Desempleo en Argentina: Magnitud del Problema y Políticas Adoptadas,* Serie Estudios no. 8 (Buenos Aires: CECE, 1995).

25. Three percent of total wages paid by employers of occasional service workers, 0.05 percent of wages paid by employers, and another 0.05 percent of wages paid by employees. The law also called for other sources of income: state contributions (a portion of which is determined annually by the National Budget), provincial contributions, and, eventually, municipal contributions. The fund, however, can also receive other income in the form of donations, inheritances, subsidies, etc. See Cetrángolo and Golbert, *Desempleo en Argentina.*

26. The percentage of the reduction varied from 30 to 80 percent, according to the jurisdiction—more for more developed regions and less for zones with relatively less development—and was contingent upon the agreement of each jurisdiction to eliminate levies on gross incomes for the sector.

27. Unions dominated, at least until 1995, the Parliamentary Legislative Commission on Labor. See Sebastián Etchemendy and Vicente Palermo, "Conflicto y Concertación: Gobierno, Congreso y Organizaciones de Interés en la Reforma Laboral del Primer Gobierno de Menem (1989–1995)," *Desarrollo Económico,* no. 148 (IDES, January–March, 1998).

28. Etchemendy and Palermo, "Conflicto y Concertación."

29. Law 24467, approved 15 March 1995.

30. Cetrángolo and Golbert, *Desempleo en Argentina.*

31. This law was passed as number 24.465/95.

32. Also approved during this year was an integral reform of the work-related accident system, a new bankruptcy law, a mediation law to reduce labor litigation, and some reforms under the title of social works. The reform of the work-related accident system involved the approval of a system of compensation for work-related accidents or illnesses that moved away from litigation towards an insurance system. An employee makes a monthly payment to a Work Risk Administrator (ART) that is responsible for any eventual accident or illness.

33. The survey by the Ministry of Labor and Social Security (MTySS) is conducted on a monthly basis and includes data from 200 firms in the private sector.

34. MTySS, *Informe de Coyuntura: Mercado Laboral* (Buenos Aires, 1996).

35. MTySS, *Informe de Coyuntura: Mercado Laboral* (Buenos Aires, 1998).

36. For a more exhaustive analysis of this topic, see Laura Golbert, *La Protección al Desempleado: Una Cuestión Pendiente,* Serie de Estudios no. 18 (Buenos Aires: CECE, May 1997).

37. Taken from MTySS, *Boletín de Estadísticas Laborales* (first semester, 1996).

38. See Cetrángolo and Golbert, *Desempleo en Argentina.*

39. In 1993 the average payment was $369, and in 1996 it was $261. MTySS, *Boletín de Estadísticas Laborales.*

40. MTySS, *Panorama de la Seguridad Social* (first quarter, 1997).

41. Today the policy of the Ministry of Labor and Social Security has changed. The current Minister of Labor proposes, in agreement with the CGT, to end the concept of "promotion contracts" (contracts that allow for promotion after a certain probationary period), to improve indemnity for those who have been fired and maintain the so-called "ultra-activity," and to shorten the probation period to one month extendable up to 180 days but with indemnity and social benefits. Regarding apprentice contracts, the proposal calls for changing their duration from two years to one year, imposing

an indemnity for cancellation, and restricting its application to only 10 percent of employees. It maintains the monopoly on representation: the union with labor representatives is the only one authorized to sign agreements. This proposal is questioned by businesses that, among other things, want to maintain the concept of "promotion contracts," fix a lower indemnity for layoffs—a ceiling of six monthly salaries, regardless of the seniority of the worker—and give priority to individual firm negotiations over industry or field negotiations.

42. In agreement with information from the media, the proposal that is being discussed incorporates, among others, the following changes: elimination of the universal basic payment (PBU) for all those who retire in the future with a pension higher than 700 pesos; recognition of a decreasing benefit scale for contributions made to the pension system (compensatory payment); elimination of the current categories of self-employed who will pay an amount in line with their real income; and an increase in the retirement age for women from 60 to 65 years. *Clarín,* April 26, 1998.

Selected Bibliography

Abalos K., Jose Antonio. *Una Puerta que se Abre: Los Organismos no Guberna-mentales en la Cooperacion al Desarrollo.* Santiago: Taller de Cooperacion y Desarrollo, 1989.

Accioly, Claudio, and Forbes Davidson. "Density in Urban Development." *Building Issues* 8, no. 3. Lund University, Lund Centre for Habitat Studies, 1996.

Adrianzen, B., and G. Graham. "The High Costs of Being Poor." *Archives of Environmental Health* 28 (June 1974): 312–315.

Altimir, O. "La Dimensión de la Pobreza en América Latina." *Cuadernos de la CEPAL,* no. 27. Santiago: United Nations, 1979.

Alvarez, Sonia, Evelina Dagnino, and Arturo Escobar, eds. *Cultures of Politics: Politics of Cultures.* Boulder, Colo.: Westview Press, 1991.

Amsden, Alice. *Asia's Next Giant: South Korea and Late Industrialization.* New York: Oxford University Press, 1989.

Andersen, Gosta Esping. "The Three Political Economies of the Welfare State." In *The Study of the Welfare State Regimes,* edited by Jon Kolberg. Armonk, N.Y.: M.E. Sharpe, 1992.

———. *The Three Worlds of Welfare Capitalism.* Princeton, N.J.: Princeton University Press, 1990.

Andraus Troyano, Annez. *Programas de Empleo e Ingresos en América Latina y el Caribe.* Lima: Oficina Internacional del Trabajo, Oficina Regional para América Latina y el Caribe, 1998.

Angell, Alan, and Carol Graham. "Can Social Sector Reform Make Adjustment Sustainable and Equitable? Lessons from Chile and Venezuela." *Journal of Latin American Studies* 27, part 1 (1995).

Arellano, J. P. *Políticas Sociales y Desarrollo, Chile, 1924–1984.* Santiago: CIEPLAN, 1985.

Argyris, Chris and Donald Schon. *Organizational Learning: A Theory of Action Perspective.* Reading, Mass.: Addison-Wesley, 1978.

———. *Organizational Learning II: Theory, Method, and Practice.* Reading, Mass.: Addison-Wesley, 1996.

Arriagada, Genero, and Carol Graham. "Chile: Sustaining Adjustment During Democratic Transition." In *Voting for Reform: Democracy, Political Liberalization, and Economic Adjustment,* edited by Stephan Haggard and Steven B. Webb. New York: Oxford University Press/World Bank, 1994.

243

Arrighi, Giovanni. "Workers of the World at Century's End," *Review: Fernand Braudel Center* 19, no. 3 (1996).

Aslund, Anders, Peter Boone, and Simon Johnson. "Why Stabilize: Lessons from Post-Communist Countries." *Brookings Papers on Economic Activity* no. 1. Washington, D.C.: Brookings Institution, 1996.

Bates, Robert. *Markets and States in Tropical Africa.* Berkeley: University of California Press, 1981.

Bates, Robert, and Paul Collier. "The Politics and Economics of Policy Reform in Zambia." In *Political and Economic Interactions in Economic Policy Reform,* edited by Robert H. Bates and Anne O. Krueger. Cambridge, Mass.: Basil Blackwell, 1993.

Batley, R. "Urban Renewal and Expulsion in São Paulo." In *Urbanisation in Contemporary Latin America,* edited by A. Gilbert et al., 231–262. Chichester, Sussex: John Wiley, 1982.

Bebbington, Anthony, and Graham Thiele. *Nongovernmental Organizations and the State in Latin America: Rethinking Roles in Sustained Agricultural Development.* London: Routledge, 1993.

Beccaria, Luis, and Ricardo Carcioffi. "Políticas Públicas en la Provisión y Financiamiento de los Servicios Sociales." In *Desigualdad y Exclusión Social: Desafíos para la Política Social en la Argentina de Fin de Siglo,* edited by Alberto Minujin. Buenos Aires: UNICEF/Losada, 1993.

Beccaria, Luis, and Nestor Lopez, eds. *Sin Trabajo.* Buenos Aires: UNICEF/Losada, 1996.

Benabou, Roland, "Inequality and Growth." *NBER Macroeconomics Annual* (forthcoming).

Bengoa, J. "La Pobreza de los Modernos." *Temas Sociales Boletín.* Santiago: Centro de Estudios Sociales y Educación SUR, March 1995.

Benhabib, J., and M. Spiegel. "The Role of Human Capital in Economic Development: Evidence from Cross-National Aggregate Data." *Journal of Monetary Economics* (1994).

Benton, Laura. "Reshaping the Urban Core: The Politics of Housing in Authoritarian Uruguay." *Latin American Research Review* 21, no. 2: 33–52.

Bigio, Anthony, ed. *Social Funds and Reaching the Poor: Experiences and Future Directions.* Washington, D.C.: World Bank, 1998.

Birdsall, Nancy, Carol Graham, and Richard Sabot, eds. *Beyond Tradeoffs: Market Reforms and Equitable Growth in Latin America.* Washington, D.C.: Brookings Institution/Inter-American Development Bank, 1998.

Birdsall, Nancy, and Estelle James. "Efficiency and Equity in Social Spending: Why Governments Misbehave." Policy, Research, and External Affairs Working Paper, no. 274. Washington, D.C.: World Bank, May 1990.

Birdsall, Nancy, and Juan Luis Londoño. "Asset Inequality Does Matter." Paper presented at the American Economics Association Annual Meetings, New Orleans, 4–6 January 1997.

Birdsall, Nancy, David Ross, and Richard Sabot. "Inequality and Growth Reconsidered: Lessons from East Asia." *World Bank Economic Review* 9, no. 3 (1995).

Bitran, E., and R. E. Saez. "Mercado, Estado y Regulación." In *Construyendo Opciones. Propuestas Económicas y Sociales para el Cambio de Siglo,* edited by R. Cortázar and J. Vial. Santiago: Ediciones Dolmen–CIEPLAN, 1997.

Bradford, Colin A., ed. *Redefining the State in Latin America.* Paris: Organization for Economic Cooperation and Development, 1994.

Braithwaite, Jeanine. "The Old and New Poor in Russia." Poverty and Social Policy Department, World Bank, Washington, D.C.: January 1995. Mimeographed.

Bruno, Michael, Martin Ravallion, and Lyn Squire. "Equity and Growth in Developing Countries: Old and New Perspectives on the Policy Issues." Policy Research Working Paper no. 1563. Washington, D.C.: World Bank, January 1996.

Buret, Eugene. "De la Misère des Classes Laborieuses en Angleterre et en France, avec l'Indication des Mayens Propres en Affranchir les Societés." (Paris: Paulin, 1840).

Campero, G. *Entre la Sobrevivencia y la Acción Política.* Santiago: Instituto Latinoamericano de Estudios Transnacionales (ILET), 1987.

Cardoso Eliana, and Ann Helwege. *Latin America's Economy: Diversity, Trends, and Conflicts.* Cambridge, Mass.: MIT Press, 1992.

Cars, Goran. "Introduction: Comparisons and Counterparts." In *Neighborhood Regeneration, an International Evaluation,* edited by Rachel Alterman and Goran Cars. London: Mansell, 1991.

Casanova, R. M. Jaén, J. C. Navarro, and J. Corredor. *La Distribución del Poder: Descentralización de la Educación, la Salud y las Fronteras.* Caracas: COPRE/UNDP, Ed. Nueva Sociedad, 1992.

CASEN: Encuesta de Caracterización Socioeconómica Nacional. CASEN Survey, 1990, Ministerio de Planificación (MIDEPLAN).

Castañeda, T. *Combating Poverty: Innovative Social Reforms in Chile During the 1980s.* San Francisco: International Center for Economic Growth, ICS Press, 1992.

Castel, Robert. *La Metamorfosis de la Cuestión Social: Una Crónica del Salariado.* Buenos Aires: Editorial Paidós, 1997.

Celedon, C., and C. Oyarzo. "Los Desafíos en la Salud." In *Construyendo Opciones: Propuestas Económicas y Sociales para el Cambio de Siglo,* edited by R. Cortázar and J. Vial. Santiago: Ediciones Dolmen–CIEPLAN, 1998.

Centeno, Miguel Angel. *Democracy within Reason: Technocratic Revolution in Mexico.* University Park, Pa.: The Pennsylvania State University Press, 1994.

Centrángolo, Oscar. *El Nuevo Sistema Previsional: ¿Una Reforma Definitiva?* Serie de Notas no. 2. Buenos Aires: CECE, August 1994.

Centrángolo, Oscar, Mario Damill, Roberto Frenkel, and Juan Pablo Jiménez. *La Sostenibilidad de la Política Fiscal en América Latina: El Caso Argentino.* Serie de Documentos de Economía no. 6. University of Palermo, Cedes, 1997.

Centrángolo, Oscar, and Laura Golbert. *Desempleo en Argentina: Magnitud del Problema y Políticas Adoptadas.* Serie Estudios no. 8. Buenos Aires: CECE, 1995.

Comité Interministerial Social (CIS). "Programa Nacional de Superación de la Pobreza: Seguimiento y Evaluación." Santiago: CIS Executive Secretariat, October 1996.

Conaghan, Catherine, and James M. Malloy. *Unsettling Statecraft: Democracy and Neoliberalism in the Central Andes.* Pittsburgh, Pa.: University of Pittsburgh Press, 1994.

Consejo Nacional de Superación de la Pobreza (CNSP). *La Pobreza en Chile. Un Desafío de Equidad e Integración Social.* Santiago: CNSP, August 1996.

Contreras, Manuel. "Génesis, Formulación, Implementación y Avance de la Reforma Educativa en Bolivia." Paper prepared for a conference on governability and human development, La Paz, Bolivia, 13 February 1996.

Cornelius, Wayne A. *Politics and the Migrant Poor in Mexico City.* Stanford: Stanford University Press, 1975.

Cornelius, Wayne A., Ann L. Craig, and Jonathan Fox. *Transforming State-Society Relations in Mexico: The National Solidarity Strategy*. San Diego: Center for U.S.-Mexican Studies, University of California, 1994.

Cornia, Giovanni Andrea, Richard Jolly, and Francis Stewart. *Adjustment with a Human Face: Protecting the Vulnerable and Promoting Growth*. New York: Oxford University Press, 1987.

Corsetti, Giancarlo, and Klaus Schmidt-Hebbel. "Pension Reform and Growth." Policy Research Working Paper no. 1998. Washington, D.C.: World Bank, June 1995.

Cortázar, R. "Necesidades Básicas y Extrema Pobreza." *Investigaciones sobre Empleo* no. 5. Santiago: PREALC, 1977.

Cortázar, R. *Política Laboral en el Chile Democrático: Avances y Desafíos en los Noventa*. Santiago: Ediciones Dolmen, 1993.

Cortázar, R., and J. Vial, eds. *Construyendo Opciones: Propuestas Económicas y Sociales para el Cambio de Siglo*. Santiago: Ediciones Dolmen–CIEPLAN, 1998.

Costa, E. "An Assessment of the Flows and Benefits Generated by Public Investment in the Employment Guarantee Scheme of Maharashtra." Working Paper no. 12. Geneva: International Labour Organisation/World Employment Programme, 1978.

Cowan, Kevin, and José de Gregorio. "Distribución y Pobreza en Chile: Estamos Mal? Ha Habido Progreso? Hemos Retrocedido?" *Estudios Públicos* 64 (Spring 1996): 27–56.

Cox, C. "La Reforma de la Educación Chilena: Contexto, Contenidos, Implementación." Colección Estudios CIEPLAN 45. Santiago: CIEPLAN, June 1997.

Cox, C., and P. González. "Educación: De Programas de Mejoramiento a Reforma." In *Construyendo Opciones: Propuestas Económicas y Sociales para el Cambio de Siglo*, edited by R. Cortázar and J. Vial. Santiago: Ediciones Dolmen–CIEPLAN, 1998.

Crispi J., and M. Marcel. "Aspectos Cuantitativos de la Política Social en Chile 1987–1993." Working paper, Ministry of Finance, Santiago: August 1993.

Cross, John. *Informal Politics: Street Vendors and the State in Mexico City*. Stanford: Stanford University Press, 1998.

Csontos, László, János Kornai, and István György Tóth. "Tax-Awareness and the Reform of the Welfare State: Results of a Hungarian Survey." Discussion Paper no. 170. Cambridge, Mass.: Harvard Institute of Economic Research, January 1997.

"Czech Republic: Surprise," *The Economist*, 8 June 1996.

De Gregorio, J., and O. Landerretche. "Equidad, Distribución y Desarrollo Integrador." In *Construyendo Opciones: Propuestas Económicas y Sociales para el Cambio de Siglo*, edited by R. Cortázar and J. Vial. Santiago: Ediciones Dolmen–CIEPLAN, 1998.

De la Cruz, R., ed. *Ruta a la Eficiencia: Descentralización de los Servicios Sociales*. Caracas: Ediciones IESA, 1995.

———. *Descentralización en Perspectiva*. Caracas: Ediciones IESA, 1998.

De la Pena, Guillermo et al. *Crisis, Conflicto y Sobrevivencia: Estudios Sobre la Sociedad Urbana en México*. Guadalajara: Universidad de Guadalajara, CIESAS, 1990.

De la Pena, Guillermo, and de la Torre. "Irregularidad Urbana, Contradicciones Sociales, y Negociación Política en la Zona Metropolitana de

Guadalajara." In *La Urbanización Popular y el Orden Jurídico en América Latina*, edited by Luis Chirinos et al., 103–136. Mexico: Universidad Nacional Autónoma de México, 1993.

Demery, Lionel, and Lyn Squire. "Poverty in Africa: The Emerging Picture." World Bank, Washington, D.C., 1995.

Deolalikar, Anil B., and Raghav Gaiha. "What Determines Female Participation in Rural Public Works? The Case of India's Employment Guarantee Scheme." Seattle: University of Washington Institute for Economic Research, 1993.

Dietz, Henry. *Poverty and Problemsolving Under Military Rule: The Urban Poor in Lima, Peru*. Austin: University of Texas Press, 1980.

Dominguez, Jorge, ed. *Technopols: Freeing Politics and Markets in Latin America in the 1990s*. University Park, Pa.: Pennsylvania State University Press, 1997.

Dornbusch, Rudiger, and Sebastian Edwards. *The Macroeconomics of Populism in Latin America*. Chicago: University of Chicago Press, 1991.

Downs, C., and G. Solimano. *Del Macetero al Potrero, o, de lo Micro a lo Macro: El Aporte de la Sociedad Civil a las Políticas Sociales*. Santiago: Oficina de Area para Argentina, Chile y Uruguay, UNICEF, 1986.

Dresser, Denise. "Neopopulist Solutions to Neoliberal Problems: Mexico's National Solidarity Program, Transforming State-Society Relations in Mexico." In *Transforming State-Society Relations in Mexico*, edited by Wayne A. Cornelius, Ann L. Craig, and Jonathan Fox, eds., La Jolla: Center for U.S.-Mexican Studies, University of California, San Diego, 1994.

D'Silva, E. H. "Effectiveness of Rural Public Works in Labour-Surplus Economies: Case of the Maharashtra Employment Guarantee Scheme." Cornell International Agricultural Monograph no. 97. Ithaca: Cornell University, 1983.

Ducci, Maria Elena. "Análisis Crítico de la Vivienda en Chile." In *Metropóli, Globalidad y Modernización*, Vol 1, edited by Augusto Bolivar Espinoza, René Coulomb, and Carmen Múñoz Bohlken. Programa Reencuentro de Dos Ciudades México-Santiago de Chile. Mexico City: Universidad Autónoma Metropolitana, 1993.

———. "La Colonia Popular, una Manifestación del Problema de la Vivienda." Master's thesis, Universidad Nacional de México, 1978.

———. "Politícas de Vivienda y Mujer." *EURE* 20, no. 59 (March 1994): 73–91.

———. "Salud y Habitat: Capítulo Chile, Informe Final." Working paper, Urban Studies Institute, 1994.

———. "Salud Mental en Mujeres de la Periferia Pobre de Santiago de Chile." Working paper, Urban Studies Institute, 1995.

Ducci, María Elena, and M. Greene. "Evaluación de Consolidación Habitacional del Programa de Vivienda Progresiva, Modalida Privada, Primera Etapa." Chile: Ministry of Housing and Urban Development (MINVU), 1994.

Eckstein, Susan. *The Poverty of Revolution: The State and Urban Poor in Mexico*. Princeton, N.J.: Princeton University Press, 1977, 1988.

———. ed. *Power and Popular Protest: Latin American Social Movements*. Berkeley: University of California Press, 1989.

———. "Urbanization Revisited: Inner-City Slum of Hope and Squatter Settlement of Despair." *World Development* 18, no. 2 (February 1990): 165–182.

Economic Commission for Latin America and the Caribbean (ECLAC). *Panorama Social de América Latina 1996.* LC/G, 1946-P. Santiago: February 1997.

———. *La Pobreza en Chile in 1990.* Santiago: 1991.

———. *Una Estimación de la Magnitud de la Pobreza en Chile, 1987.* Santiago: ECLAC, 1990.

ECLAC-UNDP. "Procedimientos para Medir la Pobreza en América Latina con el Método de la Línea de Pobreza." *Comercio Exterior* 42, no. 4. Mexico: ECLAC, April 1992.

Escobar, Arturo, and Sonia E. Alvarez, eds. *The Making of Social Movements in Latin America: Identity, Strategy, and Democracy.* Boulder, Colo.: Westview Press, 1992.

Espínola, V. *Descentralización del Sistema Escolar en Chile.* Santiago: Centro de Investigaciones y Desarrollo de la Educación (CIDE), 1991.

Espínola, V. and others. "Evaluación de la Gestión Educacional en Educación en el Contexto de la Descentralización." Estudios Sociales no. 91, first quarter. Santiago: Corporación de Promoción Universitaria, 1997.

Etchemendy, Sebastián, and Vicente Palermo. "Conflicto y Concertación: Gobierno, Congreso y Organizaciones de Interés en la Reforma Laboral del Primer Gobierno de Menem (1989–1995)." *Desarrollo Económico,* no. 148 (IDES, January–March, 1998).

Evans, Peter. *Embedded Autonomy: States and Industrial Transformation.* Princeton, N.J.: Princeton University Press, 1995.

Feldman, Jorge, Aldo Isuani, and Laura Golbert. *Maduración y Crisis del Sistema Previsional Argentino.* Argentine Political Library no. 236. Buenos Aires: Centro Editor de América Latina, 1988.

Fernández, Viviana. *International Seminar: Sustainable Urban Housing Development.* Working paper. University of Chile, 1997.

Filgueira, Fernando. "Political Environments, Sector-Specific Configurations and Strategic Devices: Understanding Institutional Reform in Uruguay." Unpublished paper prepared for an Inter-American Development Bank project, "The Political Economy of Institutional Reform in Latin America," approx. March 1998.

Foweraker, Joe, and Ann L. Craig, eds. *Popular Movements and Political Change in Mexico.* Boulder, Colo.: Lynne Rienner, 1990.

Foxley, A., E. Aninat, and J. P. Arellano. *Las Desigualdades Económicas y la Acción del Estado.* Mexico: Fondo de Cultura Económica, 1980.

Friedmann, Santiago, Nora Lustig, and Arianna Legovini. "Mexico: Social Spending and Food Subsidies During Adjustment in the 1980s." In *Coping with Austerity,* edited by Nora Lustig. Washington, D.C.: Brookings Institution, 1995.

Gaiha, Raghav. "Do Anti-Poverty Programmes Reach the Rural Poor in India?" New Delhi: Faculty of Management Studies, University of Delhi, May 1998.

Garcia, A., and M. Schkolnik, "Superación de la Pobreza. Balance y Propuestas." In *Políticas Económicas y Sociales en el Chile Democrático,* edited by C. Pizarro, et al. Santiago: CIEPLAN–UNICEF, 1995.

Garreton, M. A. "New State-Society Relations in Latin America." In *Redefining the State in Latin America,* edited by C. I. Bradford. Paris: Organization for Economic Cooperation and Development (OECD), 1994.

Geddes, Barbara. "The Politics of Economic Liberalization." *Latin American Research Review* 30, no. 2 (1995).

Gershberg, Alec Ian. "Distributing Resources in the Education Sector: Solidarity's Escuela Digna Program." In *Transforming State-Society Relations in Mexico: The National Solidarity Strategy*, edited by Wayne A. Cornelius, Ann L. Craig, and Jonathan Fox. La Jolla: Center for U.S.-Mexican Studies, University of California, San Diego, 1994.

Gilbert, A., and P. Ward. *Housing, the State, and the Poor: Policy and Practice in Three Latin American Cities.* Cambridge: Cambridge University Press, 1985.

Glewwe Paul, and Gillette Hall. "Poverty, Inequality, and Living Standards During Unorthodox Adjustment." *Economic Development and Cultural Change* 42 (1994): 689–717.

Golbert, Laura. *La Protección al Desempleado: Una Cuestión Pendiente.* Serie de Estudios no. 18. Buenos Aires: CECE, May 1997.

Goldín, Adrián. *El Trabajo y los Mercados: Sobre las Relaciones Laborales en la Argentina.* Buenos Aires: EUDEBA, 1997.

González, R. "Organismos no Gubernamentales, Políticas Sociales y Mujer: El Caso de Chile." In *Políticas Sociales, Mujeres y Gobierno Local*, edited by D. Raczynski and C. Serrano. Santiago: CIEPLAN, 1992.

Goodman, Margaret et al. *Social Investment Funds in Latin America: Past Performance and Future Role.* Washington, D.C.: Evaluation Office, Social Programs and Sustainable Development Department, Inter-American Development Bank, March 1997.

Gordon, Gary Isaac. "Mexico City's 'War of the Sidewalks': The Politics and Economics of Street Vending in Historical Perspective." Paper delivered at the Latin American Studies Association meeting, Guadalajara, Mexico, April 1997.

Gorz, Andrés. "Salir de la Sociedad Salarial." *Debates* (Valencia, Spain: December 1994).

Graham, Carol. "Macroeconomic and Sectoral Reforms in Zambia: A Stakeholders' Approach?" Brookings Institution, Washington, D.C., May 1996. Mimeographed.

———. "Mexico's Solidarity Program in Comparative Context: Demand-Based Poverty Alleviation Programs in Latin America, Africa, and Eastern Europe." In *Transforming State-Society Relations in Mexico: The National Solidarity Strategy*, edited by Wayne A. Cornelius, Ann L. Craig, and Jonathan Fox. Chap. 15, pp. 309–328. La Jolla: Center for U.S.-Mexican Studies, University of California, 1994.

———. "The Politics of Protecting the Poor During Adjustment: Bolivia's Emergency Social Fund." *World Development* 20, no. 9 (1992).

———. "Popular Capitalism Makes Headway in Peru," *Wall Street Journal*, 19 April 1996.

———. *Private Markets for Public Goods: Raising the Stakes in Economic Reform.* Washington, D.C.: Brookings Institution, 1998.

———. *Safety Nets, Politics, and the Poor: Transitions to Market Economies.* Washington, D.C.: Brookings Institution, 1994.

———. "Strategies for Enhancing the Political Sustainability of Reform in Ukraine." *PSP Discussion Papers* no. 50. Washington, D.C.: World Bank, January 1995.

Graham Carol, and Moisés Naím. "The Political Economy of Institutional Reform." In *Beyond Trade-offs: Market Reforms and Equitable Growth in Latin America*, edited by Nancy Birdsall, Carol Graham, and Richard Sabot. Washington, D.C.: Brookings Institution/IDB, forthcoming.

Greene, M., and M. E. Ducci. "Seguimiento y Evaluación del Programa de Mejoramiento de Barrios y Lotes con Servicios." Chile: Ministry of the Interior, 1997.

Grindle, Merilee S. *Challenging the State: Crisis and Innovation in Latin America and Africa.* New York: Cambridge University Press, 1996.

———. *Audacious Reforms: Institutional Invention and Democracy in Latin America.* Baltimore: Johns Hopkins University Press, forthcoming.

Haggard, Stephan, and Robert R. Kaufman, eds. *The Politics of Economic Adjustment.* Princeton, N.J.: Princeton University Press, 1992.

Hardy, C. *Organizarse para Vivir: Pobreza Urbana y Organización Popular.* Santiago: Programa de Economía del Trabajo (PET), 1988.

———. *La Reforma Social Pendiente.* Santiago: Fundación Chile 21, 1997.

Heyneman, Stephen P. "America's Most Precious Export." *The American School Board Journal* 182, no. 3 (March 1995).

———. "International Educational Cooperation in the Next Century." Paper prepared for presentation to the International Commission on Education for the Twenty-First Century, Paris, 9 February 1995.

Holt, Robert, and Terry Roe. "The Political Economy of Reform: Egypt in the 1980s." In *Political and Economic Interactions in Economic Policy Reform,* edited by Robert H. Bates and Anne O. Krueger. Cambridge, Mass.: Basil Blackwell, 1993.

Hornsby, Ann. *Pushing for Democracy in Colombia: Non-Profit Challenges to Dependence on the State.* Ph.D. dissertation, Department of Sociology, Harvard University, 1991.

Instituto Nacional de Estadísticas (INE). *Censo de Población y Vivienda Chile, 1992: Resultados Generales.* Santiago: INE, 1992.

———. *Chile. Estimaciones y Proyecciones de Población por Sexo y Edad.* Santiago: INE–CELADE, 1995.

Inter-American Development Bank (IDB). *Annual Report, Organizing Social Services to Perform.* Washington, D.C.: IDB, 1997.

———. *Economic and Social Progress in Latin America: Social Services.* Washington, D.C.: Johns Hopkins University Press, 1996.

———. *Hacia una Política Social Efectiva. Informe de la Misión Piloto del Programa Reforma Social del Banco Interamericano de Desarrollo, Grupo Agenda Social.* Washington, D.C.: IDB, 1994.

———. "The Use of Social Investment Funds as an Instrument For Combating Poverty." A Bank Strategy Paper. Washington, D.C.: IDB, July 1998.

IDB/UNDP (United Nations Development Programme). *Social Reform and Poverty: Toward a Comprehensive Agenda for Development.* Washington, D.C. and New York: IDB/UNDP, 1993.

Kane, Cheikh. "Notes on the Ukrainian Pensions System." Washington, D.C.: *Poverty and Social Policy Department,* World Bank, January 1995.

Katz, Jorge, and Alberto Muñoz. *Organización del Sector Salud: Puja Distributiva y Equidad.* Buenos Aires: Centro Editor de América Latina, 1988.

Killick, Tony. *A Reaction Too Far: Economic Theory and the Role of the State in Developing Countries.* London: Overseas Development Institute, 1989.

Kliksberg, B., ed. *El Rediseño del Estado: Una Perspectiva Internacional.* Mexico: Fondo de Cultura Económica, 1994.

Law, L. *Human Capital, Physical Capital, and Growth in the Southeast Asian Countries.* Stanford, Calif.: Stanford University Press, 1995.

Lawson, Victoria. "Workforce Fragmentation in Latin America and its Empirical Manifestations in Ecuador." *World Development* 18, no. 5 (1990).

Leon, A., and J. Martinez. "La Estratificación Social Chilena Hacia Fines del Siglo XX." In *Chile en los Años Noventa*, edited by C. Tolosa and E. Lahera. Santiago: Presidency of the Republic and Dolmen Ediciones, 1998.

Lerner, Max. Introduction to *The Prince and the Discourses*, by Niccolò Machiavelli. New York: The Modern Library, 1950.

Lewis, Oscar. *The Children of Sanchez: Autobiography of a Mexican Family*. New York: Random House, 1961.

———. *Five Families: Mexican Case Studies in the Culture of Poverty*. New York: Random House, 1959.

Lomnitz, Larissa. "The Social and Economic Organization of a Mexican Shantytown." *Latin American Urban Research* 4 (1974): 135–155.

Lowden, P. "The Escuelas Integrales Reform Program in Venezuela." In *Implementing Policy Innovations in Latin America: Politics, Economics and Techniques*, edited by A. Silva. Washington, D.C.: Social Agenda Policy Group, Inter-American Development Bank, 1996.

Lustig, Nora, "The Safety Nets Which Are Not Safety Nets: Social Investment Funds in Latin America" (draft). Washington, D.C.: 31 October 1997.

———. ed. *Coping with Austerity: Poverty and Inequality in Latin America*. Washington, D.C.: Brookings Institution, 1995.

Lustig, Nora, and Miguel Szekely. "Mexico: Economic Trends, Poverty, and Inequality." Washington, D.C.: Inter-American Development Bank, 1998.

MacDonald, Joan. "La Vivienda en Chile, Hoy." Working paper no. 12. Santiago: Corporación de Promoción Universitaria, 1989.

Machinea, José Luis, and Oscar Cetrángolo. "El Sistema Previsional Argentino: Crisis, Reforma, y Transición." Estudios del Trabajo no. 4. Buenos Aires: ASET, second semester 1992.

Maira, L. *Superación de la Pobreza: Algunas Lecciones y Aprendizajes de la Experiencia Chilena*. Santiago: Corporación de Políticas Públicas y Relaciones Internacionales, CEPRI-Perspectiva, 1997.

Malloy, James. "Policy Analysis, Public Policy, and Regime Structure in Latin America." *Governance: An International Journal of Public Policy and Administration* 2, no. 3 (1989).

Mangin, William. "Latin American Squatter Settlements: A Problem and a Solution." *Latin American Research Review* 2 (1967): 65–98.

———, ed., *Peasants in Cities: Readings in the Anthropology of Urbanization*. Boston: Houghton Mifflin, 1967.

Marcel, Mario. "Políticas Públicas en Democracia: El Caso de la Reforma Tributaria de 1990 en Chile." Colección Estudios CIEPLAN 45. Santiago: CIEPLAN, June 1997.

Marcel, Mario, and A. Arenas. "Reformas de la Seguridad Social en Chile," *Serie de Monografías* no. 5. Washington, D.C.: Inter-American Development Bank, 1991.

Marcel, Mario, and Andres Solimano. "The Distribution of Income and Economic Adjustment." In *The Chilean Economy*, edited by Barry Bosworth, Rudiger Dornbusch, and Raul Laban. Washington, D.C.: Brookings Institution, 1994.

Marcel, Mario, and C. Toha. "Reforma del Estado y Gestión Pública." In *Construyendo Opciones: Propuestas Económicas y Sociales para el Cambio de Siglo*, edited by R. Cortázar and J. Vial. Santiago: Ediciones Dolmen–CIEPLAN, 1998.

Márquez, G. "Venezuela: Poverty and Social Policies in the 1980s." In *Coping with Austerity: Poverty and Inequality in Latin America*, edited by N. Lustig. Washington, D.C.: Brookings Institution, 1995.

Martínez, J., and M. Palacios. *Informe sobre la Decencia: La Diferenciación Estamental de la Pobreza y los Subsidios Recibidos.* Santiago: Colección Estudios Urbanos, Ediciones Sur, 1996.

Merquior, João Guilherme. "A Panoramic View of the Rebirth of Liberalism." *World Development* 20, no. 8 (1993).

Mesa-Lago, Carmelo. *Changing Social Security in Latin America: Toward Alleviating the Social Costs of Economic Reform.* Boulder, Colo.: Lynne Rienner, 1994.

―――. *Social Security in Latin America: Pressure Groups, Stratification, and Inequality.* Pittsburgh, Pa.: University of Pittsburgh Press, 1978.

Middlebrook, Kevin. *The Paradox of Revolution: Labor, the State, and Authoritarianism in Mexico.* Baltimore: Johns Hopkins University Press, 1995.

Milanovic, Branko. *Poverty and Inequality in the Transition.* Washington, D.C.: World Bank, forthcoming.

Ministry of Housing and Urban Development/National Institute of Housing (INVI), Statistical Bulletin no. 223. (March 1997): 11.

Ministry of Housing and Urban Development, Division of Housing Policy, Chile, "Vivienda, una Tarea de Dignidad, Estrategia Habitacional al Año 2000." (1995).

Ministry of Labor and Social Security, *Boletín de Estadísticas Laborales.* Buenos Aires: Ministry of Labor and Social Security, first semester 1996.

―――. *Informe de Coyuntura. Mercado Laboral.* Buenos Aires: Ministry of Labor and Social Security, 1996.

―――. *Informe de Coyuntura. Mercado Laboral.* Buenos Aires: Ministry of Labor and Social Security, 1998.

―――. *Panorama de la Seguridad Social.* Buenos Aires: Ministry of Labor and Social Security, first quarter 1997.

Ministry of Planning and Coordination (MIDEPLAN), Republic of Chile, *Balance de Seis Años de las Políticas Sociales, 1990–1996.* Santiago: MIDEPLAN, August 1996.

―――. "Pobreza y Distribución del Ingreso en Chile, 1996. Resultados de la Encuesta de Caracterización Socioeconómica Nacional." Report for the Press. Santiago: MIDEPLAN, July 1997.

Minujin, A., and G. Kessler. *La Nueva Pobreza en la Argentina.* Buenos Aires: Editorial Planeta, 1995.

Montaño, Jorge. *Los Pobres de la Ciudad en los Asentamientos Espontáneos.* Mexico City: Siglo XXI Editores, 1976.

Montoya, Silvia. "El Sector Salud en Argentina: La Evaluación de la Reforma." Documento de Trabajo 13. Córdoba: Fundación Mediterranea (IERAL), April 1998.

Morley, Samuel. *Poverty and Adjustment in Venezuela.* Working Paper Series no. 156. Washington, D.C.: Inter-American Development Bank, 1992.

―――. *Poverty and Inequality in Latin America.* Baltimore: Johns Hopkins University Press, 1995.

Moser, Caroline O. "Confronting Crisis, a Comparative Study of Household Responses to Poverty and Vulnerability in Four Poor Urban Communities." ESD Studies and Monographs Series no. 8. Washington, D.C.: World Bank, 1996.

―――. "Situaciones Críticas: Reacciones de las Familias de Cuatro Comunidades Urbanas Pobres ante la Vulnerabilidad y la Pobreza." ESD Studies and Monographs Series no. 8, p. 3. Washington, D.C.: World Bank, 1996.

Murillo, Victoria. "El Sindicalismo Argentino y las Reformas del Estado." *Desarrollo Económico,* no. 147 (October–December 1997).

———. "Latin American Unions and the Reform of Social Service Delivery Systems: Institutional Constraints and Policy Choice." Working Paper. Inter-American Development Bank, Office of the Chief Economist, 1996.

Musgrave, Richard Abel. *The Theory of Public Finance.* New York: McGraw Hill, 1959.

Naím, Moisés. "Latin America's Journey to the Market: From Macroeconomic Shocks to Institutional Therapy." ICEG Occasional Paper 62. San Francisco: International Center for Economic Growth, ICS Press, 1995.

———. *Paper Tigers and Minotaurs: The Politics of Venezuela's Economic Reforms.* Washington, D.C.: Carnegie Endowment, 1993.

Navarro, Juan Carlos. "Implementing Social Reform: Lessons from the Venezuelan Experience." In *Social Policy Reform in Latin America.* Working Paper Series no. 230. Washington, D.C.: Latin American Program, Woodrow Wilson International Center for Scholars, 1997.

———. *Las Organizaciones de Participación Comunitaria y la Prestación de Servicios Sociales a los Pobres en América Latina.* Washington, D.C.: Institute of Advanced Management Studies, Inter-American Development Bank, 1994.

———. "Reforming Social Policy in Venezuela: Implementing Targeted Programs in the Context of a Traditional Pattern of Public Intervention." Inter-American Development Bank, Washington, D.C., 1994. Mimeographed.

Navarro, Juan Carlos, and R. De la Cruz. *La Organización Industrial de Servicios de Educación en Venezuela.* Working Paper, Research Centers Network, Inter-American Development Bank, Washington, D.C., 1997.

Nelson, Joan, ed. *Economic Crisis and Policy Choice: The Politics of Adjustment in the Third World.* Princeton, N.J.: Princeton University Press, 1990.

———. "The Politics of Long Haul Economic Reform." In *Fragile Coalitions: The Politics of Economic Adjustment,* by Joan Nelson and collaborators. New Brunswick, N.J.: Transaction Books, 1989.

———. "The Politics of Pension and Health Care Delivery Reforms in Hungary and Poland." Discussion Paper 52. Budapest: Collegium Budapest, November 1998.

———. "Poverty, Equity, and the Politics of Adjustment." In *The Politics of Economic Adjustment,* edited by Stephan Haggard and Robert R. Kaufman. Princeton, N.J.: Princeton University Press, 1992.

———. "Reforming Social Sector Governance: A Political Perspective." Paper prepared for a conference on "Governance, Poverty Eradication, and Social Policy," Harvard University, 12–14 November 1997.

———. "Social Costs, Social-Sector Reforms, and Politics in Post-Communist Transformations." In *Transforming Post-Communist Political Economies,* edited by Joan M. Nelson, Charles Tilly, and Lee Walker. Washington, D.C.: National Academy Press, 1997.

Nelson, Joan, and collaborators. *Fragile Coalitions: The Politics of Economic Adjustment.* New Brunswick, N.J.: Transaction Books, 1989.

Necochea, Andrés. "Los Allegados, una Estrategia de Superviviencia Solidaria en Vivienda." *EURE* 13-11, no. 39–40 (October 1987): 87.

Nickson, Andrew R. *Local Government in Latin America.* Boulder, Colo.: Lynne Rienner, 1995.

North, Douglass. *Institutions, Institutional Change, and Economic Performance.* New York: Cambridge University Press, 1990.

Oates, W. *The Political Economy of Fiscal Federalism.* Lexington, Mass.: Lexington Books, 1993.

O'Donnell, Guillermo, Philippe C. Schmitter, and Laurence Whitehead, eds. *Transitions from Authoritarian Rule: Latin America.* Baltimore: Johns Hopkins University Press, 1986.

"Old and Unaffordable," *The Economist,* 30 April 1994.

Osborne, David, and Ted Gaebler. *Reinventing Government: How the Entrepreneurial Spirit is Transforming the Public Sector, from Schoolhouse to Statehouse, City Hall to the Pentagon.* Reading, Mass.: Addison-Wesley, 1992.

Oxhorn, P. *Organizing Civil Society: Popular Organizations and the Struggle for Democracy in Chile.* University Park, Pa.: Pennsylvania State University Press, 1995.

Paul, S. *Accountability in Public Services: Exit, Voice and Capture.* Washington, D.C.: World Bank, 1991.

Perlman, Janice. *The Myth of Marginality: Urban Poverty and Politics in Rio de Janeiro.* Berkeley: University of California Press, 1976.

Persson, Torsten, and Guido Tabellini. *Monetary and Fiscal Policy. Vol. 1, Credibility.* Cambridge, Mass.: MIT Press, 1994.

Pinto, Brian, Marek Belka, and Stefan Krajewski. "The Microeconomics of Transformation in Poland: A Survey of State Enterprise Responses." World Bank, Washington, D.C., June 1992. Mimeographed.

Pizarro, Crisostomo, Dagmar Raczynski, and Joaquín Vial, eds. *Políticas Económicas y Sociales en el Chile Democrático.* Santiago: CIEPLAN–UNICEF, 1995.

Portes, Alejandro. "The Urban Slum in Chile: Types and Correlates." *Ekistics,* no. 202 (September 1972): 175–180.

Psacharopoulos, George, Samuel Morley, Ariel Fiszbein, Haeduck Lee, and Bill Wood. *Poverty and Income Distribution in Latin America: The Story of the 1980s.* Washington, D.C.: World Bank, 1997.

Putnam, Robert. *Making Democracy Work: Civic Traditions in Modern Italy.* Princeton, N.J.: Princeton University Press, 1993.

Raczynski, Dagmar. "Chile: Fondos de Solidaridad de Inversión Social (FOSIS)." In *Social Investment Funds in Latin America: Past Performance and Future Role,* edited by Margaret Goodman et al., chap. 2. Washington, D.C.: Evaluation Office and the Social Programs and Sustainable Development Department, Inter-American Development Bank, June 1997.

———. "¿Disminuyó la Extrema Pobreza Entre 1970 y 1982?" Notas Técnicas no. 90. Santiago: CIEPLAN, December 1986.

———. "La Estrategia para Combatir la Pobreza en Chile. Programas, Instituciones, y Recursos." In *Estrategias para Combatir la Pobreza en América Latina. Programas, Instituciones y Recursos,* edited by D. Raczynski. Santiago: CIEPLAN–IDB, 1995.

———. "Focalización de Programas Sociales: Lecciones de la Experiencia Chilena." In *Políticas Económicas y Sociales en el Chile Democrático,* edited by C. Pizarro et al. Santiago: CIEPLAN–UNICEF, 1995.

———. "Para Combatir la Pobreza en Chile: Esfuerzos del Pasado y Desafíos del Presente." In *Construyendo Opciones. Propuestas Económicas y Sociales para el Cambio de Siglo,* edited by R. Cortázar and J. Vial. Santiago: Ediciones Dolmen–CIEPLAN, 1998.

————. "Social Policies in Chile: Origin, Transformations and Perspectives." In *Democracy and Social Policy Series,* Working Paper no. 4. Notre Dame, Ind.: Kellogg Institute, University of Notre Dame, 1994, 1998.

————. "Social Policy, Poverty, and Vulnerable Groups: Children in Chile." In *Adjustment with a Human Face, Ten Country Case Studies,* edited by G. A. Cornia, R. Jolly, and F. Stewart. Oxford: Clarendon Press, 1987.

Raczynski, Dagmar, and others. "Proyecto de Fortalecimiento Institucional del Fondo de Solidaridad e Inversión Social (FOSIS) de Chile: Evaluación y Rediseño de Programas, Informe Final." Santiago: CIEPLAN and FOSIS, January 1996.

Raczynski, Dagmar, and P. Romaguera. "Chile: Poverty, Adjustment, and Social Policies in the 80s." In *Coping with Austerity: Poverty and Inequality in Latin America,* edited by N. Lustig, Washington, D.C.: Brookings Institution, 1995.

Raczynski, Dagmar, and C. Serrano. "Administración y Gestión Local: La Experiencia de Algunos Municipios en Santiago." *Colección Estudios CIEPLAN.* Santiago: CIEPLAN, 22 December 1987.

————. "¿Planificación para el Desarrollo Local? La Experiencia de Algunos Municipios de Santiago." *Colección Estudios CIEPLAN.* Santiago: CIEPLAN, 24 June 1988.

Ramírez, Ronaldo. *International Seminar: Sustainable Urban Housing Development.* University of Chile, 1997.

Ray, Talton. *The Politics of the Barrios of Venezuela.* Berkeley: University of California Press, 1969.

Razetto, L. *Economía Popular de Solidaridad.* Santiago: Programa de Economía del Trabajo (PET), 1986.

Reddy, Sanjay. *Social Funds in Developing Countries: Recent Experiences and Lessons.* UNICEF Staff Working Papers, Evaluation, Policy and Planning Series no. EPP-EVL-98-002. New York: UNICEF, 1998.

Reich, Michael R. "The Political Economy of Health Transitions in the Third World." In *Health and Social Change in International Perspective,* edited by L. Chen, A. Kleinman, and N. C. Ware. Boston: Harvard School of Public Health, 1994.

Roberts, Kenneth M. "Neoliberalism and the Transformation of Populism in Latin America: The Peruvian Case." *World Politics* 48, no. 1 (1996): 82–116.

Rodgers, Gerry, Charles G. Gore, and José B. Figueiredo, eds., *Social Exclusion: Rhetoric, Reality, Responses.* Geneva: International Institute for Labour Studies, 1995.

Rodríguez, Alfredo. "Cómo Gobernar a Principados que se Regían por sus Propias Leyes Antes de ser Ocupados." *SIAP* 17, no. 65 (March 1983).

Rodríguez, J., and C. Serrano. "Como Va el Proceso de Descentralización del Estado en Chile." In *Construyendo Opciones: Propuestas Económicas y Sociales para el Cambio de Siglo,* edited by R. Cortázar and J. Vial. Santiago: Ediciones Dolmen–CIEPLAN, 1998.

Rodrik, Dani. "Understanding Economic Policy Reform." *Journal of Economic Literature* 34, no. 1 (1996).

Root, Hilton L. *Small Countries, Big Lessons: Governance and the Rise of East Asia.* Hong Kong: Oxford University Press, 1996.

Rossi, Alejandro. "Reforma Previsional ¿Cómo y Por Qué?" Master's thesis, Social Sciences Research, University of Buenos Aires, n.d.

Rubio, Luis. "Mexico's New Politics." *LASA (Latin American Studies Association) Forum* 28, no. 3 (Fall 1997): 11.

Sachs, Jeffrey, and Andrew Warner. "Economic Reform and the Process of Global Integration." In *Brookings Paper on Economic Activity*, Vol. 1. 1995.

Schady, Norbert Rudiger. "Seeking Votes: The Political Economy of Expenditures by the Peruvian Social Fund (FONCODES), 1991–1995." Policy Research Working Paper, no. 2166. Washington, D.C.: World Bank, Poverty Reduction and Economic Management Network, 1999.

Scherman, J. "Techo y Abrigo: Las Organizaciones Populares de Vivienda: Chile, 1974–1988." *Colección de Experiencias Populares* 7. Santiago: PET, 1990.

Scott, James. *Seeing Like a State: How Certain Schemes to Improve the Human Condition Have Failed*. New Haven: Yale University Press, 1998.

Secretaría de Desarrollo Urbano y Ecologia (SEDUE). *Housing Reconstruction Program in Mexico City*. Mexico City: SEDUE, 1987.

Sennet, Richard. *Flesh and Stone*. New York: WW Norton & Company, 1994.

Serrano, C. "Municipio, Política Social, y Pobreza." In *Políticas Económicas y Sociales en el Chile Democrático*, edited by C. Pizarro et al. Santiago: CIEPLAN–UNICEF, 1995.

———. "Gobierno Regional e Inversión Pública Descentralizada." *Colección Estudios CIEPLAN* 42. Santiago: CIEPLAN, June 1996.

Sheahan, John. "Effects of Liberalization Programs on Poverty and Inequality: Chile, Mexico, and Peru." *Latin American Research Review* 32, no. 3 (1997): 7–38.

Skocpol, Theda, and Kenneth Finegold. "State Capacity and Economic Intervention in the Early New Deal." *Political Science Quarterly* 97, no. 2 (1982): 255–278.

Stewart, Frances, and Willem van der Geest. "Adjustment and Social Funds: Political Panacea or Effective Poverty Reduction?" In *Adjustment and Poverty: Options and Choices*, edited by Frances Stewart. London: Routledge, 1995.

Stokes, C. "A Theory of Slums." *Land Economics*, 38 (August 1962): 187–197.

Strassmann, Paul. "Home-Based Enterprises in Cities of Developing Countries." *Economic Development and Cultural Change* 36, no. 1 (October 1987): 121–144.

Subbarao, K., Aniruddha Bonnerjee, Jeanine Braithwaite, Soniya Carvalho, Kene Ezemenari, Carol Graham, and Alan Thompson. *Safety Net Programs and Poverty Reduction: Lessons from Cross-Country Experience*. Washington, D.C.: World Bank, 1997.

SUBDERE (Subsecretaría de Desarrollo Regional). *Seguimiento y Evaluación Expost de Proyectos FNDR, Período 1990–1994. Informe Final*. Santiago: Ministry of the Interior, February 1997.

Tardinico, Richard, and Rafael Menjívar Larín, eds. *Global Restructuring, Employment, and Social Inequality in Urban Latin America*. Miami: North-South Center Press, 1997.

Tendler, Judith. *Good Government in the Tropics*. Baltimore: Johns Hopkins University Press, 1997.

Tendler, Judith, (with the assistance of Rodrigo Serrano). *The Rise of Social Funds: What Are They a Model Of?* Monograph for the United Nations Development Program (UNDP), draft. Cambridge, Mass.: Department of Urban Studies and Planning, MIT, January 1999.

Thomas, John W. "Food for Work: An Analysis of Current Experience and Recommendations for Future Performance." Development Discussion Paper no. 213. Cambridge: Harvard Institute for International Development, Harvard University, 1986.

Tommasi, Mariano, and Andrés Velasco. "Where Are We in the Political Economy of Reform?" *Policy Reform* 1 (1996).

Torche, A. "Distribuir el Ingreso para Satisfacer las Necesidades Básicas." In *Desarrollo Económico para Chile en Democracia,* edited by F. Larraín. Santiago: Ediciones Universidad Católica de Chile, 1987.

Torre, Juan Carlos. *El Proceso Político de las Reformas Económicas en América Latina.* Buenos Aires: Editorial Paidós, 1998.

Trejo, Guillermo, et al. *Contra la Pobreza.* Mexico City: Cal y Arena, 1993.

Turner, John C. "Approaches to Government-Sponsored Housing." *Ekistics* 42, no. 242 (January 1976): 4–7.

———. "Housing Priorities, Settlement Patterns, and Urban Development in Modernizing Countries." *Journal of the American Institute of Planners* 34, no. 6 (1968): 354–363.

United Nations Development Programme (UNDP). *Desarrollo Humano en Chile—1998. Las Paradojas de la Modernización.* Santiago: UNDP, 1998.

———. *Human Development Report.* New York: Oxford University Press, 1991, 1996, 1997.

———. *Informe de Desarrollo Humano.* Santiago: UNDP, 1994, 1995, 1996.

———. *Report on Human Development.* World Press Editions, 1996.

Vergara, P. *Políticas Hacia la Extrema Pobreza en Chile, 1973–1988.* Santiago: FLACSO, 1990.

Verschure, Han. *International Seminar: Sustainable Urban Housing Development,* University of Chile, 1997.

Von Braun, Joachim, Tesfaye Teken, and Patrick Webb. "Labor-Intensive Public Works for Food Security in Africa: Past Experience and Future Potential." *International Labour Review* 131, no. 1 (1992): 19–34.

Von Hayek, F. "The Use of Knowledge in Society." *American Economic Review* 34, no. 4 (1945): 519–530.

Wade, Robert. *Governing the Market: Economic Theory and the Role of Government in East Asian Industrialization.* Princeton, N.J.: Princeton University Press, 1990.

Walt, Gill. *Health Policy: An Introduction to Process and Power.* London and New Jersey: Zed Books, 1994.

Ward, Peter. "The Latin American Inner City: Differences of Degree or of Kind?" *Environment and Planning* 25 (1993): 1131–1160.

———. *Mexico City: The Production and Reproduction of an Urban Environment.* New York: John Wiley & Sons, 1990.

Weyland, Kurt. *Democracy Without Equity: Failures of Reform in Brazil.* Pittsburgh, Pa.: University of Pittsburgh Press, 1996.

———. "How Much Political Power Do Economic Forces Have? Conflicts Over Social Insurance Reform in Brazil." *Journal of Public Policy* 16, no. 1 (1996).

Wiens, Thomas, and Maurizio Guadagni. *Designing Rules for Demand-Driven Rural Investment Funds: The Latin American Experience.* World Bank Technical Paper no. 407. Washington, D.C.: World Bank, May 1998.

Wiesner, E. *Fiscal Decentralization and Social Spending in Latin America: The Search for Efficiency and Equity.* Working Paper Series 199. Washington, D.C.: Inter-American Development Bank, 1994.

Williamson, John. Introduction to *Latin American Adjustment: How Much Has Happened?* Edited by John Williamson. Washington, D.C.: Institute for International Economics, 1990.

———. ed., *The Political Economy of Policy Reform.* Washington, D.C.: Institute for International Economics, 1994.

World Bank. *Averting the Old-Age Crisis.* Washington, D.C.: World Bank, 1994.

———. *Chile: The Adult Policy Challenge, a World Bank Country Study.* Washington, D.C.: IBRD, 1995.

———. *Venezuela Poverty Study: From Generalized Subsidies to Targeted Programs.* Washington, D.C.: World Bank, 1991.

———. *The East Asian Miracle: Economic Growth and Public Policy.* New York: Oxford University Press, 1993.

———. *Venezuela 2000: Education for Growth and Social Equity.* Washington, D.C.: World Bank, 1993.

———. *World Development Report.* New York: Oxford University Press, 1997, 1996, 1991.

———, Working Group for the Social Funds Portfolio Review. "Portfolio Improvement Program Review of the Social Funds Portfolio." Forthcoming as World Bank Technical Paper. Washington, D.C.

World Health Organization. *Most Recent Values of WHO Global Health-For-All Indicators* (1996). Internet search, 30 April 1998 in: http://www.who.int/whosis/hfa/c./

The Contributors

Maria Elena Ducci holds degrees in architecture from the Universidad Católica de Chile and in urban studies from the Universidad Nacional Autónoma de Mexico (UNAM). She directs the Urban Environment Program at the Instituto de Estudios Urbanos de la Universidad Católica de Chile in Santiago and is a founding member of Acción Ciudadana por el Medio Ambiente, which coordinates more than fifty NGOs working for the improvement of the environment in Santiago's Metropolitan Region. Ducci has authored several publications and has been a guest scholar at the Woodrow Wilson International Center for Scholars and a Fulbright fellow at the Latin American Program at the University of Chicago.

Susan Eckstein is professor of sociology at Boston University and past president of the Latin American Studies Association. She is the author of *The Poverty of Reduction: The State and Urban Poor in Mexico* (1977, 1988), *Back from the Future: Cuba under Castro* (1994), and *The Impact of Revolution: A Comparative Analysis of Mexico and Bolivia* (1976).

Laura Susana Golbert is a visiting researcher at the Centro de Estudios de Estado y Sociedad and professor at the Universidad Nacional de San Martín and at the Universidad Nacional de Buenos Aires. She has recently conducted research on urban violence and social cohesion for the United Nations Development Programme. Among her most recent publications are "Los Problemas del Empleo y las Políticas Sociales," in *Boletín Informativo Techint,* no. 296 (October–December 1998) and "Programas de Empleo e Ingresos en Argentina," co-authored with Claudia Giacometti, in *Programas de Empleo e Ingresos en América Latina y el Caribe* (BID/OIT, Lima, 1998).

Carol Graham is a senior fellow in the Foreign Policy Studies Program and co-director of the Center on Social and Economic Dynamics at the Brookings Institution. She is also professorial lecturer of Latin American Studies and Economics at Johns Hopkins University and an adjunct professor in Government at Georgetown University. She is the author of *Private Markets for Public Goods: Raising the Stakes in Economic Reform* (Brookings, 1998), and *Safety Nets, Politics and the Poor: Transitions to Market Economies* (Brookings, 1994). Most recently she edited, with Nancy Birdsall, *Beyond Tradeoffs: Market Reforms and Equitable Growth in Latin America* (Brookings/IADB 1998) and *New Markets, New Opportunities? Economic and Social Mobility in a Changing World* (Brookings/Carnegie 2000).

Merilee S. Grindle is Edward S. Mason Professor of International Development at the Kennedy School of Government at Harvard University and faculty fellow of the Harvard Institute for International Development. She has written extensively on the comparative analysis of policymaking, implementation, and public management in developing countries. Her most recent book is entitled *Audacious Reforms: Insitutional Invention and Democracy in Latin America.* With John W. Thomas, she co-authored *Public Choices and Policy Change,* which received the Charles H. Levine Award for the best book on public policy published in 1991.

Juan Carlos Navarro is senior principal specialist in the Ecucation Unit of the Inter-American Development Bank. He coordinated the Center for Public Policy at the Instituto de Estudios Superiores de Administración in Caracas, Venezuela, and has been a visiting scholar at Harvard University. His research focus has been on social and education policy in Latin America.

Joan M. Nelson is a senior associate of the Overseas Development Council. Since the mid-1980s she has focused on the politics of economic reform and the interactions between market-oriented reforms and democratization. Her most recent publication is "Reforming Health and Education: The World Bank, the IDB, and Complex Institutional Change" (Overseas Development Council Policy Essay no. 26, 1999). She recently co-edited (with Charles Tilly) a National Research Council volume on post-Communist transformations, and earlier directed a project comparing East European and Latin American experiences with dual transformations. Among her other publications are *Transforming Post-Communist Political Economies* (co-editor with Charles Tilly and contributor; National Academy Press, 1998) and *Intricate Links: Democratization and Market Reforms in Latin American and Eastern Europe* (1994).

Dagmar Raczynski is director of Asesorías para el Desarrollo in Santiago, Chile, and professor at the Institute of Sociology, Catholic University of Chile. Her most recent publications include *Estrategias para Combatir la Pobreza en America Latina: Programas, Instituciones y Recursos* (BID–CIEPLAN, 1995) and "The Crisis of Old Models of Social Protection in Latin America: New Alternatives for Dealing with Poverty," in V. E. Tokman and G. O'Donnell, *Poverty and Inequality in Latin America: Issues and New Challenges*, 1998.

Judith Tendler is a development economist and professor of political economy in the Department of Urban Studies and Planning at the Massachusetts Institute of Technology. Her research interests lie in the study of better-performing government and NGO programs. Her recent publications include *Good Government in the Tropics*, published by Johns Hopkins University Press in 1997, and co-published in Portuguese in Brazil by Editora Revan of Rio de Janeiro and the Brazilian National School of Public Administration (ENAP); *New Lessons from Old Projects: The Workings of Rural Development in Northeast Brazil* (World Bank, 1994); and three lead articles in *World Development*— "Tales of Dissemination in Agriculture," "Trust in a Rent-Seeking World: Health and Government Transformed in Northeast Brazil" (co-authored with Sara Freedheim), and "Small Firms and Their Helpers: Lessons on Demand" (co-authored with Mônica Alves Amorim).

Index

reforms, 178; reforms, administrative, 189–192; shantytowns, 185–188; social indicators, 25t; urban areas, 181–188
Middle class, the, 58

Neoliberal social policy, 122–124
New Zealand, 53–54
Nicaragua; Gross National Product (GNP), 23t; health care in, 152t
Nongovernmental organizations (NGOs), 114n., 134; and social funds, 99
North American Free Trade Agreement (NAFTA), 176
North, Douglass, 29

Panama; Gross National Product (GNP), 23t; income distribution, 24t; poverty, 21t; public spending, 27t; social indicators, 25t
Paraguay; Gross National Product (GNP), 23t; income distribution, 24t; poverty, 21t; public spending, 27t; social indicators, 25t
Pensions, 36–39; in Argentina, 229–234; in Chile, 64–66, 125–126. See also safety net policies; social security
Peru, 34, 36; Gross National Product (GNP), 23t; income distribution, 24t; poverty, 21t, 84n.; public spending, 27t; social indicators, 25t
Politics; citizen involvement, 30–31; in Mexico, 178–179, 192–196; and social services

reform, 39–40, 65–66
Poor, the. See poverty
Poverty, 21t, 58, 71–80, 109n.; in Chile, 119–146, 172n.; effects of social funds on, 92–95; increase, 20–22; in individual nations of Latin America, 21t, 47n., 48n.; in Mexico, 176, 180–181
Privatization, 5–6, 28–29, 124–126, 134
Psychology, entitlement, 56
Public spending, 3–5, 22–23, 48n., 78–80; in Chile, 120–129, 136t, 141t; in Venezuela, 202–203, 209–213. See also social services
Putnam, Robert, 32–33

Quality of labor, 61

Reform; and adjustment programs, 71–73; advocates, 60–62; agendas, 26–34; anti-statist, 28–29; and bureaucrats, 41–42; characteristics, 48n., 55–56; in Chile, 78–82, 125–126, 131–139; and citizens, 41; in Czechoslovakia, 81–82; and democracy advocates, 40–41; and dissensus, 38–42; economic policy, 38–39, 55, 60–62; and economists, 38–39; educational, 55–56; health care, 55–56; in industrialized nations, 53–54, 69n.; institutional, 78–80; labor, 235–237; in Mexico, 189–192; in New Zealand, 53–54; opposition to, 17–19, 30, 34–38, 51n.; pension, 62; and

About the Book

While previous analyses of public-sector reform efforts in Latin America have focused largely on strategies to redefine the role of the state in the economy, there is a growing realization that social reform—addressing such issues as poverty, inequality, and unemployment—is a condition on which economic and political stability rest. This volume provides a wide-ranging analysis of social-welfare reform in the region, examining in particular the politics involved in implementing difficult and controversial social policies that often pit the middle strata of society, represented by powerful stakeholders, against the poor.

Joseph S. Tulchin is director of the Latin American Program of the Woodrow Wilson International Center for Scholars. **Allison M. Garland** is a former senior program associate for the Latin American Program.

The Woodrow Wilson International Center for Scholars

Lee H. Hamilton, Director

About the Center

The Center is the living memorial of the United States of America to the nation's twenty-eighth president, Woodrow Wilson. Congress established the Woodrow Wilson Center in 1968 as an international institute for advanced study, "symbolizing and strengthening the fruitful relationship between the world of learning and the world of public affairs." The Center opened in 1970 under its own board of trustees.

In all its activities the Woodrow Wilson Center is a nonprofit, nonpartisan organization, supported financially by annual appropriations from the Congress and by the contributions of foundations, corporations, and individuals. Conclusions or opinions expressed in Center publications and programs are those of the authors and speakers and do not necessarily reflect the views of the Center staff, fellows, trustees, advisory groups, or any individuals or organizations that provide financial support to the Center.